Standard Library Edition

AMERICAN STATESMEN

IN FORTY VOLUMES
VOLUME XXX

THE CIVIL WAR
CHARLES SUMNER

Charles Sumner

American Statesmen

STANDARD LIBRARY EDITION

The Home of Charles Sumner

HOUGHTON MIFFLIN COMPANY

American Statesmen

CHARLES SUMNER

BY

MOORFIELD STOREY

The Riverside Press

BOSTON AND NEW YORK
HOUGHTON MIFFLIN COMPANY
The Riverside Press Cambridge

The Riverside Press
CAMBRIDGE · MASSACHUSETTS
PRINTED IN THE U.S.A.

CONTENTS

ILLUSTRATIONS

CHARLES SUMNER

CHAPTER I

BIRTH AND EDUCATION

CHARLES SUMNER came of typical Massachusetts stock. His family on both sides was of English origin, but his ancestors left England very soon after the landing of the Pilgrims, and dwelt in the neighborhood of Boston for nearly two centuries before his birth. Roger Sumner, his lineal ancestor in the eighth generation, died and was buried at Bicester in Oxfordshire. William, the only son of Roger, came to America about 1635, and settled in Dorchester, which adjoined Boston on the south. He became at once a land-owner and was made a freeman in 1637. He was admitted to the church in 1652; was a deputy to the General Court, a selectman, a commissioner to try small causes, and in other ways showed himself an active and public-spirited citizen. He brought three children with him from England, and two more were born afterward. Roger, his second son, was born in England. He married Mary Josselyn, of Lancaster, in Massachusetts, and became an in-

habitant of that town in 1660, but when Lancaster
was destroyed by the Indians he removed to Milton,
where he died. George, the third son of William,
was the ancestor of Increase Sumner, a justice of
the Supreme Judicial Court of Massachusetts, and
governor of the Commonwealth. William, the
fourth son of Roger, had many children, of whom
one, Seth, was married twice. A son of the first
marriage was the grandfather of Major-General
Edwin V. Sumner, who commanded a corps in the
Army of the Potomac under McClellan and Burn-
side. A son of the second marriage, Job, was the
father of Charles Pinckney Sumner, and the grandfather of Charles Sumner.

The Sumners had been for the most part farmers, but Job was resolved to obtain a liberal education, and entered Harvard College in November,
1774, at the age of twenty. The shots fired at
Concord and Lexington changed the current of his
ambition, and in May, 1775, he joined the American army at Cambridge. He was a lieutenant at
Bunker Hill and during the siege of Boston, and
his conduct in several actions earned him a commission as captain, given him by vote of Congress
in 1779, to date from July 1, 1776. He was com-
missioned a major in 1783, and was second in command of the force which protected New York during the evacuation by the British in that year. It
was from soldiers under his command that Washington received the last salute of the revolutionary
army. After the war, on July 7, 1785, the cor-

poration of Harvard College gave him the degree of A. M., as a member of his class, by a vote which recited that he had " during the war behaved with reputation as a man and as an officer." In 1785 he was appointed a commissioner to settle the accounts between the Confederation and the State of Georgia, and he resided in Georgia until he died. He is said to have been a candidate for governor, and to have been defeated by only a few votes. He was apparently a man of the world, who lived expensively and entertained freely. He died in New York of a fever, in his thirty-sixth year, and was buried in St. Paul's churchyard on Broadway, where stands his tombstone, erected by the Society of the Cincinnati.

His son, Charles Pinckney Sumner, was born in Milton, and brought up on a farm. He went to Phillips Academy at Andover, and graduated at Harvard College in 1796, where he formed a friendship with Joseph Story which exercised an important influence on his son's career. After graduating he taught school for a while, but in 1799 he entered the office of Josiah Quincy, and in 1801 was admitted as an attorney. He took an active interest in politics as a supporter of Jefferson, and his first political speech, made in 1804, was an argument against disunion. He was clerk of the House of Representatives in 1806–7 and 1810–11. He was married in 1810, and in 1819 he accepted the office of deputy sheriff, having been unsuccessful in practice. From 1825 till just before his death in 1839 he was the sheriff of Suffolk County, and while his political activity ended when he became sheriff, he was interested in the temperance question and in the anti-Masonic movement, though he had been a Mason. He was an anti-slavery man in feeling, though not prominent in the 'agitation. He delivered a number of public addresses at various times, but was not conspicuous as an orator. He was high-minded, courageous, scholarly, extremely conscientious and faithful in the discharge of every duty, but formal, reserved, grave, and stern; somewhat narrow also, and without his father's social charm. He foresaw the inevitable result of the agitation against slavery, and in 1820 said: " Our children's heads will some day be broken on a cannon-ball on this question." It is from him that Charles Sumner may well have derived his unbending conscience and his intense earnestness.

Charles Pinckney Sumner married Relief Jacob of Hanover in Massachusetts, a descendant from Nicholas Jacob, who came to America in 1633, and after settling in Watertown, removed to Hingham in 1635. Her grandfather was a man of property and one of the Committee of Public Safety at the time of the Revolution, but the family were generally farmers of the solid New England type. Her father was evidently in narrow circumstances, and before her marriage she supported herself by her needle. She was a woman of even temper and great good sense, who probably did much to temper her husband's austerity in the family life. She had nine children, and died in 1866 at the age of eighty-one.

Such was the ancestry of Charles Sumner. He and his twin sister Matilda, the first children of their parents, were born on January 6, 1811, at the corner of Revere and Irving streets in Boston. His childhood was in no way remarkable; he was educated in the schools of Boston, and was an amiable, quiet, refined, and studious boy. Among his schoolmates at the Public Latin School were Robert C. Winthrop, who was older, and Wendell Phillips, who was younger than himself. He won several prizes for translations from Latin, for a Latin poem, and for an English theme; but while taking respectable rank, he seems to have been more remarkable for knowledge acquired by general reading than for striking ability. Though apparently never ill his health was not robust, and having little inclination for sports he early acquired the tastes and habits of a scholar.

His father at first did not intend to give him a college education, and it is a little curious that Sumner himself, in later years the champion of peace, wished to enter the military academy at West Point. His application for a cadetship failed, and the father's opportune appointment as sheriff, with a larger income, enabled the son to enter Harvard College in September, 1826. Lovers of speculative inquiry may be interested to consider what sort of a soldier was thus lost to the country.

Sumner's college class was not so rich in distinguished men as its brilliant predecessor, the famous class of '29, and he was among the youngest members. He devoted his time to history, literature, and the classics, in which he excelled, but his dislike for mathematics and physics prevented his taking high rank, and abandoning this ambition he gave himself up to the studies that he loved. A classmate tells us that he was "one of the best declaimers in the class," showing "a great degree of earnestness with an entire freedom from any effort to make a dash." "It was the same type of subdued eloquence, inseparable from the man," which he afterward displayed, and already he was self-possessed and easy on the stage. He received minor parts at college exhibitions and Commencement, and he won a second Bowdoin prize by an essay on "The Present Character of the Inhabitants of New England," which, we are told, showed copious reading and immense industry, but lacked condensation and clearness. He was fond of discussion, persistent and possibly somewhat aggressive in argument. Socially he was frank, kindly and genial, but possessed a native dignity which became him well. His life at college was a period of healthy and natural growth before anything had occurred to awaken strong feeling.

The year after Sumner's graduation was spent at home. He took time to decide what his work in life should be, and meanwhile, rising early and working late, he read the classics, poetry, general literature and history, and attacked mathematics with better success than in college. He taught school for a few weeks, wrote an essay on commerce for a prize offered by a Boston society, of which Daniel Webster was the president, and received the award from his hands. This success gratified his friends and we may suppose gave him a certain reputation. Except that, in natural sympathy with his father, his feelings were enlisted against Freemasonry, he seems to have taken little interest in public questions during this year, which was spent in desultory labor. At this time he saw little of society ; he was pondering carefully the question of his future occupation, and it was after much deliberation and with many misgivings that he decided to study law.

Sumner entered the Harvard Law School in September, 1831, where he was brought under the influence of Judge Story, who had been sitting on the Supreme Bench of the United States for twenty years and was just beginning the series of treatises which gave him his great international reputation. Story's enthusiasm and personal charm made him a stimulating teacher. As an old friend of Sumner's father he took a kindly interest in the son, which ripened into friendship, and Sumner was soon a constant visitor at his house. Simon Greenleaf, who was appointed a professor about six months before Sumner left the school, also became his friend, and the two eminent lawyers inspired him with the strongest devotion to his profession.

Sumner remained in the Law School until the end of December, 1833, applying himself to study with ardor and persistency. For the first time he felt a definite ambition, for the first time his work satisfied and inspired him. He wrote to one of his classmates: " A lawyer must know everything. He must know law, history, philosophy, human nature; and if he covets the fame of an advocate he must drink of all the springs of literature, giving ease and elegance to the mind and illustration to whatever subjects it touches." His plan of life was: "Six hours, namely, the forenoon, wholly and solely to law; afternoon to classics; evening to history, subjects collateral and assistant to law, etc. . . . Recreation must not be found in idleness or loose reading."

Possessed with this theory he read law, classics, history, literature, rising early and working late, until his inflamed eyes and clouded complexion showed the effects of excessive labor. Yet he was never ill and seemed independent of sleep and exercise. He treated his mind as a reservoir and into it steadily pumped learning of every kind, which his strong memory retained. He became librarian of the school, and was given a room in Dane Hall, where he acquired a remarkable familiarity with the books under his charge. He won a Bowdoin prize by an essay on the subject, " Are the most important Changes in Society effected Gradually or by Violent Revolutions?" He wrote two articles for the " American Monthly

Review," and before he left the Law School became a contributor to the "American Jurist." His style gained in clearness and conciseness, but his writings were more learned than original. The impression which he made upon his contemporaries at this time was very pleasant. Thus President Quincy's daughter, Mrs. Waterston, speaks of seeing at one of her mother's receptions, "the tall spare form and honest face of Charles Sumner," and adds: "This youth, though not in the least handsome, is so good-hearted, clever, and real, that it is impossible not to like him and believe in him."

Judge Story's son, William W., who was some eight years younger than Sumner, writes: "He used to come to our house some two or three evenings in the week, and to his long conversations I used to listen night after night with eager pleasure. His simplicity and directness of character, his enthusiasm and craving for information, his lively spirit and genial feeling, immediately made a strong impression on me. My father was very fond of him, and treated him almost as if he were a son; and we were all delighted to welcome him to our family circle. He was free, natural, and naïve in his simplicity, and plied my father with an ever-flowing stream of questions, and I need not say that the responses were as full and genial as heart and mind could desire. . . . He was at this time totally without vanity, and only desirous to acquire knowledge and information on every subject. . . .

Though he was an interesting talker, he had no lightness of hand. He was kindly of nature, interested in everything, but totally put off his balance by the least persiflage; and if it was tried on him his expression was one of complete astonishment. He was never ready at a retort . . . and was at this time almost impervious to a joke. He had no humor himself and little sense of it in others, and his jests, when he tried to make one, were rather cumbrous. But in 'plain sailing' no one could be better or more agreeable."

Another characteristic is described by a friend, who says: " A peculiar life-and-death earnestness characterized even then all that Sumner did and said."

His years at the Law School gave him a definite ambition, and for the first time he distinguished himself from his fellows and showed promise of future eminence, while the favorable opinion of Judge Story and Mr. Greenleaf gave him a reputation at the very outset of his career. In those days the community was small, and the world outside was ready to welcome a man who made his mark at Cambridge.

In January, 1834, after leaving the Law School, Sumner entered the office of Benjamin Rand, an eminent lawyer of Boston, where he continued to write for the " Jurist," becoming one of its editors in May. In February he went to Washington for a month, making on his way short visits in Philadelphia and New York. Through the introductions of Judge Story, Sumner enjoyed on this trip rare opportunities to become acquainted with the distinguished men of the day. A letter from Professor Greenleaf introduced him to Chancellor Kent, and it is amusing to find Kent saying that he "thought Jackson would ruin us; wanted to go to Washington, but if he went should be obliged to see much company, call upon Jackson and dine with him, perhaps, all of which he could not consent to do." This was a time when men took political differences seriously, and did not condone in social intercourse conduct which they condemned in public speech. It is amusing, also, to find Sumner writing: "Kent's conversation is lively and instructive, but grossly ungrammatical."

During this visit he saw much of Judge Story; was introduced to President Jackson; met the judges of the Supreme Court at their Sunday dinner, he being the only guest; secured what he "may almost call a place in the court;" dined repeatedly with Horace Binney; made the acquaintance of Henry Wheaton and Francis Lieber, afterward his intimate friend; and heard many distinguished lawyers address the Supreme Court. The country was convulsed at the time by the removal of the deposits from the Bank of the United States, and the debates in Congress were especially interesting. Webster gave Sumner a card admitting him to the floor of the Senate, so that he heard the greatest orators of the country, — Webster, Clay, and Calhoun, for once on the same side. It was a memorable visit, and it would seem that in scenes of such excitement, and under the influence of such men, the political instincts of Sumner must have been aroused. Yet he wrote to his father: "Calhoun has given notice to-day that he will speak to-morrow on Mr. Webster's bank bill. I shall probably hear him, and he will be the last man I shall ever hear speak in Washington. I probably shall never come here again. I have little or no desire ever to come again in any capacity. Nothing that I have seen of politics has made me look upon them with any feeling other than loathing. The more I see of them the more I love law, which I feel will give me an honorable livelihood."

To see what manner of man he then was we may borrow the eyes of a young lady who saw him in Philadelphia, a daughter of Mr. Peters, the reporter : —

"He was then a great, tall, lank creature, quite heedless of the form and fashion of his garb; 'unsophisticated,' everybody said, and oblivious to the propriety of wearing a hat in a city, going about in a rather shabby fur cap; but the fastidiousness of fashionable ladies was utterly routed by the wonderful charm of his conversation, and he was carried about triumphantly and introduced to all the distinguished people, young and old, who then made Philadelphia society so brilliant. No amount of honeying, however, could then affect him. His simplicity, his perfect naturalness, was what struck every one, combined with his rare culture and his

delicious youthful enthusiasm. . . . Every one was
sorry when he left town, and from that time his
name was really a household word with us. There
was a sweetness and tenderness of character about
him, and an entire unworldliness, that won all hearts,
while his delightful culture completed the charm."

A witness of the opposite sex describes him as
"modest and deferential, attracting attention by
his remarkable attainments and manly presence."

After his return, Judge Story offered him the
position of an instructor in the Law School, but he
declined it, and in September, 1834, was admitted
to the bar. For a little more than three years he
practiced law in Boston, forming a partnership in
November, 1834, with George S. Hillard. Professor Greenleaf kept a desk in the rooms, and
Judge Story was a frequent caller, with others
then prominent in literary or legal life. Sumner
was not the man to acquire a large general practice. He lacked the readiness and quick perception essential to success before juries, and he had
not yet shown any great power as a speaker. He
had a number of suits which he conducted with
success, but his arguments were learned essays
rather than that forcible presentation of the case
which is most effective in getting a judgment.
Indeed, his copious learning was rather an incum-
brance in active practice, since he was disposed
to overestimate the value of what had cost him
so much labor, and to rely on quotations rather
than on his own ideas, often better suited to the

immediate occasion. The defect which Doctor
Holmes points out in saying that he had " little
imagination, wit, or sense of humor" was a serious handicap, the outward sign of that great disqualification, the inability to put oneself in another's place. He stood ready to undertake any
work which came, but could not seek business, and
apparently did not attract clients. He did as well,
probably, as most young lawyers, but the reputation which he brought from the school and the
commendations of l is friends led him to expect
more, and he was naturally disappointed.

Yet he was always occupied. The literary work
for which he was fitted sought him constantly.
In January, 1835, he became an instructor in the
Law School, during Judge Story's absence, and
again in 1836--37. He was substantially in charge
of the school at one time, and though he did not
fail as a teacher, he was not brilliantly successful.
In 1835 Judge Story selected him to report his decisions in the Circuit Court, of which he published
three volumes. He assisted Greenleaf in his Maine
Digest, and prepared the index for Story's " Equity
Jurisprudence." He was an editor of the " Jurist,"
and a constant contributor to it, but dealt more
with the literary aspects of the law than with practical questions. He helped Dunlap in revising
for the press his work on " Admiralty Practice,"
and he prepared the forms which are added to
it. He wrote for the " North American Review,"
and delivered some lectures, but they were essays

on legal subjects which gave him no popular re‧
putation.

During these years he did not make any effort
to enter general society, but he enlarged his acquaintance with eminent men and made some lifelong friendships.   His connection with the "Jurist" brought him into correspondence with leading
lawyers all over the country and with foreign
writers on jurisprudence.   He became intimate
with Cornelius C. Felton, afterwards the President
of Harvard University, Henry W. Longfellow,
and Henry R. Cleveland, a company of scholars
who met with Hillard and Sumner almost weekly,
calling their society " The Five of Clubs."   His
circle was not large, but it was of the best, and his
associates were mostly older than he.

Devoted to his work, he showed little interest in
the questions of the day, while his friends were taking part in politics.   He became acquainted with
Dr. William Ellery Channing, and later felt his
influence strongly, but as yet his sense of public
duty was not awakened.   Winthrop and Hillard
went to the legislature, and Phillips, his intimate
friend, had already won reputation as a speaker,
but he was still absorbed in law and literature.
Only two references to slavery are found in his
published letters.   On February 24, 1834, in writing to his parents of his journey from Baltimore
to Washington, he says: " For the first time I
saw slaves, and my worst preconception of their
appearance and ignorance did not fall as low as

their actual stupidity. They appear to be nothing more than moving masses of flesh, unendowed with anything of intelligence above the brutes. I have now an idea of the blight upon that part of our country in which they live."

Nearly two years later, on January 9, 1836, he writes to Lieber, then in Columbia, S. C.: "You are in the midst of slavery. . . . What think you of it? Should it longer exist? Is not emancipation practicable? We are becoming abolitionists at the North fast; the riots, the attempts to abridge the freedom of discussion, Governor McDuffie's message, and the conduct of the South generally have caused many to think favorably of immediate emancipation, who never before inclined to it."

Sumner had subscribed to the "Liberator" in 1835, and had read it since, but these letters show only a languid interest in the question. Nor was it sympathy with the sufferings of slaves, but indignation at the attempts to impair the liberties of white men, which roused him, and began to change the kindly scholar into the insistent and uncompromising foe of slavery.

CHAPTER II

EUROPEAN EXPERIENCE

SUMNER had long felt an overmastering desire to visit Europe, and in 1837 he determined to go, although his friends with few exceptions counseled against the journey, as an interruption of his professional career. His own funds were insufficient, but Judge Story and two other friends lent him what he needed, and with excellent letters of introduction he sailed on December 8, 1837. He was well prepared for his new experiences. He had learned to be nice in his dress, and the impression which he made upon strangers may be gathered from the description of him given by one who met him just before he started. "He appeared with a right royal presence, his countenance characterized by a genuine warmth and great readiness; in a word it was that of a highly bred, well-informed gentleman of a somewhat older school than I was in the way of meeting." He was "handsomely dressed, erect, easy, conscious of his strength." The "shabby fur cap" of a few years before had disappeared with all that it implied.

The years which he spent in Europe enlarged his horizon, added to his knowledge, filled his

memory with a wealth of associations, and made
him a citizen of the world. No other American
had been received so cordially or offered such
opportunities. In a biography intended to present Sumner as a statesman and to show what
influence he exerted upon the government of his
country, there is room only for such a sketch of his
journey as will indicate what it contributed to the
education with which he entered public life. It
was now that he established personal relations with
leading foreigners, and gained an influence which
later was of great value in the conduct of our
foreign affairs.

Landing at Havre, he spent five months in
France, almost entirely in Paris. He was then in
England for ten months, again for four weeks
in Paris, and then made a tour through France to
Italy, where he remained five months; thence to
Germany, where he saw the principal cities, stay-
ing in Vienna, Berlin, and Heidelberg, about a
month in each. He saw the Rhine and the Low
Countries, and in March, 1840, returned to London for about three weeks, after which he sailed
for home. His journey was an unbroken success.
His spectacles were rosy, and Europe was full of
enchantment for him.

In Paris he called at once on his correspondent
Foelix, editor of the " Revue Etrangère," but only
to find his own knowledge of French insufficient
for conversation. Therefore he took lodgings on
the unfashionable side of the Seine, studied with

two teachers, and supplemented their instruction
by attending lectures at the Sorbonne and the
Ecole de Droit, and by visiting the theatres, where
he followed the play with book in hand. In less
than a month he was able to engage in a conversation on American politics and make himself
understood in French. Early in March he took
lodgings near the boulevards, and presented his
letters of introduction. His life in Paris was no
vacation; about the middle of April he wrote to
Greenleaf that he had heard " one hundred and
fifty or two hundred lectures on all branches of
jurisprudence, belles-lettres, and philosophy," that
is to say, "two or three lectures of an hour or
more each " every morning, delivered by the great
scholars and scientific men of France. In the
hospitals he saw the best surgeons of the day at
work; at the theatres and the opera he enjoyed
Grisi, Lablache, Dejazet, Mars; he visited the
museums, the galleries, and the historic places; he
attended the Chambers of Deputies and Peers, and
from a reserved tribune in the former heard a
great debate and saw the statesmen of France.
He made the acquaintance of leading lawyers and
was given especial privileges in the courts. He
studied French procedure in operation, talked with
the judges, learned to know their system of law,
heard arguments by the most eminent advocates,
and watched important trials. He went into society
and met many eminent persons, — Cousin, Demetz,
the Duc de Broglie, Michel Chevalier, Madame

Murat, Pardessus, David.　He saw and had a long conversation with Sismondi.　Nor did he forget to study the people, in the streets and at the fêtes. The knowledge which he thus gained of the French language was of great service during the civil war, when, as chairman of the Senate committee on foreign relations, he wished to talk freely with foreign ministers.

When on May 29, 1838, he left Paris for England, he was not twenty-eight and had as yet no reputation.　Of his attitude towards English society he wrote to Judge Story: " Since I have been here I have followed a rigid rule with regard to my conduct; I have not asked an introduction to any person; nor a single ticket, privilege, or anything of the kind from any one; I have not called upon anybody (with one exception) until I had been first called upon or invited."　None the less he was received everywhere and given a rare opportunity to see everything and know everybody, so that a brief statement of his doings in England becomes almost a catalogue of names and places.

His first interest was in his profession, and there was scarcely an eminent lawyer or judge whom he did not meet.　He went the circuits, was the guest of the bar, attended their dinners and mingled with barristers on terms of close acquaintance, and sat on the bench.　He stayed with Lord Brougham and became familiarly acquainted with him.　He was the guest of Denman, Vaughan, Parke, Alderson, Langdale, Coltman, and other judges, and in his letters to Judge Story and Greenleaf he describes every judge and every prominent lawyer. With the attorney-general, Campbell, with Follett, Talfourd, Rolfe, Wilde, Crowder, Sir Frederick Pollock, Dr. Lushington, Charles Austin, Hayward, Adolphus, and many others he established cordial relations, and his ten months in England gave him a more extended acquaintance with English lawyers than he had with those of his own country.

Of literary men he met Carlyle, Wordsworth, Macaulay, Sydney Smith, Hallam, Parkes, Senior, Grote, Jeffrey, Rogers, Whewell, Landor. Leigh Hunt, Theodore Hook, Thomas Campbell, and others. Among his associates were Monckton Milnes, Robert Ingham, Basil Montagu, John Kenyon. He was the guest of Lord Durham, Inglis, Cornewall Lewis, Hume, and Roebuck among political leaders, and of Lords Fitzwilliam, Lansdowne, Wharncliffe, Leicester, Holland, and Carlisle among the peers. Lord Morpeth, the son of the Earl of Carlisle, became his close friend and a constant correspondent in later years. Miss Martineau, Mrs. Shelley, Mrs. Grote, Mrs. Norton, the Duchess of Sutherland, Joanna Baillie, Mrs. Jameson, and Lady Blessington were among the ladies whose acquaintance he made, and as Mrs. Parkes, the granddaughter of Dr. Priestley, wrote: " It was said, after Mr. Sumner's northern journey, that he made the acquaintance of all the principal Whig families going north and of the Tories on his return. He was wondrously popular, almost like a meteor passing through the country. Young, agreeable, full of information and animation, he enchanted every one; and he bore the ovation well and modestly." He witnessed the coronation of Queen Victoria and heard her first speech from the throne. In Parliament he heard Peel, Sheil, O'Connell, Lord John Russell, Lord Lyndhurst, Lord Brougham, Sir Edward Sugden, and other leaders of the day. He was toasted at various public dinners and replied with success. He even rode to hounds, with an immunity from disaster which is not the least remarkable fact in his foreign experience.

There is abundant testimony from independent sources to Sumner's brilliant success in English society and to the reasons for it. Mr. Abraham Hayward spoke of his "entire absence of pretension," and said: "Sumner's social success at this early period, before his reputation was established, was most remarkable. He was a welcome guest at most of the best houses both in town and country, and the impression he uniformly left was that of an amiable, sensible, high-minded, well-informed gentleman."

Lady Wharncliffe wrote: "I never knew an American who had the degree of social success he had; owing, I think, to the real elevation and worth of his character, his genuine nobleness of thought and aspiration, his kindliness of heart, his absence of dogmatism and oratorical display, his genuine amiability, his cultivation of mind, and his appreciation of England without anything approaching to flattery of ourselves or depreciation of his own country."

These statements of English people show that Sumner must have possessed very unusual attractions for men and women of intelligence, cultivation, and character. He carried good letters, but he presented very few, and letters at best only offer an opportunity. A man is liked or disliked for himself, not for his introductions.

He left England on March 22, 1839, for a month in Paris. Here he showed that his sojourn in England had not affected his love for America. General Cass, the American minister, thought that the American position on the northeastern boundary question should be stated, as it was not understood in Europe, and at his request Sumner prepared for " Galignani's Messenger " an elaborate article, conciliatory in tone, which added to his reputation on both sides of the water.

He next visited Italy, and spent three months in Rome, studying Italian literature, and learning to speak Italian fluently if not with entire correctness. Here first awoke the love of art from which in later years he derived much pleasure, and he became the warm friend of Crawford the sculptor. In Florence he met some Italian men of letters and saw something of Florentine society. He visited Venice and Milan, and entered Germany early in October. He spent a week in Munich, and a

month in Vienna, where Prince Metternich received
him graciously and, contrasting the youth of America with the age of Europe, said: " Mais laissons
nous jouir de notre vieillesse." Thence by Prague,
Dresden, and Leipsic, he came to Berlin, where he
made the acquaintance of Raumer, Ranke, Hum-
boldt, and Savigny, and was well received by the
Crown Prince. During five weeks in Heidelberg
he studied German industriously, learning to understand and to converse "tolerably." He saw
much of Mittermaier and Thibaut, and still ambi-
tious to be a jurist he made the most of his opportunities to meet these great teachers of the law and
the other scholars at Heidelberg. He next made
the trip down the Rhine, saw Cologne, Brussels,
and Antwerp, and returned to London, March 17,
1840. His final fortnight in London was full of
pleasure. In his last letter to Hillard before sailing he wrote : " London is more bewitching than
ever," and breaks off with "I must now go to
breakfast with Sydney Smith: to-morrow with
Rogers: next day with dear Sir Robert Inglis: the
next with Milnes." It is not strange that he was
loath to exchange a life so full of charm for the
work of a lawyer in Boston.

Judge Story, Mr. Greenleaf, and other friends
expressed their doubts and advised his return.
They told him that they wished to have him as
a colleague at the Law School, but he replied that
he needed a larger income than the school could
offer. To Longfellow he wrote on November 10,

1839: "I now begin to think of hard work, of long days filled with uninteresting toil and humble gains. I sometimes have a moment of misgiving when I think of the certainties which I abandoned for travel and of the uncertainties to which I return. But this is momentary, for I am thoroughly content with what I have done. . . . I hope people will not say that I have forgotten my profession and that I cannot live contented at home. Both of these things are untrue. I know my profession better now than when I left Boston, and I can live content at home." But the misgivings of his friends were well founded. Sumner was by nature a student and a scholar, with little aptitude for the life of a practicing lawyer. By perseverance he might have overcome some of his disqualifications, but his journey only widened the breach between him and his office. He had learned to love a fuller and freer life. If his trip did not fit him better for the law, however, it completed his preparation for the part which he was to take in the affairs of his country.

It is strange, however, that he still had no prevision of what awaited him. During his years in Europe the slavery question had become a burning issue. On the day of his departure Wendell Phillips, his intimate friend, delivered the speech in Faneuil Hall which made him famous; yet Sumner's letters do not refer to it and betray no interest in political questions, dealing only with the private life of his friends, and with literary subjects.

He talks with Sismondi of slavery; doubtless he discussed it with Miss Martineau, the Duchess of Sutherland, and others who strongly opposed it; but his own feelings are not expressed, and his own zeal is not aroused.

CHAPTER III

PROFESSIONAL LIFE

On May 3, 1840, Sumner landed in New York, and in September he resumed practice in earnest. He brought out the third volume of Story's Reports and was engaged in several cases, some involving the validity of patents. He was retained with Hillard by the British consul in actions against British officers who had searched American ships suspected of being slavers. He did his best to prove that his professional enthusiasm was not dampened by his foreign experience, but not with entire success. To Lieber he wrote: " My mind, soul, heart, are not improved or invigorated by the practice of my profession ; by overhauling papers, old letters, and sifting accounts in order to see if there be anything on which to plant an action. The sigh will come for a canto of Dante, a rhapsody of Homer, a play of Schiller. But I shall do my *devoir*." Yet he was not less devoted to America by reason of his attachment to his foreign friends, and in reply to a suggestion that, after making a fortune, he might like to settle in England, he wrote: " I never expect to be rich. . . . If I were so, however, I should prefer to live among

my own kindred, near the friends to whom I have
grown and in sight of objects that have become as
dear as they are familiar. Believe me when I say
that I have no hankering after England or English people."

He found the society of Boston very pleasant,
and was welcomed cordially in a circle which included Judge Story, Jeremiah Mason, Washington
Allston, Dr. Channing, Rufus Choate, Prescott,
Bancroft, Longfellow, Felton, Dr. Howe, the Nor-
tons, and others. In short, in 1840–41 he led an
agreeable but not very productive life, enlarging
his acquaintance, and devoting himself to his profession.

When the Harrison campaign of 1840 deeply
stirred the whole community, he did not share the
excitement, and it is not entirely certain how he
voted, though probably for Harrison. His letters
to his brother George just before and just after the
election prove him a very early opponent of the
spoils system, but singularly indifferent to the
issues of the contest. The influence of his father
and Judge Story, both Democrats, and the example
of the conservative men with whom he lived may
have promoted this apathy ; but whatever the cause,
at thirty Sumner was a cultivated and scholarly
gentleman, with slight interest in politics. His
ambition was not active, and the success for which
he hoped was purely professional.

He could not, however, live among men and
not concern himself in their problems. He was

essentially unselfish, and one is struck, in reading his letters between 1841 and the summer of
1845, with the breadth of his sympathies, the
warmth of his feelings, the catholicity of his tastes.
He corresponded constantly with his friends on
both sides of the ocean. He interested himself in
all their projects, lent them cordial assistance,
rejoiced in their success, and was ever ready to
praise them generously. He spoke ill of none, and
showed no trace of jealousy nor of the selfishness,
indolence, or preoccupation which leads men to
neglect the calls of private or public duty. To
help Crawford he raised the money to buy his
Orpheus for the Boston Athenæum, and secured
him many commissions. He brought substantial
aid to Horace Mann in his struggle to improve the
methods of education in Massachusetts. He was
strongly interested in Dr. Howe's work for the
blind. He rejoiced in the success of Longfellow's
poems, of Hillard's oration before the Phi Beta
Kappa society at Cambridge, of Prescott's "Conquest of Mexico," and in his letters he recounts with
sincere delight the praises which they received. Dr.
Howe, who was one of Sumner's warmest friends,
wrote to him: —

"I know not where you may be or what you may
be about; but I know what you are *not* about.
You are not seeking your own pleasure or striving
to advance your own interests; you are, I warrant
me, on some errand of kindness — some work for
a friend or for the public."

It was thus intellectually impossible for Sumner not to be interested in every great question which divided the community, and soon we find in his letters decided views on slavery and the questions arising from anti-slavery agitation. He was drawn into the contest gradually, and only by his sense of public duty.

After the treaty of 1841 between Great Britain, Russia, Austria, and Prussia for the suppression of the slave trade, the slavers often hoisted the American flag to avoid arrest and search. Any vessel belonging to the treaty powers might easily defy their authority if this ruse protected it against search, and England therefore claimed the right to stop and examine suspected vessels. If they were found to be American, no right to interfere with them was asserted. This claim led to a diplomatic discussion, and Sumner supported the English contention in two careful articles. On the same side were Kent, Story, Prescott, and Rufus Choate; but Webster, then secretary of state, took the opposite view, and England tacitly waived her claim.

About this time a number of slaves on the way from Hampton Roads to New Orleans in the brig Creole mutinied, and carried the vessel into Nassau. There by English law the slaves became free, and the British government refused to surrender them. Mr. Webster maintained that, as their freedom was won by mutiny, the British government was bound by the comity of nations to aid the officers of the ship in asserting their authority and not to interfere with the status of persons on board. Dr. Channing in a vigorous pamphlet attacked this position, and Sumner, who assisted in preparing it for the press, was strongly enlisted in support of Dr. Channing, and expressed his views in conversation, in letters, and in the press.

He followed with admiration and sympathy the course of John Quincy Adams in his heroic and persistent struggle for the right of petition. He was as yet only a student, but his study of the questions which constantly arose was rapidly preparing him to act.

When the Boston " Advertiser " took the ground that slavery was a local institution concerning only the inhabitants of the slave States, Sumner replied on January 10, 1843, saying: —

" The opponents of slavery in the free States recognize the right of all States to establish within their own borders such institutions as they please; and they do not seek, either through their own legislatures or through Congress, to touch slavery in the States where it exists. But while they abstain from all *political* action in these States, they do not feel called upon to suppress their sympathy for the suffering slave, nor their detestation of the system which makes him a victim. . . . Slavery is, on several grounds, distinctly within the jurisdiction of the United States, of which the free States are a part. It is a *national* evil, for which to a large extent the *nation* and all its parts are responsible, and which to a large extent the *nation* may remove."

As legitimate subjects of discussion in the free States he named slavery in the District of Columbia, slavery in the territories, the slave trade between our own ports, the rendition of fugitive slaves, the laws of the slave States abridging the rights of colored persons who were citizens of the free States, the conditions to be made on admitting new States, and the amendment of the Constitution.

" It cannot be doubted," he said, " that the Constitution may be amended so that it shall cease to render any sanction to slavery. The power to amend carries with it the previous right to inquire into and discuss the matter to be amended, and this right extends to all parts of the country over which the Constitution is spread, — the North as well as the South."

This is a clear statement of the lines within which Sumner's action against slavery was always confined.

Early in 1844 he undertook to edit Vesey's Reports, in twenty volumes with original notes, agreeing to prepare a volume every two weeks. This was a tremendous undertaking, under which his health broke down. In 1843 and 1844 he suffered from despondency, and after completing four volumes of the Reports, he became seriously ill in June, 1844. In July his friends thought that he was dying of consumption, the disease which had proved fatal to others of his family. At the end of the month, however, he began to recover, and regained his strength so rapidly that in November we find him trying an important patent case against Franklin Dexter, which he won after eleven days of trial and an argument of ten hours. His spirits did not immediately revive with his strength, for we find him in August writing to Dr. Howe: —

"Since my convalescence I have thought much and often whether I have any just feeling of gratitude that my disease was arrested. Let me confess to you that I cannot find it in my bosom. . . . Why was I spared? For me there is no future, either of usefulness or happiness."

His illness doubtless helped to keep him a spectator during the great campaign of 1844. He had no sympathy with the Whigs in their position on the tariff, but he shared the views of men like Adams and Giddings on the slavery question, and regarding this as the important issue he hoped for the election of Clay. Late in 1844 he resumed his work upon Vesey, of which a part had been edited by others during his illness, and completed it in the spring of 1845. With this his career as a lawyer practically closed. He had reached the threshold of his public life.

CHAPTER IV

ENTRANCE INTO PUBLIC LIFE

SUMNER'S opportunity came when he was invited
to deliver the annual oration in Boston on the
Fourth of July, 1845. He accepted the invitation,
and his oration gave him at once a new position
in the community. He stated his subject thus :
" What in our age are the true objects of national
ambition — what is truly national honor, national
glory; what is the true grandeur of nations ? "
The political situation at the time gave the subject
" an urgent interest," for wars with Mexico about
Texas, and with England over the northwestern
boundary were then threatened. "Mexico and
England," he said, " both avow the determination
to vindicate what is called the national honor ;
and our government calmly contemplates the arbit-
rament of war, provided it cannot obtain what is
called an honorable peace." Hence he was brought
to consider the question, " Can there be in our age
any peace that is not honorable, any war that is not
dishonorable ? "

His oration was an argument against war, in
which its horrors, its failure to accomplish its objects, its wickedness, its waste, its absurdity, were

all set forth. A speech in praise of peace would doubtless have passed unchallenged, but Sumner's method excited warm opposition. Seeking to be clear, he spoke to an audience as he thought to himself, without reserve or regard for the feelings of others. He stated the truth as he saw it, never thinking that the truth upon a public question could offend any one. The address was carefully prepared: it was enriched with quotations and illustrations from the history and literature of every nation and every time, and inspired throughout with a lofty purpose and sincere moral enthusiasm. Its statements were true and its arguments sound. It was more rhetorical perhaps than suits the taste of to-day, but its views were in harmony with those of Franklin, whose famous saying, "There never was a good war or a bad peace," has left no stain on his reputation for rare wisdom.

But among Sumner's auditors were officers of the army, navy, and state militia, while the Washington Light Guard, in full uniform, sat directly before him. These gentlemen, conscious of their becoming raiment, were irritated when they heard the orator say: " Peaceful citizens volunteer as soldiers, and affect in dress, arms, and deportment 'the pride, pomp, and circumstance of glorious war;'" and when he spoke of such warriors as men " closely dressed in padded and well-buttoned coats of blue ' besmeared with gold,' surmounted by a huge mountain cap of shaggy bear-skin, with a barbarous device typical of brute force, a tiger painted on oilskin, tied to their backs."

The regular officers felt themselves personally insulted by his questions : " What use is the standing army of the United States ? What use is the navy of the United States ?" Not even the famous passage, which showed that the annual cost of the battleship Ohio would support four institutions like Harvard College, found favor in their ears, and their criticism of the speaker was sharp.

The oration was received on both sides of the ocean with every variety of approval and disapproval, but all agreed that Sumner had shown rare courage, high purpose, and marked eloquence. From that time he was strong in the support of generous youth. He had learned his own power as an orator, until then not suspected ; he had found that there was an audience ready to sympathize with his highest aims, and he stepped at once into the position of a recognized leader.

While he was delivering his address in the Tremont Temple, the convention was assembling in Texas to ratify her annexation to the United States, and to frame her constitution. The great contest which was to end in the civil war was just beginning. " The hour and the man " were both come.

A brief review may recall the political situation. From the adoption of the Missouri Compromise in February, 1821, until January, 1836, slavery excited no serious discussion in Congress. The wise, however, knew that the conflict between freedom and slavery was irrepressible. On May 1. 183\

Andrew Jackson, fresh from crushing nullification, wrote: " The tariff was only the pretext, and dis-union and a Southern Confederacy the real object. The next pretext will be the negro or slavery question." The great political parties ignored the issue, but forces were at work beyond their control. Lundy and Garrison began an agitation which led to the formation of anti-slavery societies. In a convention held at Baltimore in 1826, eighty-one such societies were represented, of which seventy-three were in slaveholding communities. In January, 1831, Garrison began to publish " The Liberator " in Boston. In November the New England Anti-Slavery Society was founded. In 1833 the New York Anti-Slavery Society was formed, and a convention at Philadelphia established the American Anti-Slavery Society. These societies took the ground that slavery was wrong and should at once be abolished ; that the existing States had the exclusive right to legislate within their own limits, but that Congress had and should exercise the power to suppress the slave trade between the States, and to abolish slavery in the District of Columbia and in the territories. A single sentence from the declaration of principles adopted by the American Society summed up their position : —

" We also maintain that there are at the present time the highest obligations resting upon the people of the free States to remove slavery by moral and political action, as prescribed in the Constitution of the United States."

Thus a few private citizens of little influence and small means undertook to grapple with a gigantic evil, supported by the political, social, and business powers of the country. They were individually pure, kindly, law-abiding, actuated only by a lofty patriotism : they saw the wrong clearly and they spoke very plainly. This force operating steadily upon the conscience of the country began to make itself strongly felt about twelve years after the Missouri Compromise.

In August, 1831, occurred the slave insurrection in Virginia led by Nat Turner, in which some sixty-one white persons were killed. It was promptly suppressed, but it left all over the South a sense of insecurity, " a suspicion, " as one Southern speaker said, " that a Nat Turner might be in every family," and that the materials for insurrection " were spread through the land, and were always ready for a like explosion." While, therefore, the methods of the abolitionists were peaceful and lawful, they were none the less irritating to the slaveholders, both because they felt the difficulty of defending slavery on moral grounds, and because they dreaded the effect of agitation upon their slaves.

Many Southern men were opposed to slavery ; but the majority of the people, everywhere, were willing to acquiesce in a system which it seemed impossible to change without a disastrous disturbance of business and political relations. Many thought with Edward Everett that " the great relation of servitude in some form or other, with greater or less departure from the theoretic equality of men, is inseparable from our nature;" that "it is a condition of life as well as any other, to be justified by morality, religion, and international law;" and that it was right "to abstain from a discussion which by exasperating the master can have no other effect than to render more oppressive the condition of the slave; and which if not abandoned there is great reason to fear will prove the rock on which the Union will split." To these men the abolitionists seemed reckless incendiaries, endangering the Union and inviting general calamity without benefit to the slaves.

The abolitionists held meetings and circulated papers attacking slavery. Their meetings were broken up, their houses were sacked, their presses were destroyed, their buildings burned. Garrison was dragged through the streets of Boston, Lovejoy was killed in Illinois, and anti-slavery agitation was met by mob violence in almost every Northern State. These demonstrations were encouraged by the press, and in many cases by respectable citizens, though such violence was an admission that the abolitionists were breaking no law. They were mobbed, because they could not be prosecuted. Southern postmasters took anti-slavery publications from the mails. The Postmaster-General, Amos Kendall, admitted that this was illegal, but declined to condemn his subordinates for their acts, saying: "By no act or direction of mine, official or private, could I be induced knowingly to aid in giving circulation to papers of this description, directly or indirectly."

The anti-slavery men sent petitions to Congress praying for such action against slavery as Congress had power to take, and these led to the struggle over the right of petition, in which John Quincy Adams won a new claim to the gratitude of his countrymen. The Twenty-fourth Congress, on May 26, 1836, after prolonged and bitter contest, adopted the rule, that all petitions, memorials, or papers relating in any way to slavery, be laid on the table without being debated, printed, read, or referred, and that no action be taken thereon. Against this rule Mr. Adams waged unrelenting war until, in the second session of the Twenty-eighth Congress, it was abandoned.

The legislatures of the Southern States called upon the Northern States to pass laws which should make anti-slavery agitation criminal, but such efforts to abridge the rights of citizens fed the flame of abolition, and attempts to enforce the Fugitive Slave Law intensified the popular feeling on both sides. The laws of Southern States, under which free colored men were imprisoned who were employed in vessels visiting their harbors, caused great indignation, which was very much increased when Samuel Hoar, sent by Massachusetts to test the validity of such imprisonment, was expelled from South Carolina. The practical result of the abolition movement from 1830 to 1845 was to create wrath on both sides, to enlist against slavery many excellent men who opposed it because it wronged the slaves, and many others because it endangered the rights of free citizens. The slaveholders, dreading discussion, undertook to prevent it, and hence attacked freedom of speech, the right of petition, the inviolability of private correspondence, and finally the right to a hearing in court. There was no escape from their dilemma. They could not prevent the discussion of slavery without depriving their fellow citizens of constitutional rights. They could not permit it without exposing slavery to the force of public opinion, which must inevitably destroy it.

From the beginning the supporters of slavery saw that they must keep their power in the Senate, where States counted, not voters. Hence they resisted the admission to the Union of any free State, unless at the same time a slave State was added; and Texas, large enough for several States, naturally tempted them. No sooner was its independence proclaimed in 1836 than Mr. Calhoun declared in favor of annexing it. Slavery had been abolished in Mexico in 1829, when Texas was a part of that country; but Texas had been settled largely by emigrants from the Southwestern States, who took their slaves with them, so that slavery existed there when it became independent. The election of President Harrison in 1840 delayed the agitation for annexation, but in 1843 President Tyler's administration was found friendly to the scheme, and the movement began in earnest. Mr. Upshur, the

secretary of state, in August, 1843, wrote to our
diplomatic representative in Texas that "few
calamities could befall this country more to be
deplored than the abolition of slavery in Texas;"
and three months later he said: "We regard annexation as involving the security of the South."
Mr. Calhoun succeeded Mr. Upshur in March,
1844, and on April 12 he concluded a treaty of
annexation, which was defeated in June, after a
discussion which aroused great public excitement.
The election of 1844 resulted in the choice of Mr.
Polk, upon a platform which favored annexation
at the earliest possible moment. President Tyler
in his annual message urged immediate action, and
at the next session of Congress a joint resolution
annexing Texas was passed, receiving the President's approval on March 2, 1845. Every friend
of slavery regarded the result as a great victory;
every friend of freedom was cast down. The
Whig party as a whole had opposed the measure,
while the Democrats supported it.

It was in the autumn of 1845, after the annexation of Texas and before the struggle over her
admission as a State, that Charles Sumner entered
the arena. The friends of slavery had succeeded
in moving him, when the abolitionists had failed.
His attitude was described by himself a few years
later: —

"I have ever entertained a strong attachment
for the Constitution and the Union. I am a Con-
stitutionalist and a Unionist, but have felt it to

be our duty at the North, according to the words
of Franklin, to step to the 'very verge of the Constitution in discouraging every species of traffic in
our fellow men.' . . . In the autumn of 1845,
when the question arose of the annexation of
Texas with a slaveholding constitution, I spoke at
a meeting called in Faneuil Hall to oppose it.
This was the first political meeting in which I had
ever taken any part; nor had I ever before sought
to express in public my opposition to slavery. In
short, there had never before been any occasion in
which I was disposed to participate. I had no
relish for the strife, nor did I coincide in views
with those who conducted the anti-slavery movement."

The autumn of 1845 was a critical time. As
the free States had a majority in the House, many
Whig leaders felt that the admission of Texas as a
slave State could be prevented. Early in that year
the Massachusetts legislature had denied the law-
fulness of the annexation, and had declared the
opposition of the State to the extension of slavery.
The most conservative classes supported this position. Up to this time the Whigs of Massachusetts
had been substantially united. When, however, the
resolution of annexation had passed, differences at
once appeared. The Whig leaders desired to take
up other questions, as was indicated by Mr. Winthrop's toast on the Fourth of July, " Our Country, however bounded : " but the younger members
of the party, led by Charles Francis Adams, John

G. Palfrey, Henry Wilson, E. R. Hoar, R. H. Dana, Jr., and others were determined to oppose the admission of Texas with a slave constitution. Sumner was made a member of a state committee appointed to organize the opposition. In the work of this committee, he took an active part, and drew the resolutions presented at a meeting in Faneuil Hall, on November 4, 1845. These resolutions, which were his first contribution to the anti-slavery contest, are characteristic. His whole argument, unchanged thereafter during his life, rested on his first proposition: that "the Government and Independence of the United States are founded on the adamantine truth of *Equal Rights and the Brotherhood of All Men*, declared on the 4th of July, 1776, a truth receiving new and constant recognition in the progress of time, and which is the great lesson from our country to the world."

Among the other recitals appear in immediate sequence the following : " *And whereas* the slaveholders seek annexation for the purpose of increasing the market of human flesh and for extending and perpetuating slavery; —

" *And whereas* by the triumph of this scheme, and by creating new slave States within the limits of Texas, the slaveholders seek to control the political power of the majority of freemen represented in the Congress of the Union."

The first statement presents the view and uses the language of the abolitionists, the second the argument which appealed to the Whigs as a po-

litical party.   The resolutions were a vigorous protest against annexation on every moral and political ground, and Sumner supported them in a
temperate speech, important only as being the first
public statement of his opposition to slavery.

The movement failed of its immediate object,
for in the December following Texas was admitted as a slave State.   But its political consequences were far-reaching, for it divided the
Whigs of Massachusetts into two parties, sometimes called the " Conscience Whigs " and the
" Cotton Whigs," and the breach constantly
widened until the birth of the Republican party.
Sumner appreciated the situation fully.   In November, 1845, he wrote: " The spirit of anti-
slavery promises soon to absorb all New England.
Massachusetts will never give her vote for another
slaveholder.   The cotton lords will interfere, but
they will at last be borne away by the rising tide."

Events moved rapidly, and annexation was
speedily followed by the Mexican war.   General
Taylor's advance into Mexican territory led to a
slight skirmish; whereupon the President sent a
message to Congress saying that " war exists, and,
notwithstanding all our efforts to avoid it, exists by
the act of Mexico herself," and asking for money.
An appropriation bill, reciting that " by the act of
the Republic of Mexico a state of war exists between that government and the United States,"
was passed, with only fourteen dissenting votes in
the House and two in the Senate.   John Davis of

Massachusetts voted against it in the Senate, and in the House, J. Q. Adams, with all the other Massachusetts members present except two, of whom one was Robert C. Winthrop.

The Whigs who voted for the bill were condemned by many leaders of the party, and nowhere more strongly than in Massachusetts. Winthrop, whose inherited position and natural abilities had early given him prominence, was especially criticised and his action was contrasted with that of Adams. This feeling was first expressed publicly in an editorial written by Charles Francis Adams in the " Daily Whig." The " Advertiser," the recognized champion of the Whig organization, replied, and then at the request of friends Sumner took part in the discussion, but with reluctance, for his relations with Winthrop had been pleasant, and he did not enjoy personal criticism. He felt strongly, however, and once enlisted he wrote as he felt. He expressed for Winthrop the " personal regard, justly due to his accomplishments and his many virtues," but condemned his vote and questioned his motives, saying : " I cannot doubt the integrity of his character ; but I fear that some thoughts little worthy of a Christian statesman have intruded upon his mind. I fear that he was unwilling to be found alone in the company of truth ; or that he would not follow truth in the company of those few men who bore the stain of anti-slavery ; or that the recollection of the unpopularity of those who opposed the late war with England frightened him from his propriety."

The "Advertiser" retorted, and Sumner in the "Courier" repeated his condemnation. These articles were not signed, but Sumner wrote to Winthrop avowing his authorship, and expressing his hope that differences on a public question would not affect their private relations. Winthrop replied that Sumner had done him injustice, and apparently had intended to be personally offensive; adding that he regretted the disturbance of their relations, and hoped that changed circumstances might reëstablish them.

Sumner's reply was so characteristic that a few words may be quoted : " In the great public questions, on which we are for the moment separated, I had hoped, perhaps ignorantly and illusively, that an honest, conscientious, and earnest discussion, such as the magnitude of the occasion seemed to require, might be conducted without the suggestion of personal unkindness on either side. . . . But the act with which your name has been so unhappily connected is public property. Especially is it the property of your constituents, whose conscience you represented. I do feel, my dear sir, that holding the sentiments on this subject which I do, and which seem to be general in our community, it was a duty to direct them distinctly, unequivocally, and publicly against the act."

After this note was written, and before Winthrop replied, Sumner published a third article, in which

he said that Winthrop's vote had " given his sanction to one of the most important acts, as it is
unquestionably the most wicked act, in our history," and after describing the terrible concomi-
tants and consequences of war, proceeded: " All
this misery has the sanction of your vote, Mr.
Winthrop. Every soldier is nerved partly by you.
. . . Surely this is no common act. It cannot
be forgotten on earth ; it must be remembered in
heaven. Blood! blood! is on the hands of the representative from Boston. Not all great Neptune's
ocean can wash them clean."

It is not surprising that Winthrop, in reply,
charged Sumner with not only criticising his acts,
but attacking his motives, and with proceeding
" upon the offensive assumption that under some influence of ambition or moral cowardice " he had
" knowingly and deliberately committed an unworthy and wicked act." He declined further
personal relations with one who had questioned his
integrity, adding, " My hand is not at the service of any one who has denounced it with such
ferocity as being stained with blood." With this
letter the correspondence ended, and for twenty
years they never spoke to each other. Sumner
continued his strictures, and the discussion widened
the breach in the Whig party.

Space is given to this incident only for the
light which it throws upon Sumner's character
and methods. It is impossible not to share Winthrop's feeling, that Sumner's language was incon-

sistent with the continuance of their personal relations. With many men, the desire to retain such relations in private, while making such attacks in public, would imply insincerity. But Sumner really thought that such language might properly be used where men of equal integrity differed on a public question; that he could discuss whether his opponent was governed by expediency or coward-ice, and that his opponent would regard it as an impersonal question of general human interest. This inability to realize his adversary's feelings led him often to use strong expressions appro-priate to the action attacked, and as often to be surprised that his words were considered offensive. His nature was affectionate and kindly, and he was absolutely sincere, but he lacked the sense of humor, and this perhaps explains why he so innocently gave such bitter offense. Living the life of a student, and much alone, he occupied in thought the historical standpoint; he applied to current events and contemporary men the historical treat-ment, and what he thought in his closet he said openly, unconscious apparently that no living man wished to anticipate the adverse verdict of history. The controversy with Winthrop changed his personal relations with many whose friendship he had valued, but who sympathized with his adver-sary. Many such ruptures ensued, especially hard for Sumner to bear, both because as a bachelor he stood more in need of friends, and because he enjoyed his social relations. But keenly as he felt the coldness of former friends, it never affected his public action.

Sumner's next noteworthy speech was delivered before the Phi Beta Kappa Society, at Cambridge, on August 27, 1846, just after his last letter from Mr. Winthrop. In this he "took advantage of the occasion to express himself freely, especially on the two great questions of slavery and war," but his address was in form a tribute to John Pickering, Judge Story, Washington Allston, and William Ellery Channing, four members of the society who had lately died. He sheltered himself behind these names in the hope of saying what he thought without offending his hearers; and his success was triumphant. Emerson wrote in his journal: "At Phi Beta Kappa, Sumner's oration was marked with a certain magnificence which I do not well know where to parallel;" and Everett said: "It was an amazingly splendid affair. I never heard it surpassed; I don't know that I ever heard it equaled."

In September, 1846, for the first time he went to a caucus, and on the 23d attended as a delegate the Whig state convention. It was his first appearance as a member of a political organization. The convention was controlled by those who wished to unite the party on economic and other issues of general policy. The anti-slavery Whigs were determined to array it against slavery. The managers had arranged that Winthrop should address the convention, but loud calls from the floor brought

up Sumner, and in a powerful speech he contended
that it was "the duty of Whigs, professing the
principles of the fathers, to express themselves
openly, distinctly, and solemnly against slavery —
not only against its further extension, but against
its longer continuance under the Constitution and
laws of the Union." He added, "While it is
their duty to enter upon this holy warfare it should
be their aim to temper it with moderation, with
gentleness, with tenderness towards slaveholders.
These should be won if possible, rather than
driven, to the duties of emancipation. But emancipation should always be presented as the car-
dinal object of our national policy." Winthrop,
in reply, emphasized the questions upon which
the Whigs were united, the tariff, care of the public money, internal improvements; and the two
speeches brought the views of the two factions
into sharp contrast. The resolutions were then
presented, and the anti-slavery Whigs offered an
amendment expressing the views of Sumner, which
was defeated after a heated debate.

Sumner's speech gave him a new position. It
was a time when anti-slavery utterances were
rare, and his temperate but unequivocal declaration of principles came with the ring of sincerity from one who thought only of his cause and
not of his own fortunes. It appealed to a rapidly
growing party who were tired of compromise and
anxious to attack slavery vigorously, and it won
for Sumner many friends among the young. The

effect of the debate may be read in Whittier's poem, " The Pine Tree," written immediately after reading it.

Winthrop was a candidate for reëlection in the autumn of 1846, and on October 25 Sumner, in an open letter, arraigned him with increased severity for his vote on the Mexican war bill. Those Whigs, who were dissatisfied with Winthrop, decided to nominate a candidate against him, and their convention, in which Charles Francis Adams presided, and John A. Andrew was chairman of the committee on nominations and resolutions, selected Sumner. The suggestion, however, having been made that his attacks on Winthrop had been prompted by a desire to succeed him, Sumner felt that he could give no color to this suspicion and declined the nomination, saying : " I have never on any occasion sought or desired public office of any kind. I do not now. My tastes are alien to official life." Dr. S. G. Howe was then nominated, but Winthrop was elected by a large majority. Sumner took a prominent part in the campaign and made a speech justifying the opposition to the Mexican war. This must interest all, who believe that a patriot is not always bound to support the government of his country in war, for it quotes from speeches of Chatham, Burke, Fox, and Englishmen like these during the American Revolution, in which the true duty of a patriot is defined by men whose sincere patriotism has never been doubted.

Thus in a single year, from a private citizen little interested in politics, Sumner had become an anti-slavery leader in Massachusetts. He could not be half-hearted, and already in January, 1847, friends were counseling moderation. He continued to practice law, but his heart was in the contest for freedom. During 1847 he wrote in the newspapers against the war and against slavery. On February 4, in Faneuil Hall, he urged the immediate withdrawal of our troops from Mexico. A fortnight later he delivered a lecture on " White Slavery in the Barbary States," in which, while painting the horrors of white slavery, he made it clear that it was not the color of the victim which made slavery abominable, and answered the familiar pro-slavery arguments by showing that when used by Algerines their fallacy was evident. He dealt solely with the slavery of whites, only alluding to the fact that the Algerines still had many black slaves enduring the same hardships. It was an adroit and very effective object lesson.

The year 1847 was important politically as the year preceding a presidential election. The Mexican war was in successful progress and its opponents were strongly aroused. Sumner had prepared some resolutions against it in the spring, though his authorship was unknown, and these with slight amendments had been adopted by the legislature. He offered substantially the same resolutions at a Whig meeting in Boston. They declared the war unconstitutional, unjust, and detestable, opposed further expenditure for it, called for the withdrawal of our troops, and opposed the annexation of any territory either by conquest or indirectly as indemnity. Sumner and C. F. Adams supported them, but they were laid on the table. Sumner, however, was placed at the head of the delegation, numbering more than one hundred members, which was sent by the meeting to the state convention.

On September 29, when the convention met Daniel Webster was present, a candidate for the next presidential nomination and seeking the indorsement of his own State. In a speech to the convention, he took ground against the extension of slavery, but was evidently averse to affirmative anti-slavery action. The resolutions declared the unalterable opposition of Massachusetts to any acquisition of territory unless on condition that slavery should be prohibited therein; but the anti-slavery forces were not satisfied, and John G. Palfrey, a member of Congress, offered a resolution, prepared in conference with Sumner and others, " that the Whigs of Massachusetts will support no men for the office of president and vice-president but such as are known by their acts or declared opinions to be opposed to the extension of slavery." This was done, as Sumner subsequently stated, " in the hope of making opposition to the extension of slavery a political test at the next presidential election." Adams and Sumner supported Palfrey, and Winthrop opposed because the resolution would divide the party and elect a Democratic president. The convention followed Winthrop, but the purpose of the minority was not affected. Palfrey's resolution contained the principle upon which a new party was soon to be founded, and in his speech Sumner said : " Be assured, sir, whatever the final determination of this convention, there are many here to-day who will never yield support to any candidate for presidency or vice-presidency who is not known to be against the extension of slavery, even though he have received the sacramental unction of a ' regular nomination.' We cannot say, with detestable morality, ' Our party, *right* or *wrong*.' The time has gone by when gentlemen can expect to introduce among us the discipline of a camp.   Loyalty to principle is higher than loyalty to party." This contest ended the struggle within the Whig party. The time was ripe for independent action.

When Congress met in December Winthrop was the Whig candidate for Speaker, and was elected, though Giddings, Palfrey, and Tuck, anti-slavery Whigs, refused to support him. Palfrey was attacked sharply in Massachusetts for voting against Winthrop and also for voting against removing the postmaster of the House, who was a Democrat, and Sumner warmly defended both votes, stating the true principle of civil service reform most concisely.

" It is proper that with a change of policy, as indicated by a change of parties, the important functionaries, who may impress their peculiar opinions upon the country, should be changed. But it is not just or proper that the humbler office-holders, who cannot in any way influence those matters on which parties hinge, should be driven with every political change from the duties to which they have just become accustomed, and in this way, perhaps, be deprived of their daily bread."

Early in 1848 the Mexican war was ended by the treaty of Guadeloupe Hidalgo, which ceded to the United States New Mexico and Upper California in return for a payment of fifteen million dollars. Should this new area be free or slave soil? This question had been raised early in the war. The President in his message of August 8, 1846, asking for an additional appropriation, indicated that the war would result in a change of boundaries, and when the appropriation bill came before the House David Wilmot, a Democrat, offered as an amendment the famous " Wilmot Proviso," prohibiting slavery forever in any territory acquired from Mexico. This gave rise to a contest between the House and the Senate which lasted through two sessions of Congress. The result left the question undecided, and when the new territory, nearly as large as the thirteen original States, became ours, the presidential campaign of 1848 had begun. The territory came to us free. Should it remain so? This was the most important question before the country. Whigs and Democrats alike recognized that a decided position would alienate some of their followers, for there was serious disaffection in both parties.

The Democratic convention nominated Lewis Cass, who had declared against the Wilmot Proviso, on a platform which did not deal with the question, but denied the power of Congress to interfere with or control the domestic institutions of the States. The Whig convention was even more diplomatic. It nominated General Taylor, at once a successful general and a Southern slaveholder, and adjourned without adopting any platform, — silent on the great question of the day. A resolution in favor of the Wilmot Proviso was voted down. Taylor was put forward as " the people's candidate," " without regard to party limits or party questions," and he claimed " the right to look to the Constitution and the high interests of " the country " and not to the principles of a party " for his " rules of action." The Whig party thus sought to evade the real issue and to achieve party success by ignoring principles. Clay and Webster, themselves candidates, felt the ignominy of the situation and did not disguise their feelings. Lowell in the " Biglow Papers " stated Taylor's position thus : —

> " Ez to my princerples, I glory
>   In hevin' nothin' o' the sort ;
> I aint a Wig, I aint a Tory,
>   I 'm jest a canderdate, in short."

To the conscientious opponents of slavery this surrender by the Whig party was the signal for immediate revolt, announced by Charles Allen and Henry Wilson in the convention itself.

In Massachusetts the result had been anticipated. A conference of representative anti-slavery Whigs held in May decided that if the party nominated Taylor or any candidate whose opposition to the extension of slavery was not assured, they would oppose the nominees and call a state convention. A call was issued so soon as the result was known, and on the list of signers Charles Francis Adams was first and Sumner second. The convention, at Worcester, was attended by five thousand people. Sumner was very active in all the preliminary steps, and his speech at the convention was eloquent and inspiring.

"In the coming contest," he said, "I wish it understood that I belong to the party of freedom, — to that party which plants itself on the Declaration of Independence and the Constitution of the United States. I hear the old political saw, that 'we must take the least of two evils.' . . . For myself, if two evils are presented to me I will take neither. . . . There are matters legitimately within the range of expediency and compromise. . . . But the question before the country is of another character. This will not admit of compromise. It is not within the domain of expediency. *To be wrong on this is to be wholly wrong.* . . . But it is said that we shall throw away our votes and that our opposition will fail. Fail, sir! No honest, earnest effort in a good cause can fail. It may not be crowned with the applause of men ; it may not seem to touch the goal of immediate worldly success, which is the end and aim of so much in life. But it is not lost. . . . Fail! . . . Did the three hundred Spartans fail when in the narrow pass they did not fear to brave the innumerable Persian hosts, whose very arrows darkened the sun? Overborne by numbers, crushed to earth, they left an example greater far than any victory, and this is the least we can do. Our example will be the mainspring of triumph hereafter. It will not be the first time in history that the hosts of slavery have out-numbered the champions of freedom. But where is it written that slavery finally prevailed?"

These words, uttered at the outset of Sumner's political career, state the rule of his life. They express the feelings, too, of those who led the greatest independent movement in our history, and give their reply to the argument by which all such movements are discouraged.

Sumner threw himself into the contest with enthusiasm. At Buffalo, on August 9, a national convention nominated Martin Van Buren and Charles Francis Adams. Sumner, though not a delegate, was present and prominent in the councils. He presided at a ratification meeting in Faneuil Hall, where he said that " a new party " had been formed whose leading principle was opposition to the extension of slavery and to its longer continuance wherever the national government was

responsible for it, thus early stating the position
soon to be taken by the Republican party.

In the following campaign he was very active.
He headed the list of delegates from Boston to the
state convention of the Free-Soil party, and was
made the chairman of the state campaign committee.   During the campaign he spoke all over
Massachusetts, and his speeches added greatly to
his reputation.   Sometimes he spoke for three hours
at a time without wearying his hearers, if we may
judge from contemporary testimony, and such attention is the best proof of eloquence.

The Free-Soilers nominated him for Congress
against Winthrop, and in accepting the nomination
he said : " It has been my desire and determination
to labor in such fields of usefulness as are open to
every private citizen, without the honor, emolu-
ment, or constraint of office.   I would show by
example (might I so aspire !) that something may
be done for the welfare of our race without the support of public station or the accident of popular
favor."   Defeat was certain, but he felt bound to
lead the forlorn hope, and his letter may well be
commended to all who doubt the wisdom of independent action or feel uncertain as to the duty of
a private citizen.

After his nomination and before his acceptance
Longfellow wrote in his diary : —

" Sumner stands now, as he himself feels, at just
the most critical point of his life.   Shall he plunge
irrevocably into politics, or not ?   That is the ques-

tion, and it is already answered. He inevitably will do so, and after many defeats will be very distinguished as a leader. . . . From politics as a career he still shrinks back. When he has once burned his ships, there will be no retreat. He already holds in his hands the lighted torch."

He was defeated, but the campaign gave him wide influence and national reputation. He had met or corresponded with Free-Soilers in other States, and was recognized as the most eloquent among the leaders in Massachusetts, while he had acquired a strong hold upon men in every part of that State. But the loss of friends continued, and while some thought of Sumner charitably, others shared the views of a former friend who wrote : " You and I never can meet on neutral ground. I can contemplate you only in the character of a defamer of those you profess to love, and an enemy to the permanency of the Union."

The year 1848 was a year of hope. All over the civilized world men believed that the old heaven and the old earth were passing away. It was a period of moral and political enthusiasm, and no one sympathized with the feeling of the hour more keenly than did Sumner. He hailed the revolution in France and the similar outbreaks in other countries as parts of a great movement for freedom, of which the anti-slavery agitation in America was another part. He anticipated its speedy triumph, but as we look around us his millennium still seems remote. Such hopes as his belong to youth. The old are apt

to question whether man does improve, and whether
history will not repeat itself indefinitely.

The year 1849 was quiet, politically. The Free-
Soil party kept its organization, and Sumner called
its annual convention to order with a brief speech,
adapting the splendid " *Ubi libertas ibi patria* "
by saying, " Where liberty is, there is my party."
As chairman of a committee he prepared an address
to the people of Massachusetts in which the party
was " explained and vindicated," and which put the
Free-Soil argument with a power and directness
well fitted to arouse public opinion. Sumner had
laid aside the florid diction of his early orations, and
spoke with unfaltering conviction in deadly earnest.
He said of his cause : " It can no longer be avoided
or silenced. To every man in the land it now says
with clear, penetrating voice, ' Are you for freedom,
or are you for slavery ? ' and every man in the land
must answer this question when he votes."

The Free-Soil position was stated thus : " Wherever we are responsible for slavery, we oppose it.
Our opposition is coextensive with our responsibility. In the States slavery is sustained by local
law. . . . We are not responsible for it there. . . .
But slavery everywhere under the Constitution of
the United States, everywhere under the exclusive jurisdiction of the national government, everywhere under the national flag, is at our own par-
ticular doors. . . . Nor will this responsibility cease
so long as slavery continues to exist in the District
of Columbia, in any territories of the United States,

or anywhere on the high seas, beneath the protecting flag of the Republic."

The campaign of 1849, though involving only state and local offices, cemented the Free-Soil organization, and kept the national issue clearly before the people. The direct appeal to the New England conscience developed anti-slavery feeling, with the important result that the Free-Soilers and Democrats began to combine and thus elected many members of the state legislature. Sumner fostered this inevitable union as a step in the formation of the new party. It was by skillfully using the balance of power that the Free-Soilers accomplished results. With the Whigs they sent John P. Hale to the Senate from New Hampshire, and with the Democrats they chose Salmon P. Chase senator from Ohio. These signal victories presaged that breaking down of party lines which made the Republican party possible.

During the years after his Fourth of July oration Sumner often lectured in various towns throughout New England. The lyceum was then in its glory, with its opportunities for educating public opinion. In May, 1849, he spoke before the American Peace Society on the " War System of the Commonwealth of Nations," his last studied argument against war. In the same year he argued strongly before the Supreme Court of Massachusetts, that under the state constitution no discrimination on account of race or color could be made between children entitled to the benefit of

the common schools.   The court held otherwise, but
the discrimination was removed by statute a few
years later. His professional practice does not
seem to have grown during the years from 1845 to
1849.   He was learning to realize his true voca-
tion, and in obedience to the strong impulses of
his nature was changing from a lawyer into a
political reformer. Gradually, half unconsciously
and at first with great reluctance, he was recognizing his real work in life.

CHAPTER V

THE friends of slavery had hoped to extend the area of slave territory by the annexation of Texas, but they were doomed to bitter disappointment. Gold was discovered in California early in 1848, and an enormous immigration followed. Among the newcomers were many from the free States who had no love for slavery, and many from the slave States who, expecting to enrich themselves by their own toil, had no wish to compete with slave labor. There came also such throngs of lawless adventurers that a strong government became necessary, and thus California was occupied by a large anti-slavery population demanding stable government.

When, after the election of General Taylor, the second session of the Thirtieth Congress met in December, 1848, President Polk's message stated that California and New Mexico were still subject to the provisional governments created during the war, but that the condition of affairs was such as to require the immediate establishment of permanent governments. Thus the question, which the Whig party had endeavored to evade, confronted its representatives as soon as the victory was won.

The President suggested that the line of the Missouri Compromise should be extended to the Pacific, to which there should be no serious objection, since the climate and soil of these regions were such that slavery could not exist there. This argument, afterwards so often reiterated, assumed that slaves could be used only in a climate like that of the Southern States, and in such agricultural labor as they performed there. This was a pure assumption and was not accepted by either side.

Douglas offered bills admitting California as a State and organizing Minnesota, Nebraska, and New Mexico as territories. The bill admitting California said nothing about slavery, but left the inhabitants to deal with it as they chose, and they seemed distinctly opposed to it. Shortly after the session began Mr. Benton presented to the Senate a petition from the people of New Mexico assembled in convention, asking for the establishment of a civil government, and saying: "We do not desire to have domestic slavery within our borders; and until the time shall arrive for our admission into the Union as a State, we desire to be protected by Congress against their introduction among us."

The proposition of Douglas did not satisfy the Southern slaveholders, who wished to carry their slaves into the newly acquired territory for which they had fought the war, and were not willing to be deprived of this right by the action of the local population; nor did it please the anti-slavery men, who had insisted upon the power and duty of Congress to exclude slavery from this territory whatever the wishes of the local population, and were not likely to recede at the moment when such a population begged to be protected against slavery. The anti-slavery men were determined and aggressive. Though the House refused Palfrey permission to introduce a bill abolishing all laws concerning slavery and the slave trade in the District of Columbia, a motion made by Gott of New York instructing the committee on the District of Columbia to bring in a bill forbidding slavery in the District was passed by a majority of ten votes, though it was afterwards reconsidered, and the committee on territories was instructed to bring in bills organizing California and New Mexico as territories, with provisions prohibiting slavery.

Nor were the friends of slavery idle. In the hope of uniting the South against the North, Calhoun prepared an address which was signed by forty members of Congress and which indicated the questions on which battle was shortly to be joined. It was an attack on the North for its aggressions on the South, asserting that the North had systematically disregarded its obligation to return fugitive slaves, insisting that slaveholders had a constitutional right to carry their slaves into the territories, which Congress had denied, and stating the position of the slavery party in these words : " We hold that the federal government has no right to extend or restrict slavery, no more than to establish or abolish it ; nor has it any right to distinguish between the domestic institutions of one State or section and another, in order to favor the one or discourage the other." This address pointed out the danger that slavery would be abolished by constitutional amendment, and that thus the owners of slaves would be driven from the country. Therefore it urged a union of Southerners to protect themselves and their property.

Calhoun's attempt was defeated by Southern opposition. Indeed, for the moment slavery was losing ground, even in its own territory. A convention in Kentucky, composed of delegates from twenty-four counties, pronounced it "injurious to the prosperity of the Commonwealth, inconsistent with the fundamental principles of free government, contrary to the natural right of mankind, and adverse to a pure state of morals," and declared " that it ought not to be increased, and that it ought not to be perpetuated in the Commonwealth." A Richmond newspaper announced that " two thirds of the people of Virginia are open and undisguised advocates of ridding the State of slavery." The like feeling was gaining ground in Missouri and other border States, and making a lodgment even further South. A strong pro-slavery man wrote : " Maryland, Virginia, North Carolina, Tennessee, Kentucky, and Missouri are pervaded with a feeling of hostility to the institution." Such were the conditions just before the struggle of 1850.

The last session of the Thirtieth Congress left

the territorial question untouched. President Taylor, who entered office without a policy, undertook in the absence of Congress to deal with California as its people wished, — a course which seemed natural to a man of simple and direct character, unfamiliar with politics. He suggested to the people that they organize their own government, adopt a constitution, and then seek admission as a State. A convention was called by the military governor, a constitution prohibiting slavery was adopted, the people accepted it and chose officers, the legislature met on December 15, and a few days later the state government was turned over to the officers thus elected. The result was entirely satisfactory to Taylor, and he wished to proceed in the same way with New Mexico.

The Thirty-first Congress met on December 3, and after a long contest Howell Cobb was chosen Speaker of the House. The President's message at once introduced the unsettled question by stating that California and probably New Mexico would shortly apply for admission to the Union. The action of California had increased the difficulty of the situation for the South, and slavery was clearly losing ground. On December 31 the anti-slavery leaders renewed the motion passed by the House at the last session, which instructed the committee on territories to bring in bills organizing California and New Mexico with slavery prohibited. On the other side Mason introduced a new fugitive slave law, while Benton brought in a bill fixing the boundaries of Texas and authorizing the payment of a considerable sum to that State for the release of her claims outside these limits. The Southern leaders began to threaten loudly that the passage of the anti-slavery measures would make secession inevitable. The student of history will find much that is instructive in their violent language, for their threats were not mere idle bluster. The great mass of the Southern people indeed was not affected, but the purpose of the leaders was genuine, and the experience of the country in 1861 and on other occasions has shown how easy it is for a body of determined men, controlling a political organization and aided by the press, to carry the people into a movement which they do not favor. A disorganized majority in such a case is like a mob against a regiment.

It is not surprising that the cry of disunion produced an effect on men in every walk of life, and that a strong sentiment was created in favor of some compromise. Under these circumstances, on January 29, 1850, Henry Clay brought forward his famous proposition of compromise, embodied in eight resolutions, which proposed to admit California without reference to slavery; to establish territorial governments in the other territory taken from Mexico, without permitting or excluding slavery; to fix the western boundary of Texas on the Rio Grande; to pay a certain amount of her debt for the relinquishment of her claims beyond that boundary; to declare inexpedient the abolition of slavery in the District of Columbia; to forbid the importation of slaves into the District to be sold there or carried to other markets; to pass a more stringent fugitive slave law, and to declare that Congress had no power to prohibit the slave trade between States. This meant the abandonment of the Wilmot Proviso, to which the legislatures of all the free States save Iowa stood committed; it intrenched slavery in the District of Columbia; sanctioned the interstate slave trade; enabled the owner to recover fugitive slaves more easily; left a large territory, then free, open to the attacks of slavery; and in return only recognized the fact that the population of California had made it a free State. The new Fugitive Slave Law empowered a commissioner of the United States, without a jury, to deliver a man into slavery upon the evidence of two witnesses that a slave had escaped, and an affidavit of identity, which was required to contain "a general description of the person so escaping with such convenient certainty as may be." The alleged slave was not allowed to testify, and thus a man could be deprived of his liberty upon evidence which would not have been admitted, and by a procedure which would not have been legal, if he had been charged with the slightest misdemeanor. The bill contained other severe provisions. It is unnecessary to repeat the history of the struggle in Congress. The measures, at first defeated as a whole, were afterward passed separately, and substantially as Clay proposed them.

Thus the South won a victory more fatal to its cause than defeat could have been.

The most important feature of the struggle, so far as it affected Sumner, was the course of Webster. In his famous speech of March 7, 1850, avowedly for " the preservation of the Union," Webster supported the compromise, declaring that he would not vote to exclude slavery from California and New Mexico because it was already excluded by nature, and he would not " reënact the will of God." He sustained the new Fugitive Slave Law " with all its provisions to its fullest extent." He condemned the opponents of the law and all agitators against slavery with unsparing violence, and instead of standing as the representative of freedom he became in the eyes of many the apologist of slavery. The speech alienated members who had looked to him for guidance, and caused the deepest sorrow and indignation among antislavery men. It was a powerful influence in breaking up the Whig party, and it opened the door of the Senate to Sumner.

President Taylor opposed the compromise, firmly believing that California should be admitted at once with the constitution adopted by her citizens, and that New Mexico should be allowed to follow. An open rupture between him and leading Southern Whigs was imminent, when his sudden death, on July 9, 1850, made Millard Fillmore president. Fillmore appointed Webster secretary of state, and from that time the whole power of the administration was used in favor of the compromise. Winthrop was appointed senator in Webster's place, and this created a vacancy in the House, for which Samuel A. Eliot was nominated by the Whigs and Sumner by the Free-Soilers. Webster's great influence held the social and commercial powers of Boston to their party allegiance, and Eliot was elected in time to vote for the compromise measures.

The Free-Soilers of Massachusetts threw their whole influence against the compromise from the outset, and Sumner took a prominent part in the movement. On February 27 in Faneuil Hall they passed resolutions, drawn by a committee of which he was a member, insisting that Congress must prohibit slavery in the territories without concession. They tried hard to make the legislature declare against the compromise, but the Whigs, who were in control, stood by Webster. Sumner's feeling is apparent in his correspondence. In February he wrote to his brother: "The bluster of the South is, I think, subsiding, though as usual the North is frightened and promises to give way. I hope to God they will stand firm. There is a small body at Washington who will not yield, — the Free-Soilers." After Webster's speech: "Webster has placed himself in the dark list of apostates." In May: "I am sick at heart when I observe the apostasies to freedom. There is one thing needful in our public men, — *backbone*."

It was late in September when the contest in

Congress ended, and its members returned to face the issues of the autumn campaign. In Massachusetts the question was, whether or not the State should approve the compromise and the course of Webster. On one side was the Whig organization, dominated by Webster and represented by Winthrop, who was a candidate for reëlection to the Senate. The merchants and manufacturers, the capitalists, the leaders of the several great professions, men like Rufus Choate and B. R. Curtis, men of letters like Ticknor, Everett, and Prescott, with all the influence which such a combination could command, were enlisted in its support, and they made their disapproval of their opponents felt in business and in society.

On the other side were Charles Francis Adams, Josiah Quincy, Horace Mann, Palfrey, Dana, Theodore Parker, Samuel Hoar and his sons, Emerson, Lowell, Whittier, Sumner, Henry Wilson, and a host of others who represented the moral forces of Massachusetts. Perhaps nothing better illustrates their feeling than Emerson's remark about Webster : "Every drop of blood in this man's veins has eyes that look downward."

The Fugitive Slave Law created intense indignation throughout the North, which was increased by attempts to enforce it. Knowing that public opinion was against them, those who were charged with its execution moved with a haste and secrecy absolutely inconsistent with Anglo-Saxon ideas of liberty, and every time that a human being was seized and hurried back to slavery under the forms of law, but without any real opportunity to defend himself, men were taught to hate slavery. In Massachusetts this feeling was especially strong. Meetings were held all over the State, the most important, perhaps, being that at Faneuil Hall "for the denunciation of the law and the expression of sympathy and coöperation with the fugitive."

At the Free-Soil convention held on October 3, Sumner was a member of the committee on resolutions, and was reëlected to the state committee. A question of practical politics was at once presented. There were in both great parties strong opponents of slavery, who sympathized with the Free-Soilers, though unwilling to abandon their party. As Sumner writes after his defeat by Eliot : " A leading and popular Whig said to me on the morning of the election, 'I must go and vote against you, though I will say I should rather at this moment see you in Congress than any person in Boston; but I stick to my party.'"

The bitter feeling of the Whig leaders drew the party line on that side very sharply. On the other hand the Democrats, some from sympathy with the Free-Soil movement, others perhaps because they saw an opportunity to overthrow the Whig domination, were willing to coöperate with the Free-Soilers. In September, 1849, the Democratic state convention had pronounced against " slavery, in every form and color." The question was whether Democrats and Free-Soilers, united upon the great issue of the campaign, should act together. Similar coöperation in other States had won important victories for freedom, and Henry Wilson, chairman of the Free-Soil state committee, favored it in Massachusetts. At a meeting of prominent Free-Soilers to consider its expediency, Adams, Palfrey, Dana, Samuel Hoar, and others opposed coalition, while Wilson and others favored it. It was finally decided that no action should be taken committing the party, but that each member should be at liberty to act according to his own sense of propriety. Sumner wrote to Wilson, saying: —

"I see no objection in point of principle to unions in towns, and also in counties, such as took place last autumn. . . . But it seems to me a step of questionable propriety for our state committee or any number of Free-Soilers to enter into an arrangement or understanding with the Democrats as to the disposition of offices. As at present advised I should be unwilling to be a party to any such bargain."

It was impossible at such a time to keep men who thought alike from acting together. The Democrats had accepted the principles of the Free-Soilers, and the latter accepted their votes. In towns and senatorial districts the combination was general and the campaign was thorough and intense. Sumner spoke in various parts of the State, but his most important speech was made at Faneuil Hall on November 6. Of it he himself says: "It is sometimes said to have made Mr.

Sumner senator.   More than anything else it determined his selection by the Free-Soil party shortly
afterwards as their candidate.   On the other hand
it was often pronounced 'treasonable,' and in subsequent discussions at Washington, sometimes in
newspapers and repeatedly in the Senate, it was
employed to point the personalities of slave masters and their allies."   It put into clear and
strong words what anti-slavery men were thinking ; reflected the intense feeling of the hour, and
showed the people a leader with courage and ability
to speak for them.

He began by stating his position on the coalition
as follows : —

" At the outset let me say that it is because I
place freedom above all else that I cordially concur in the different unions or combinations throughout the Commonwealth. . . . The friends of freedom may arbitrate between both the old parties,
making freedom their perpetual object, and in this
way contribute more powerfully than they otherwise could to the cause which has drawn us together."

He denounced the monstrous provisions of the
Fugitive Slave Law, and declared it unconstitutional
for reasons which he stated at length.   His counsel
to resist it was often brought up against him, and
should be quoted : —

" *I cannot believe that this bill will be executed
here.* . . . But let me be understood ; I counsel no
violence.   There is another power stronger than

any individual arm which I invoke : I mean that irresistible public opinion, inspired by love of God and man, which, without violence or noise, gently as the operations of nature, makes and unmakes laws. Let this public opinion be felt in its might, and the Fugitive Slave bill will become everywhere among us a dead letter. No lawyer will aid it by counsel, no citizen will be its agent; it will die of inanition, like a spider beneath an exhausted receiver.

" It rests with you, my fellow citizens, by word and example, by calm determination and devoted lives, to do this work. From a humane, just, and religious people will spring a public opinion to keep perpetual guard over the liberties of all within our borders. . . . It shall prevent any slave hunter from ever setting foot in this Commonwealth. . . . I would not touch his person. Not with whips and thongs would I scourge him from the land. The contempt, the indignation, the abhorrence of the community, shall be our weapons of offense. Wherever he moves he shall find no house to receive him, no table spread to nourish him, no welcome to cheer him. . . . Villages, towns, and cities shall refuse to receive the monster."

In answer to the argument of the Whigs that the compromise ended the slavery contest, he said : —

" We are told that the slavery question is settled. Yes, *settled — settled*, — that is the word. *Nothing, sir, can be settled which is not right.*

Nothing can be settled which is against freedom."

His declaration of principles may be quoted, as the people of Massachusetts in effect made it their platform when they sent Sumner to the Senate.

" We demand, first and foremost, the instant repeal of the Fugitive Slave bill.

" We demand the abolition of slavery in the District of Columbia.

" We demand of Congress the exercise of its time-honored power to prohibit slavery in the territories.

" We demand of Congress that it shall refuse to receive any new slave State into the Union.

" We demand the abolition of the domestic slave trade, so far as it can be constitutionally reached, but particularly on the high seas under the national flag.

" And generally we demand from the national government the exercise of all constitutional powers to release itself from responsibility for slavery.

" And yet one thing further must be done. The slave power must be overturned, so that the national government may be put openly, actively, and perpetually on the side of freedom."

A few extracts from a single other passage are always pertinent: " The friends of freedom cannot lightly bestow their confidence. They can put trust only in men of tried character and inflexible will. Three things at least they must require: the first is *backbone ;* the second is *backbone ;* and the third is *backbone*. When I see a person of upright character and pure soul yielding to a temporizing policy, I cannot but say, *He wants backbone*. When I see a person talking loudly against slavery in private, but hesitating in public and failing in the time of trial, I say, *He wants backbone*. When I see a person leaning upon the action of a political party and never venturing to think for himself, I say, *He wants backbone*. When I see a man careful always to be on the side of the majority, and unwilling to appear in a minority, or, if need be, to stand alone, I say, *He wants backbone*. Wanting this they all want that courage, constancy, firmness, which are essential to the support of principle. Let no such man be trusted."

The campaign resulted in the triumph of the coalition. There was indeed no choice for governor; but the combined Democrats and Free-Soilers had a majority in the legislature. Never had the Whig party of Massachusetts known so crushing a defeat. From the outset the object of the Free-Soilers had been to elect a senator, and now, when the victory was won, Sumner was their choice. The newspaper organ of the party said that this was "because, while true as the truest to Free-Soil principles, he was supposed to be less obnoxious than any prominent Free-Soiler in the State to the Democratic party. He was never identified with any of the measures of the Whig party, except those relating to slavery. He never entered

a Whig state convention except to sustain the sentiment, not of the Whig party alone, but of Massachusetts against the annexation of Texas and the Mexican war."

Sumner's confidential letters, and the contemporary judgment of those who knew him best, fortified by the opinion of political opponents, leave no doubt that he had never desired the place. To Charles F. Adams, with whom he was in the closest relations, he wrote: "My dreams and visions are all in other directions. In the course of my life I have had many, but none have been in the United States Senate. In taking that post I must renounce quiet and repose forever; my life henceforward would be in public affairs. I cannot contemplate this without repugnance." But from his associates in Massachusetts, from Free-Soilers elsewhere, from leaders like Chase and Giddings in Washington, came a pressure which he could not resist, and when the Free-Soil members of the legislature by unanimous vote, or according to another account by eighty-four votes out of eighty-five, selected him as their candidate, he consented to stand.

The failure to elect the state officers by the people threw the election into the legislature, and the Free-Soilers and Democrats at separate caucuses chose committees to determine how the votes of the two parties should be cast. It was decided that the Democrats should name the state officers with some exceptions, and also the senator for the short

term which expired March 4, 1851, while the
Free-Soilers should name the senator for the long
term of six years. The belief, however, that Sumner was more acceptable to the Democrats than
any other Free-Soiler proved unfounded. His advanced position on the slavery question, and especially his speech against the Fugitive Slave Law,
made some Democrats very reluctant to accept him,
lest they might hazard their relations with the national organization by helping to elect a man whom
the Democratic journals of Boston described as "a
disunionist." He secured a two thirds vote in the
Democratic caucus and his nomination was made
unanimous with only a few dissenting votes, but
after the other officers had been elected by the
combined votes of Free-Soilers and Democrats, it
was found that enough Democrats in the House to
prevent his election refused to vote for him.

There followed a struggle from January 14 till
April 24, 1851. During the contest he was opposed bitterly by the Whigs, who denounced the
coalition as an iniquitous conspiracy, and, smarting under their recent defeat, spared no pains to
take from the Free-Soilers the prize of victory.
Webster exerted all his influence and seems to
have been joined by Lewis Cass, who represented
a certain number of Democrats. Caleb Cushing
led the Democratic opposition in the House, and it
often seemed that this combination would be successful. But the Democrats did not feel satisfied
with their position in refusing to carry out their

agreement after all their own candidates had been elected, and they attempted to meet the difficulty by offering to vote for some other Free-Soil candidate like Stephen C. Phillips. Governor Boutwell urged a change, and some of Sumner's own supporters were inclined to accept the suggestion. Sumner himself wrote to Wilson : "In this matter, I pray you, do not think of me. . . . Abandon me, then, whenever you think best, without notice or apology. The cause is everything. I am nothing." The Free-Soilers, however, stood firm, believing Sumner their best man, and also fearing that a change might give the Democrats an excuse for breaking the compact.

Failing with his supporters, his opponents next sought some concession from Sumner himself. He was asked by the editor of the " Times," a Democratic journal of Boston, to write a letter modifying his speech against the Fugitive Slave Law, so as to make it easier for the Democrats to support him. He declined, and when the editor asked him how he would like to see that speech reprinted in the " Times," replied that nothing would give him greater pleasure. The speech was published the next day, with the statement that it contained Mr. Sumner's deliberate opinions and the expression of a hope that the Democratic members of the legislature would read it, " and then consider whether it is not their duty to vote for some other person." The Free-Soil organ accepted the issue, and likewise published the speech, adopting every word of it with enthusiastic approval. Individual Democrats and committees urged him to give some assurance that he would not agitate the slavery question in the Senate, or would give other questions precedence; but he replied that he had not sought the office, and if it came to him, it must come to an absolutely independent man whose opinions were known, and who would go to the Senate resolved to assert them. This inflexible determination of Sumner's supporters, with considerable pressure from the constituencies, finally triumphed, and so many of Sumner's opponents yielded as to secure his election.

The New York "Tribune," then in close alliance with the Whig party, thus spoke of his victory: —

"We do not know the man who has entered the Senate under auspices so favorable to personal independence as Mr. Sumner. He has not sought the office, has not made an effort for its acquisition. No pledge has he given to any party or any person upon any question or measure."

Sumner received the news of his election at the house of Mr. Adams, "with as perfect calmness and absence of any appearance of excitement as was possible. There was no change in his face or in his manner, and the latter was one of perfect quiet and self-possessed dignity." On the same day Longfellow writes: "He is no more elated by his success than he has been depressed by the failure heretofore, and evidently does not desire the office."

Geo. S. Boutwell

All over the State and the country the result was hailed with the greatest enthusiasm by the opponents of slavery. It was justly regarded as a signal victory for freedom.

It was the unique beginning of a remarkable public career. The next campaign in Massachusetts presented for approval the result of the coalition. Winthrop was the candidate of the Whigs for governor, while the Democrats renominated Governor Boutwell. Sumner took no part in the contest, both because the propriety of his own election was involved, and because he desired to shun further personal conflict with Winthrop. The excitement was intensified by the feeling over the Fugitive Slave Law, and again the coalition carried the State. Boutwell was reëlected by the legislature, and those Democrats who had refused to support Sumner were defeated. When, therefore, he took his seat in the Senate on December 1, 1851, he went there the fully accredited representative of Massachusetts.

CHAPTER VI

FIRST YEARS IN THE SENATE

The anti-slavery cause had two unfaltering supporters in the Senate before Sumner entered it, John P. Hale of New Hampshire and Salmon P. Chase of Ohio. Hale had great ability and courage, firm principles, and a caustic wit which made him a power in debate, but as compared with Sumner he was critical, not aggressive. The character of Chase is well known. He had far more skill as a politician than Sumner, and, though he was an earnest and uncompromising Free-Soiler, the contest was to him more like a game. William H. Seward was still identified with the Whigs, though his speeches showed a clear grasp of the situation and did much to create and develop anti-slavery feeling. Sumner brought into the Senate a new force. In the language of Von Holst, " The rigid fidelity to principle and the fiery-spirited moral earnestness of abolitionism, united to the will and capacity to pursue political ends with the given political means, received in him their first representative in the Senate." He was no politician in the ordinary sense. He saw clearly what was right, and he devoted his life with absolute singleness of purpose and unwavering courage to the pursuit of the ends which his conscience approved. To intense conviction he added a certain lightness of heart, a serene confidence of ultimate success. It was not so much that he weighed and disregarded the obstacles and the personal consequences which daunted other men, as that they did not present themselves to him. His gaze was fixed on a distant goal, and he did not stoop to look at what lay in the path.

When Congress met in December, 1851, more than a year had elapsed since the passage of the compromise measures, and meanwhile the Administration and the leaders of both parties — Clay and Webster agreeing with Cass, Buchanan, and Douglas — had exerted all their influence to unite the country in support of the compromise. The great material and political forces of the nation, with too much assistance from the church, were all arrayed on the same side. In January, 1851, forty-four members of Congress, headed by Clay, issued a manifesto written by Alexander H. Stephens, declaring that they would support no man for any prominent office who was not known to condemn disturbance of the compromise and further agitation of the slavery question.

Never was there a more determined effort to "cry 'Peace' when there is no peace." Never was clearer proof of Sumner's rule that "nothing can be settled which is not right." In both Houses petitions for the repeal of the Fugitive Slave Law were presented, and the law was bitterly denounced by Giddings, Horace Mann, Hale, and others, while Senator Butler of South Carolina declared his conviction that the attempt to prevent agitation of the slavery question was absolutely idle. The abuses attending the attempts to recover fugitive slaves kept the public excited. Free persons were seized and deported as slaves. Murders, mob violence, and lawlessness on both sides aroused the deepest indignation. The rescue of Shadrach in February, 1851, while under arrest in Boston as a fugitive slave, led the President to issue a proclamation calling upon all well-disposed citizens to aid in enforcing the law, and the secretaries of war and of the navy issued instructions in aid. Mr. Clay introduced resolutions calling for information, to which the President responded by a special message reciting the facts and his action, upon which ensued a bitter debate in the Senate.

Nor was it only at the North that the compromise had failed. In South Carolina a convention declared in May, 1851, that "the State of South Carolina cannot submit to the wrongs and aggressions which have been perpetrated by the federal government and the Northern States without dishonor and ruin, and that it is necessary for her to release herself therefrom, whether with or without the coöperation of the Southern States." Like feeling was strong in Mississippi; but the majority of the Southern people were not ready for secession, and all attempts to secure action in this direction failed. An active minority, however, refused to regard the compromise as final.

It was easier to stay the rising tide than to stop
the discussion of slavery by paper proclamations,
in the face of events like these.   It was the indignation excited by the Fugitive Slave Law — the
public resolve that it should be repealed — which
sent Charles Sumner to the Senate, and which he
went there to express.

When he took his seat the exasperation on both
sides was steadily growing, and the final contest
was beginning.   He made his entrance upon the
stage just as Henry Clay was retiring, for the latter
never entered the Senate after the first day of the
session.

On the same day with Sumner, Hamilton Fish
of New York and Benjamin F. Wade of Ohio also
entered the Senate.   Chase was already his friend,
and his relations with the families of Seward and
Fish were cordial from the beginning.   He took a
chair on the Democratic side next to Chase.   Before him sat Butler of South Carolina, and behind
Chase was James M. Mason of Virginia.   Cass,
who presented his credentials, was an old friend,
and Sumner was received very pleasantly by other
senators, by the diplomatic corps, and by many
residents, so that he found himself amid agreeable
surroundings.   The social antipathies of Boston
were not felt in the capital, and Boston heard of
his " triumphant success in Washington, social
and otherwise."   In the arrangement of committees he was placed at the foot of those on revolutionary claims and on roads and canals, which

gave him scant opportunities. His first speech was made upon a resolution of welcome to Kossuth, when he came to this country after the failure of the Hungarian revolution. It was a graceful tribute to the great Magyar, and in it he took ground against any departure from our policy of non-intervention in the affairs of other nations, a position which many strong supporters of freedom disapproved.

His next appearance was in support of a bill granting land to the State of Iowa " in aid of the construction of certain railroads," a position which made him friends in the West and Southwest, but was used against him at home. Cheaper ocean postage and other questions of general interest engaged his attention, but it was not until the end of May that he said anything even remotely relating to slavery. He felt it wise to become familiar with his colleagues and his surroundings, with the rules and atmosphere of the Senate, and to show that he was not " a man of one idea," — a fanatic at once unreasonable and unpractical. Indeed, nothing could have injured Sumner's influence in the Senate or gratified his enemies more than his rushing prematurely into a debate, or endeavoring to interject a speech against slavery into a discussion of some other subject. He did not, however, forget the cause to which he owed his election. He meant to be heard before the session closed, but at his own time, and not until the necessary preparation had been completed.

His silence was misinterpreted. Before the session was three months old the Whig journals began to taunt their opponents with Sumner's failure to attack slavery. Garrison, at an anti-slavery meeting, introduced a resolution condemning him, and Phillips, though opposing it and expressing his implicit confidence in Sumner, said, " I think his course at Washington impolitic and wrong." Other friends assured him of their perfect faith, but none the less impressed on him the importance of breaking his silence.

As he wrote to John Jay : —

" Had I imagined the impatience of friends, I would have anticipated their most sanguine desires. . . . I fear nothing. I am under no influences which can interfere with this great duty. From the time I first came here I determined to speak on slavery some time at the end of June or in July, and not before unless pressed by some practical question. No such question has occurred, and I have been left to my original purposes."

It soon became apparent that an opportunity to speak would not readily be given to him. On May 26 he presented a memorial against the Fugitive Slave Law, but on seeking to say a few words he was interrupted by the president, and only allowed to proceed on his assurance that he did not propose to enter into any discussion. He simply announced his purpose to address the Senate at a later day. when he hoped for a hearing.

The two great parties held their national con-

ventions in June, and, differing on other questions,
declared their support of the compromise and their
opposition to any agitation of the slavery question
in almost identical language.   Under these circumstances Sumner was obliged to make his own opportunity, and when for this purpose he offered,
on July 27, a resolution requesting the committee on the judiciary to consider the expediency of
reporting a bill for the immediate repeal of the
Fugitive Slave Law, both parties were determined
to prevent his speaking.   Sumner's appeal to the
courtesy of his associates fell on deaf ears, and his
motion was defeated, even Hamilton Fish voting
against it.

This action made it very doubtful whether Sumner would be allowed to deliver his speech.   Mason
told him that he might have an opportunity "next
term," but not at the current session.   Politicians
of both parties were anxious that he should not
speak before the presidential election, and especially that he should not be able to put certain
senators on record as to the Fugitive Slave Law.
His failure increased the anxiety of his friends at
home, and he was thus between two fires.   But he
never changed his purpose, and in the last days of
the session he secured the floor in the only way
possible.   The Civil and Diplomatic appropriation
bill was under consideration, when Hunter of Virginia moved an amendment for the payment of unusual expenses in executing the laws of the United
States.   Sumner, who was prepared, at once moved

the following amendment, "provided that no such
allowance shall be authorized for any expenses incurred in executing the act of September 18, 1850,
for the surrender of fugitives from service or labor,
which said act is hereby repealed," and upon this
he made a speech which occupied nearly four hours.
It stands in his works under the title so often
quoted, "Freedom National, Slavery Sectional."

This speech and its reception by his opponents
are full of instruction. It is far from being an in-
flammatory harangue, or even the ordinary speech
of a political partisan. The present Senate on far
less exciting questions is much more violent. It is
an argument such as a thorough student of constitutional law and history might address to a court
of justice. It is free from all suspicion of personal
bitterness, and it contains no word which could
offend a slaveholder, except as any attack upon
slavery might irritate its supporters. The speaker
did not dilate on the horrors of slavery, nor recite
the crimes of slave masters. The whole subject
was lifted above the plane of political contest into
the serener air of eternal principles, — the atmosphere of an ideal senate. As Sumner said in his
introductory remarks: "Slavery I must condemn
with my whole soul; but here I need only borrow
the language of slaveholders; nor would it accord
with my habits or my sense of justice to exhibit
them as the impersonation of the institution — Jefferson calls it the ' enormity ' — which they cherish.
Of them I do not speak. But without fear and

without favor, as without impeachment of any person, I assail this wrong."

He showed by abundant authority that slavery
was not recognized in the Constitution, and that
Congress had no power to establish it. Thence
he argued that it could not legally exist where the
jurisdiction of the national government was exclusive. He traced the history of the provision as
to persons "held to service or labor," arguing that
it was not among the compromises of the Constitution, but that it was only a compact between
the States like the kindred provision for the extradition of criminals, and that Congress had no
power to enforce it. He took the ground that the
Constitution only prevented the States from making laws which should discharge from service or
labor a person held thereto in any other State, and
that the States alone had power to pass laws for
the rendition of such persons. For these reasons
and because it committed the great question of
personal liberty "to the unaided judgment of a
single petty magistrate," denying a trial by jury,
he contended that the Fugitive Slave Law was
unconstitutional. He cited authority for the proposition that an unconstitutional law need not be
obeyed, and insisted that a law which could not be
enforced without outraging the public conscience
and exciting dangerous commotions should not be
left upon the statute-book, quoting with approval
the remark of Senator Butler of South Carolina,
that "a law which can be enforced only by the
bayonet is no law."

In conclusion he maintained that a law which required men to stifle their natural sympathy with a fugitive slave was contrary to the divine law and not to be obeyed; but it was passive, not active, resistance which he counseled.

" By the supreme law which commands me to do no injustice, by the comprehensive Christian law of brotherhood, *by the Constitution which I have sworn to support*, I am bound to disobey this act. Never, in any capacity, can I render voluntary aid in its execution. Pains and penalties I will endure, but this great wrong I will not do."

The speech was fortified by copious quotations from the leaders of human thought; it tried slavery and the Fugitive Slave Law by unchangeable principles of law, morals, and religion, and it was characterized throughout by loftiness of spirit and deep conviction. It was a thoroughly dignified presentation of the speaker's case, yet its delivery demanded high courage.

A debate followed in which several Southern senators were offensively personal, but nothing indicated that the speech had aroused any serious bitterness. It was received by Sumner's Free-Soil colleagues, and by the opponents of slavery on both sides of the water, with great enthusiasm, and it made many converts. From this time he was the acknowledged representative in the Senate of the moral forces opposed to slavery, — the embodied conscience of the anti-slavery movement.

The adjournment of Congress a few days later

set the leaders of the two parties free to enter the presidential campaign of 1852. Dividing upon all other issues, they united in declaring that the slavery question was finally settled by the compromise of 1850. The campaign tested severely the conscience of the country, for the feeling against slavery was shared by Whig and Democrat alike, yet no one could vote either party ticket without pledging himself, so far as a vote could pledge him, to do nothing against it. The Free-Soilers had formed alliances here with the Whigs and there with the Democrats on the question of freedom. In certain localities these alliances promised the election of anti-slavery candidates, but how could Free-Soilers act with men committed by their party platforms to oppose any one willing even to discuss slavery?

From the beginning Sumner consistently favored independent action both in private and in public. This view prevailed, and in August the Free-Soilers in national convention nominated John P. Hale and George W. Julian for president and vice-president. Two weeks after Congress adjourned the Free-Soilers of Massachusetts nominated an independent state ticket. At this convention Sumner made his first appearance after his speech in the Senate, and in a short but very effective address advocated a new party, " a party of freedom," encountering the time-dishonored argument, that in this country there can be only two parties, so insistently put forth by the politician to hold his wavering followers, saying : —

" At the present time in our country there exists a deep, controlling, conscientious feeling against slavery. You and I, sir, and all of us, confess it. . . . If not *through* the old parties then *over* the old parties this irresistible current *shall* find its way. It cannot be permanently stopped. If the old parties will not become its organs they must become its victims. The party of freedom will certainly prevail."

Seward did not share his views, but actively supported the Whig candidates, and after the election said : " No new party will arise, nor will any old one fall. The issue will not change. We shall go on much as heretofore, I think, only that the last effort to convert the Whig party to slavery has failed."

Mr. Seward with his varied and great abilities lacked prophetic instinct; yet the campaign of 1852 seemed to justify his opinion. The Free-Soilers, weakened by the return of the " Barn-Burners " in New York to the Democratic party, cast hardly more than half as many votes as they had four years before, losing ten thousand votes in Massachusetts. The Whigs carried only Vermont, Massachusetts, Kentucky, and Tennessee, though in the popular vote they were but two hundred thousand behind the Democrats. In Massachusetts a certain alliance with the Democrats continued, but the Whigs secured a small majority in the legislature and elected all the members of Congress save two. They therefore secured the state offices and elected Edward Everett to the national Senate. But in many districts the vote was close and the victory was not overwhelming.

Sumner took no part in the contest after his speech at the convention. Campaign speaking was naturally distasteful to him, and not being a practical politician he was slow to recognize the claims which his political associates made upon their leader. His inaction gave rise to many complaints from his supporters, and for a while his hold upon some of them was weakened.

At the next session of Congress the question of slavery was not discussed, and Sumner preserves in his works only two contributions to the debates. One of these was a short speech in support of resolutions offered by Chase against secrecy in proceedings of the Senate, in which he said: —

" Executive sessions with closed doors, shrouded from the public gaze and public criticism, constitute an exceptional part of our system, too much in harmony with the proceedings of other governments less liberal in character. The genius of our institutions requires publicity."

His first Congress established his position and demonstrated his courage and ability, and at its close he was able to say, " With most of the Southern men my relations have been pleasant." Perhaps his opponents were more ready to treat him with indulgence because he was one of an insignificant minority, while they were in control of the government. This good feeling, however, in the nature of things could not endure.

Though the Whigs elected the legislature of Massachusetts in 1852, the Democrats and the Free-Soilers carried a proposition to call a constitutional convention. The primary object was to change the existing basis of representation, under which the city of Boston elected forty-four representatives on a general ticket, to the great advantage of the Whigs who controlled the city; but the convention was called upon to deal with many other propositions. It met early in May, and finished its work on August 1, 1853. Among its members were many of the ablest men in the State, and its discussions were interesting. Marshfield, the home of Daniel Webster,'chose Sumner as its representative by a very large majority over Webster's son, a result which was hailed with satisfaction as the verdict of his townsmen on Webster. Sumner's principal contribution to the discussions was a speech in favor of dividing the State into equal districts according to population, and letting each district choose its representative. In this he differed from his party associates and his views did not prevail, though the district system was adopted not many years afterward and is still in force. He advocated the abolition of all distinctions of race or color in the militia, and as chairman of the committee on the bill of rights, he made an instructive speech in regard to the history and utility of such declarations. He was not a leader in the convention; though it enlarged his acquaintance throughout the State, and corrected the impression of many that he was a man of one idea, who was not readily accessible.

. The state campaign in the autumn of 1853 turned on the adoption of the new constitution, and Sumner threw himself into it with vigor, speaking almost every evening after he began, and in all the principal cities. His speech was much admired, and his exertions effaced entirely the feeling caused by his inaction a year before. The campaign ended in a Whig victory and the defeat of the constitution by some five thousand votes. This result was due to several causes and it ended the alliance between Democrats and Free-Soilers, which was replaced in a short time by a union of anti-slavery men in the party of Freedom. The Whigs were offensively triumphant and the Free-Soilers were correspondingly depressed. Neither dreamed of the political revolution which was impending.

CHAPTER VII

THE REPEAL OF THE MISSOURI COMPROMISE

WHEN the Thirty-third Congress met on December 5, 1853, the situation was discouraging to the Free-Soilers. Chase and Sumner stood alone in the Senate, for Hale had given place to a Democrat. The country, by the concurrent action of both parties, had decided that slavery should not even be discussed. The pro-slavery party, controlling every branch of the government, was able to make, to execute, and to interpret laws. It wielded the whole patronage of the nation, and its purpose to use this power had been declared by the new secretary of state in the offensive phrase, "To the victors belong the spoils." Indeed, it was the darkest moment of the struggle, not because the slave power was then most aggressive, but because there was the least resistance to slavery and the conscience of the country seemed dead. The Whig party had fallen "like Lucifer, never to hope again," but the Free-Soilers had lost rather than gained strength by its fall. Yet it is in the history of the next twelve years that the believer in free government must always find abundant justification for his faith, for it was during these that apathy gave place to the consuming fire in which slavery perished.

The President's message assured the country that the prevailing peace would not be disturbed during his administration, and everything promised a dull session. Nor was it the enemies of slavery who renewed the contest. The blow which in the end proved fatal to it came from its friends. Intoxicated with their victory they thought to win even greater triumphs. Slavery had gained peace but not territory by the compromise, and its friends knew that when it ceased to expand it began to die. Convinced that the surrender of the North was final, they resolved to assert the equal right of slavery in all the territories of the United States and to repeal the Missouri Compromise, which had consecrated to freedom all the territory acquired from France which lay north of latitude 36° 30′.

On December 14 Mr. Dodge of Iowa introduced a bill to organize the territory of Nebraska, which was in the usual form, with no reference to slavery. Nebraska was part of the territory from which slavery was forever excluded by the Missouri Compromise. The bill was referred to the committee on territories, and on January 4 was reported to the Senate with amendments, which copied from the statutes organizing the territories of Utah and New Mexico the provision, that any States formed from the territory should be admitted into the Union, whether their constitutions prohibited or permitted slavery. The accompanying report said: "It is a disputed point whether slavery is prohibited in the Nebraska country by valid enactment. The decision of this question involves the constitutional power of Congress to pass laws prescribing and regulating the domestic institutions of the various territories of the Union." This question the committee did not discuss, preferring to follow the policy adopted with New Mexico and Utah by the compromise of 1850. The report questioned the power, which Congress had exercised for years, of regulating the domestic institutions of the territories and of prescribing the conditions upon which States should be admitted, and it set aside the provisions of a statute designed to be a permanent compact between North and South, and so regarded for a generation.

As originally printed the bill contained twenty sections, but a few days later it was again printed with an additional section, said to have been omitted by the copyist. This declared the intent of the bill to be that all questions as to slavery in the territories, and States to be formed therefrom, should be left to the decision of the people residing therein ; that all cases involving title to slaves and questions of personal freedom should be referred to the local tribunals, with a right of appeal to the Supreme Court of the United States ; and that the fugitive slave laws should be executed in the territories as in the States. These propositions were said to be established by the compromise of 1850.

Some two weeks later Mr. Dixon of Kentucky

proposed an amendment that the existing prohibition of slavery "shall not be so construed as to apply to the territory contemplated by this act, or to any other territory of the United States ; but that the citizens of the several States or territories shall be at liberty to take and hold their slaves within any of the territories of the United States or of the States to be formed therefrom." This amendment, if adopted, established slavery everywhere except in the existing free States.

The next day Sumner offered an amendment expressly providing that the act should not be construed " to abrogate or in any way contravene the act of March 6, 1820," known as the Missouri Compromise. That is to say, the anti-slavery leader sought to maintain the existing law, while his opponents wished at a blow to give slavery the widest possible extension. On January 23, Douglas, from the committee on territories, submitted a substitute bill, which divided the territory into two, Kansas and Nebraska, and in terms declared that the Missouri Compromise " was superseded by the principles of the legislation of 1850, commonly called the Compromise Measures, and is hereby declared inoperative." This measure was approved by the President, and Douglas moved its immediate consideration. It was postponed, however, till January 30, when it was made the special order from day to day until disposed of.

The claim of Douglas that the Missouri Compromise was in any way affected by the compromise of 1850 was a brazen assumption. In the exercise of its power to govern the territories, Congress had, in 1820, determined that slavery should be prohibited in certain territory of the United States, and should be permitted in certain other territory. In 1850 it had authorized the organization of territorial governments in Utah and New Mexico, without settling the question of slavery while they remained territories; but had provided that, when admitted as States, they should be received " with or without slavery." Both measures asserted the power of Congress to deal with the question, and between them was no inconsistency.

Nothing in the situation of Kansas and Nebraska made it important to organize these territories at once. The Indian commissioner in his official report of November 9, 1853, made this statement: " On the 11th of October, the day on which I left the frontier, there was no settlement made in any part of Nebraska. From all the information I could obtain there were but three white men in the territory, except such as were there by authority of law, and those adopted by marriage or otherwise into Indian families." General Houston, who was well informed, said that there was not a white man in Kansas, and by treaty with the Indians large parts of the territory were given up to them, from which whites were excluded. It was therefore only a political exigency which led to the introduction of the Kansas-Nebraska bill. As Douglas is said to have confessed subsequently, " his party,

in the election of Pierce, had consumed all its pow-
der, and therefore, without a deep-reaching agitation, it would have no more ammunition for its
artillery."

The full meaning of the proposed measure was
not immediately appreciated by the Free-Soilers,
and in order to arouse public opinion, Chase, Sumner, Joshua R. Giddings, Edward Wade, Gerrit
Smith, and Alexander DeWitt, calling themselves
"the Independent Democrats in Congress," issued
an address to the country. This document, drawn
by Chase, was a strong statement of the situation
and a powerful appeal to the moral sense of the
people. Douglas felt its force, and doubtless it
opened his eyes to the character of the contest
which he had provoked. In opening the debate he
denounced the signers with great bitterness, calling
them " abolition confederates," and accusing them
of misrepresentation and calumny. His ill-temper
was perhaps increased by the recollection that, not
five years before, he had said that the Missouri
Compromise " had become canonized in the hearts
of the American people as a sacred thing which
no ruthless hand would ever be reckless enough to
disturb." An uneasy conscience, as is often the
case, added venom to his attacks on his opponents.

In reply to Douglas, Chase defended the appeal,
and Sumner supported him with a few words,
saying that the signers had discharged a public
duty. His principal speech against the bill was
made on February 15, and discussed the measure

itself, expressly declining to engage in any personal controversy with Douglas. The speech was singularly dispassionate, a literary and historical treatment of the question prepared in the closet, and not an argument glowing with the heat of debate. He made the character of the Missouri Compromise as a binding compact clearly apparent; he insisted that it be maintained, and showed the gradual change in public sentiment on the slavery question, until, as he said, " the original policy of the government is absolutely reversed. Slavery, which at the beginning was a sectional institution, with no foothold anywhere on the national territory, is now exalted as national, and all our broad domain is threatened by its blighting shadow."

He was studious to state his position without flinching, yet so as to conciliate rather than offend his opponents. This he accomplished, and his speech was approved by his supporters as a clear and strong statement, while even opponents as bitter as the Webster Whigs complimented him.

Sumner took no further part in the debate except twice to deny accusations made against himself, and the bill passed on March 4. In the House the Senate bill could not be reached under the rules, so an identical bill was introduced and passed there. This was sent to the Senate in May, and Sumner spoke briefly against it just before its passage. He took the opportunity to present remonstrances from various bodies of citizens, including some from clergymen of all denominations. A protest from three thousand New England ministers had been presented by Mr. Everett earlier in the debate, and in this, as in some of those presented by Sumner, the signers protested " in the name of Almighty God and in his presence." This language was denounced as blasphemous by Douglas and his supporters, and in answer to their attacks Sumner spoke with dignity and power. He paid a just tribute to the clergy of New England. Then keenly appreciating the situation and accurately forecasting the future he continued : —

" Ah, sir, senators vainly expect peace. Not in this way can peace come. In passing such a bill as is now threatened, you scatter from this dark midnight hour no seeds of harmony and good will, but broadcast through the land dragon's teeth, which haply may not spring up in a direful crop of armed men, yet I am assured, sir, will fructify in civil strife and feud. . . .

" Sir, the bill you are about to pass is at once the worst and best on which Congress has ever acted. Yes, sir, *worst* and *best* at the same time.

" It is the worst bill inasmuch as it is a present victory of slavery. In a Christian land, and in an age of civilization, a time-honored statute of freedom is stricken down, opening the way to all the countless woes and wrongs of human bondage. . . .

" Sir, it is the best bill on which Congress ever acted, *for it annuls all past compromises with slavery and makes any future compromises impossible.*

Thus it puts Freedom and Slavery face to face, and bids them grapple. Who can doubt the result? It opens wide the door of the future, when at last there will really be a North and the slave power will be broken. . . . Everywhere within the sphere of Congress the great *Northern Hammer* will descend to smite the wrong, and the irresistible cry will break forth, 'No more Slave States!'"

This lofty defiance, this confident prophecy, so free from any passion or bitterness, in the very moment of slavery's greatest triumph, exactly represented the rising feeling of the North, and the speech was cordially applauded.

Up to this time nothing had occurred to disturb his personal relations with his associates, but the "dragon's teeth" sprang up sooner than he thought. On the evening of May 24 Anthony Burns was seized as a fugitive slave in Boston, and on the evening of the 26th a meeting of abolitionists was held in Faneuil Hall. Immediately after this a body of citizens, among whom were some who had been prominent at the meeting, attacked the court-house where Burns was detained, and in the conflict one of the guards was killed. This created intense feeling in Washington, where the news was received while the memory of Sumner's speech was fresh in men's minds. In fact the speech did not reach Boston till the morning after the riot, but it was felt that the trouble had been inspired by the abolitionists, and it was easy to claim that Sumner's speech was responsible for it, especially as he came from

the city where it had occurred. The organs of
the Administration attacked him fiercely, and some
of the articles suggested personal violence.

Sumner was warned to be on his guard, but he
continued to walk from his rooms to the Capitol
regardless of the threatened danger. At a restau-
rant where he dined he was menaced, though no
actual assault was attempted. But the feeling of
hostility to him, the idea of holding him personally
responsible for the acts of abolitionists and in-
flicting upon him physical punishment, had been
planted in the minds of men who were approaching the time when

> "The war of tongue and pen
>   Learns with what deadly purpose it was fraught."

In Boston the majesty of the law was vindicated,
and through crowded streets, but in deep silence
and between files of soldiers, Anthony Burns was
carried back to slavery. For many a spectator
the sight gave a new meaning to the word " slavery," and the incident made many determined abolitionists. Massachusetts and especially Boston
were stirred to their depths.

Supporters and opponents of the compromise
united in a petition for the repeal of the Fugitive
Slave Law, which, bearing many influential names
and twenty-nine hundred signatures, was presented in the Senate by Julius Rockwell, who
had succeeded Everett. On June 26 this petition
was referred to the committee on the judiciary
after some debate, in the course of which Sumner

spoke in answer to Jones of Tennessee, who had threatened disunion if the law should be repealed, and had attacked Massachusetts and her citizens with some bitterness.

Sumner made a spirited reply in which he alluded to her revolutionary history, and among other things said : " The senator says that Boston is filled with traitors. That charge is not new. Boston of old was the home of Hancock and Adams. Her traitors now are those who are truly animated by the spirit of the American Revolution. In condemning them, in condemning Massachusetts, in condemning these remonstrants, you simply give proper conclusion to the utterance on this floor that the Declaration of Independence is ' a self-evident lie.' "

Mr. Butler of South Carolina at once replied, claiming that the Revolution was carried through by slaveholding States, and characterizing Sumner's speech as "a species of rhetoric intended to feed the fires of fanaticism in his own State," but " vapid " and unworthy of a scholar. Touching upon the constitutional duty of the States to return fugitive slaves, he first asked Sumner's colleague, Rockwell, whether Massachusetts "would send fugitives back to us after trial by jury or any other mode," and receiving no reply he turned to Sumner and said, " Will this honorable senator tell me that he will do it ? " Sumner answered, " Is thy servant a dog, that he should do this thing ? " This reply excited Butler, and the

debate became bitterly personal. He attempted
to state Sumner's position somewhat incoherently,
when Sumner, interrupting, said: "The senator
asked me if I would help to reduce a fellow man
to bondage. I answered him." To which Butler
replied: "Then you would not obey the Constitution. Sir, standing here before this tribunal,
where you swore to support it, you rise and tell
me that you regard it the office of a dog to enforce it. You stand in my presence as a coequal
senator, and tell me that it is a dog's office to execute the Constitution of the United States."

Mason of Virginia followed in an insolent vein
beginning: "I say, sir, the dignity of the American
Senate has been rudely, wantonly, grossly assailed
by a senator from Massachusetts, — and not only
the dignity of the Senate, but of the whole people,
trifled with in the presence of the American Senate,
either ignorantly or corruptly, I do not know which,
nor do I care." Pettit of Indiana compared Sumner and Webster as a jackal and a lion, or a buzzard
and an eagle. On a later day Clay of Alabama
described Sumner as "a sneaking, sinuous, snake-
like poltroon," and used other like epithets, con-
cluding: "If we cannot restrain or prevent this
eternal warfare upon the feelings and rights of
Southern gentlemen, we may rob the serpent of his
fangs, we can paralyze his influence, by placing him
in that nadir of social degradation which he merits."

Sumner could afford to despise the coarse epithets
of such opponents as Clay and Pettit, but their at-

tacks followed the speeches of more important men
like Mason, whose insolence, reflected as it doubtless was in the behavior of many senators, was extremely irritating. In fact, the Southern leaders
had so long adopted a domineering manner in debate, and had assumed for themselves such social
superiority, that men were anxious to have them met
with their own weapons. Public feeling in the
North demanded a champion able to assert at least
the equality of Northern men with their Southern
fellow citizens, and Sumner perhaps felt that his
own position in the Senate and in the country would
be weakened if he seemed unable or unwilling to
face his antagonists. Whatever were the controlling considerations, he departed in this instance
from his previous course, and met personality with
personality. He replied to the claims of Mason
and Butler by facts from the history of their States.

Thus Butler had said : " Yes, sir, the independence of America, to maintain republican liberty,
was won by the arms and treasure, by the patriotism and good faith, of slaveholding communities."

To this Sumner's reply was crushing. He showed
by indisputable evidence that Massachusetts alone
not only furnished to the army of the Revolution
thirteen times as many men as South Carolina, but
more than all the Southern States together, though
the populations of the Northern and Southern States
were then substantially equal. Not stopping here
he showed by the memoirs of General Moultrie
and by other South Carolina authorities, that when

the British were threatening Charleston, the governor and council proposed that South Carolina should remain neutral during the war, and " the question whether the State shall belong to Great Britain, or remain one of the United States, be determined by the treaty of peace between those two powers."   He concluded by proving from Southern sources that the failure of the South to do its share in the Revolution was caused by slavery, quoting from the Secret Journals of the Continental Congress, —

" That the State of South Carolina . . . is unable to make any effectual efforts with militia by reason of the great population of citizens necessary to remain at home to prevent insurrection among the negroes, and to prevent the desertion of them to the enemy."

He pointed out that Butler had challenged the comparison, and proceeded : —

" For myself, sir, I understand the sensibilities of senators from ' slaveholding communities ' and would not wound them by a superfluous word. Of slavery I speak strongly, as I must, but thus far, even at the expense of my argument, I have avoided the contrasts founded on detail of figures and facts, which are so obvious between the free States and ' slaveholding communities.' . . . God forbid that I should do injustice to South Carolina. I know well the gallantry of many of her sons. . . . I have little desire to expose her sores; I would not lay bare even her nakedness. But the senator in his vaunt for 'slave-holding communities' has made a claim for slavery so derogatory to freedom, and so inconsistent with history, that I cannot allow it to pass unanswered. . . . I speak here for a commonwealth of just renown, but I speak also for a cause which is more than any commonwealth, even that which I represent; and I cannot allow the senator to discredit either. Not by slavery, but in spite of slavery, was independence achieved. Not *because*, but *notwithstanding* there were 'slaveholding communities,' did triumph descend upon our arms."

Then addressing himself to Mr. Mason: —

" With imperious look and in the style of Sir Forcible Feeble, that senator undertakes to call in question my statement that the Fugitive Slave Act denies the writ of *habeas corpus;* and in doing this he assumes a superiority for himself which, permit me to tell him in his presence, nothing in him can warrant. Sir, I claim little for myself; but I shrink in no respect from comparison with that senator, veteran though he be. Sitting near him, as has been my fortune since I had the honor of a seat in this chamber, I have come to know something of his conversation, something of his manners, something of his attainments, something of his abilities, something of his character, — ay, sir, and something of his associations; and while I would not disparage him in any of these respects, I feel that I do not exalt myself unduly, that I do not claim too much for the position which

I hold or the name which I have established, when I openly declare that as senator from Massachusetts and as man I place myself at every point in unhesitating comparison with that honorable assailant.   And to his peremptory assertion that the Fugitive Slave Act *does* *not* deny the *habeas corpus*, I oppose my assertion, peremptory as his own, that it *does*, and there I leave that issue."

These extended quotations have been made to show the character and purpose of a speech which was an important event in Sumner's life.   It increased the personal hostility to him felt by the pro-slavery party, and it made him more distinctly the leader of the anti-slavery forces in Congress. The feeling in the Senate was so strong that a proposition to expel him was seriously considered.   On the other hand, the applause from the North was general.   The feeling of the time is illustrated not so much by the enthusiastic plaudits of the active abolitionists as by the verdict of conservative men, from many of whom he received letters of warm approval.

Sumner had won that cordial and enduring respect which Americans always feel for a man " that ain't a-feared."   He had shown himself not only a polished scholar and idealist, but a fearless fighter also ; he had met and withstood the champions of the Senate on their own grounds.   It was a triumph for his cause, for his State, and for himself, and it drew from Whittier the lines " To C. S.," which describe him as

"One
Who, momently by Error's host assailed,
Stands strong as Truth, in greaves of granite mailed;
And, tranquil-fronted, listening over all
The tumult, hears the angels say, Well done ! "

During the remainder of the session nothing very important occurred. There were occasional references to his view of his constitutional obligations, but he was treated as a rule with entire respect and courtesy by his opponents. His reply to Mason and Butler had discouraged further attacks, and cleared the atmosphere of the Senate.

The answer of the North to the repeal of the Missouri Compromise was the Republican party. Anti-slavery men were to be found in every political organization, but upon the question of slavery none of these organizations could be trusted. No party with a Southern wing would alienate Southern votes. When, therefore, the Kansas-Nebraska bill brought the country face to face with the danger that slavery would be extended over all the territories of the United States and thus control the government, resistance to this extension became the paramount duty of the hour, and men who differed on other questions united for the common defense. All over the North a new party was demanded. The party existed: it only needed to be recognized by its own members. In Washington some thirty members of the House met on the morning after the passage of the bill, and concluded that a new party was necessary. The

name "Republican," which, indeed, had been suggested previously at a small meeting in Wisconsin,
was discussed and agreed upon. In Massachusetts
the Free-Soilers held a convention, and the sentiment of the meeting was expressed by Henry
Wilson: "We go with none who do not wear
our principles upon their foreheads, and have them
engraved on their hearts."

Conferences followed, and after a preliminary
meeting, at which the name "Republican" was
adopted, a state convention of delegates was held
at Worcester on September 7, and at this Sumner
made his first public appearance after his return
from Washington. He addressed himself to the
duty of Massachusetts, and made a powerful argument for a new party. The speech did not smell
of the lamp like some of his earlier ones; he did
not stop to consider phrases; he was still hot from
the battle. Of the Burns case he said: "In those
streets where he had walked as freeman Anthony
Burns was seized as slave, under the base pretext
that he was a criminal, — imprisoned in the court-
house, which was turned for the time into fortress
and barracoon, — guarded by heartless hirelings,
whose chief idea of liberty was license to wrong,
— escorted by intrusive soldiers of the United
States, — watched by a prostituted militia, — and
finally given up to a slave hunter by the decree of
a petty magistrate, who did not hesitate to take
upon his soul the awful responsibility of dooming
a fellow man, in whom he could find no fault, to

a fate worse than death. . . . In doing this deed of woe and shame, the liberties of our citizens, white as well as black, were put in jeopardy, the mayor of Boston was converted to a tool, the governor of the commonwealth to a cipher, the laws, the precious sentiments of religion, the pride and glory of Massachusetts, were trampled in the dust, and 'you and I and all of us fell down' while the Slave Power flourished over us."

He insisted that to every scheme of slavery Massachusetts must send forth an "*everlasting No;*" that she must by proper laws secure for her people the rights of trial by jury and *habeas corpus;* that she must choose to office "men who, at Washington, will not shrink from conflict with slavery, and also other men who at home in Massachusetts will not shrink from the same conflict when the slave hunter appears," and that this could only be done by a new party.

He urged that all existing laws for the protection of freedom must be enforced, and that new laws must be enacted where the old laws were inadequate, saying: "Massachusetts will do well in following Vermont, which by special law places the fugitive slave under the safeguard of trial by jury and the writ of *habeas corpus.* . . . A simple prohibition, declaring that no person holding the commission of Massachusetts as justice of the peace or other magistrate shall assume to act as a slave-hunting commissioner or as counsel of any slave hunter, under some proper penalty, would go far to render the existing slave act inoperative. There are not many so fond of this base trade as to continue it when the commonwealth sets upon it a legislative brand."

He justified this counsel, which would have placed Massachusetts in direct conflict with the United States, by the familiar argument that every man was bound only to support the Constitution as he understood it. He pointed out that the judgment of the Supreme Court was final in each case, but as a precedent was not binding on the court itself and therefore could not bind coördinate branches of the government. In the same vein he reminded his hearers that all human tribunals are liable to err, recited historical instances of judicial error, and summed up his advice as follows: "No man who is not lost to self-respect, and ready to abandon that manhood which is shown in the Heaven-directed countenance, will voluntarily aid in enforcing a judgment which in conscience he believes wrong. He will not hesitate 'to obey God rather than man' and calmly abide the peril he provokes."

This was strong doctrine for an eminent lawyer and a senator of the United States to preach in a law-abiding community. It was the most extreme speech that Sumner had made. It brushed aside all respect for law, and appealed directly to the consciences of men, to that law which is above magistrates. It advocated a course of conduct which, if adopted in the ordinary affairs of life,

would make our " government of laws " impossible.
He was preaching revolution. When the decisions
of courts cannot be reconciled with the great principles of right and wrong; when they find no support in the consciences of men, their authority is
gone, and a refusal to obey them may be justified
by the same arguments that make resistance to
other tyrants " obedience to God." In each case
the question of acquiescence or resistance is a
question which each man in the last resort must
decide for himself according to his conscience, sub-
mitting to the penalties with fortitude if he fails to
make his resistance good.

The judgment of a majority in many Northern States sustained Sumner's opinion that the
time for resistance had come. Chase and Seward applauded his speech, and the legislature of
Massachusetts at the next session followed his
advice. He was perhaps the first of the national
leaders to advocate the laws known as " personal
liberty bills " and the similar statutes, by which
Northern States undertook in effect to nullify
the Fugitive Slave Law. His fundamental proposition was, that the provision of the Constitution touching the rendition of " persons held to
service or labor " did not confer any power on the
national government " to establish a uniform rule
for the rendition of fugitives," but was " merely
a compact between the States with a prohibition
on the States, *conferring no power on the nation*,"
like the provision for the extradition of fugitives

from justice. From this he drew the conclusion that, "as a compact, its execution depends absolutely upon the States without any intervention of the nation. *Each State in the exercise of its own judgment will determine for itself the precise extent of obligation assumed.*" When he first asserted this position in the Senate he contented himself with the inference that Congress had no power to pass the Fugitive Slave Law, but he suggested no action by the States. Now, however, he went further, and called upon the States to act so as to secure for their citizens claimed as fugitive slaves the right of trial by jury and the privilege of *habeas corpus*, and to render the execution of the Fugitive Slave Law difficult if not impossible. Upon the legal proposition, that the States were at liberty to construe the Constitution and to pass any laws which their construction of that instrument permitted, rested the whole body of statutes passed by the free States for this purpose, and Sumner's argument was doubtless largely influential in procuring their enactment.

The Republican party, however, was not immediately triumphant. Strong as was the feeling excited by the Kansas-Nebraska bill and the Fugitive Slave Law, it was not strong enough to dissolve party ties in Massachusetts. The convention which Sumner addressed was composed mostly of Free-Soilers. The Whig leaders, elated by their recent victory, were unwilling to unite with men whom they had just been opposing especially when to do so was to confess that their opponents had been right. The aspect of the slavery question had not changed enough to make these men forget so recent a contest. An unexpected political movement accomplished that for which Sumner and his associates were laboring. A secret order, organized in New York to resist the influence of foreign-born voters, especially such as were Catholics, spread rapidly over the country, and many anti-slavery men joined it, notably Henry Wilson of Massachusetts. He was well acquainted with the secrets of the new party, which named itself "American," but was popularly called "Know-Nothing," and we may safely rely upon his statement that "hundreds of thousands, who cared less for its avowed principles than for the higher claims of justice and humanity, and had little faith in its permanency, were willing to use its machinery to disrupt the Whig and Democratic parties, in the confident hope that out of the disorganized masses there would come a great political party, antagonistic to the dominating influences of the slave power." [1]

What the party leaders had attempted to prevent was accomplished. While the political armies were seemingly intact, the privates were secretly in revolt and deserted on the battlefield. When the election took place the Know-Nothings chose the entire state ticket, — all the members of Congress, all the state senators, and nearly all the representa-

[1] Wilson's *Rise and Fall of the Slave Power*, ii. 419, 420.

tives, — and so dominant was the anti-slavery
sentiment in the legislature that Wilson was sent to
the Senate as Sumner's colleague.

The rise of the new organization left Sumner
without a party, and after his speech at Worcester
he took no part in the campaign.   He was absolutely opposed to the attitude of the " Know-Nothings " towards foreign voters, and he never favored secrecy in political action.   With his hatred
of intolerance or oppression and his essentially
frank nature, no other position was possible for
him.   So far, however, as the result was due to the
anti-slavery feeling, Sumner's speeches in the Senate and elsewhere had helped to secure it.   As a
movement against religious freedom and the equality of men, the new party failed ignominiously and
deservedly.   As a movement for freedom, it succeeded, and by shattering the Whig organization
opened the way for the Republican party, which,
abandoning the secrecy and the intolerance of the
" Know-Nothings," became a true party of freedom.

It is interesting to observe that it was the Whig
and not the Democratic party which delayed the
formation of the Republican party.   Until the
Whig party was destroyed, the new organization
was feeble.   The general respectability of the
Whigs, and the party spirit which made them unwilling to recognize the weakness of their own position, while they were keenly alive to the faults of
Democrats and Free-Soilers, kept their party together long after it had ceased to be a useful

political tool. Of the two great parties, it was essentially the anti-slavery party, but political expediency and the constant desire of its leaders to win the next election kept it from taking strong ground on the issue of the day. By offering a shelter to the timid, by appearing to be the better of the two powerful parties while it did not work effectively for righteousness, it divided the anti-slavery forces, created a bitter difference between men who thought alike, and was therefore a worse enemy of freedom than the Democratic party, as a false friend is more dangerous than an open foe. While the Whig party endured, there was no harmonious and strong opposition to the slave power. When it was destroyed, the knell of slavery was sounded. Such conditions are not uncommon in the history of parties; and when they prevail the real obstacles to progress are often those who think themselves its friends, but whose action is paralyzed by cowardice or selfishness, and who neither work heartily themselves nor give place to others who will do so. The political field must be cleared of such effete organizations, which live on their past and prize victory for its spoils, whenever any great political object is to be attained or any great reform accomplished.

The second session of the Thirty-third Congress met in December, 1854, and began peacefully. Sumner offered resolutions on various subjects of general interest, such as the amendment of the law relating to the fisheries, and mediation in the Cri-

mean war. He introduced a bill securing to seamen their wages in case of wreck, which he supported by a speech ; and he wrote against capital
punishment to a committee of the Massachusetts
legislature. But such calm could not continue.
The legislation in the Northern States against
the Fugitive Slave Law provoked retaliation, and
in February, 1855, the committee on the judiciary reported a bill " to protect officers and other
persons acting under the authority of the United
States ; " which provided that any one tried in a
state court for an act done under any law of the
United States might have the suit removed 'to the
federal court. It was recognized at once as an attempt to defeat the recent legislation of the Northern States and to aid in enforcing the Fugitive
Slave Law, and when it was taken up an active
debate ensued, in which Mr. Benjamin said :
" The whole course of Northern legislation for the
past few months has been a course of direct war
with the South ; and the bill now before the Senate is a measure, not of aggression, but of defense."
Sumner closed the debate by a speech in which he
repeated some of his arguments against the consti-
tutionality of the Fugitive Slave Law. In answer
to the question of Butler, whether, if there were
no federal laws on the subject, he would recommend
Massachusetts to pass any law for the rendition of
fugitive slaves, he replied, " Never," thus for himself at least repudiating any obligation to regard
this provision of the Constitution. In closing he

offered an amendment repealing the Fugitive Slave Law, for which nine senators, including Chase and Seward, voted, but which was defeated by the adverse votes of thirty. The bill passed the Senate, but was not taken up in the House, and Sumner's speech was his only conspicuous contribution to the anti-slavery cause during the session.

Shortly after his return home, he delivered a carefully prepared address on the needs of the hour, entitled " The Anti-Slavery Enterprise, its Necessity, Practicability, and Dignity, with Glances at the Special Duties of the North." It was the closing lecture in an anti-slavery course at Boston, and was afterwards repeated elsewhere, and finally in the city of New York itself, where it was received, said the " Tribune," with enthusiasm " by the largest audience yet gathered in New York to hear a lecture." It was at once repeated in Brooklyn, and again in Niblo's Theatre in New York. When we recall the persecution to which the early anti-slavery men were exposed in that city, and the demonstrations which attended their meetings, this reception of Sumner indicated a wonderful change in public opinion. He placed the argument against slavery on the highest plane, and said of the anti-slavery movement : " With the sympathies of all Christendom as allies, already it encompasses the slave masters by a *moral blockade*, invisible to the eye, but more potent than navies, from which there can be no escape except in final capitulation." In this sentence he touched the essential weakness of slavery. Its friends felt keenly the " moral blockade," and knew that slavery must extend or die.

Towards the end of May, 1855, Sumner made his first journey to the West, and while in Ohio he visited Chase. In all he "traversed eleven free States and three slave States." During this journey, in a letter of June 18, he stated the political situation : " The country is approaching a crisis on the slavery question, when freedom will triumph in the national government or the Union will be dissolved. At moments latterly I have thought that the North was at last ready for a rising, and that it would be united in the support of a truly Northern man for president. Perhaps the wish is father of this thought. It is evident that the Know-Nothings cannot construct a national platform on which they can stand at the North and South ; their failure will make way for a Northern combination."

Again, as often, the idealist saw with far clearer vision than did the practical politician. The Know-Nothing National Council, which met on June 5 at Philadelphia, divided hopelessly on slavery and the organization was shattered, though the Know-Nothings still retained sufficient coherence to delay the advent of the Republican party for a year. In Massachusetts a vigorous attempt was made to draw the anti-slavery Whigs and Know-Nothings into union with the Republicans for the autumn campaign of 1855. Mr. Winthrop and other

Whigs were urged to take the lead in the new party. Mr. Winthrop declined, but Julius Rockwell, who had been Sumner's colleague in the Senate, became the Republican candidate for governor, and the ranks of the party were recruited from both organizations, though each nominated its own candidates. Nevertheless, the Know-Nothings carried the State by a large plurality.

Sumner took an active part in the campaign. He put to the voters the direct question, "Are you for freedom, or are you for slavery?" arguing that neither the Democratic nor the Whig party represented the cause of freedom, and that the exigency required a new party. Though the Know-Nothings controlled the State and professed anti-slavery opinions, he took decided ground in a careful speech, alike against their distinguishing principle and their methods, saying: "The special aims which this party proposes are in harmony with the darkness in which it begins." He denounced religious intolerance, unwilling that "the children of the Pilgrims of a former generation" should "turn from the Pilgrims of the present," and concluded: "A party which, beginning in secrecy, interferes with religious belief, and founds a discrimination on the accident of birth, is not the party for us."

Sumner was splendidly consistent in rejecting the assistance of those who, while opposing slavery, were also opposing freedom of thought and speech. He felt the need of every ally in his great contest, yet he did not hesitate to uphold the principles upon which our government rests, even against anti-slavery men. His attacks upon their party led some of the Know-Nothings to oppose his reëlection, but they were not successful.

CHAPTER VIII

THE BROOKS ASSAULT

THE first session of the Thirty-fourth Congress began December 3, 1855. Only eighteen months earlier Sumner had warned his colleagues that they were scattering " broadcast through the land dragon's teeth, which . . . will fructify in civil strife and feud." His prophecy was already realized.

The Missouri Compromise had been repealed in order to make new slave States; but to cloak this purpose the act declared that it was intended " not to legislate slavery into any territory or State, nor to exclude it therefrom, but to leave the people thereof perfectly free to form and regulate their domestic institutions in their own way." The law transferred the struggle from the halls of Congress to the plains of Kansas, and made them the battlefield on which the contest was to be won or lost. Nothing could be done unless the Kansans themselves decided, or appeared to decide, in favor of slavery, and therefore, to insure slave States in the new territory, the first requisite was pro-slavery population.

The friends of the Kansas-Nebraska Act had

expected such an immigration from Missouri as would give Kansas the necessary voters. They did not realize the deep feeling in the North, which from its larger population could easily send more emigrants. Emigration societies were at once formed in Massachusetts and other Northern States, whose purposes and methods were entirely legal; but the South saw in them evidence of a purpose which, backed by adequate resources, meant the inevitable defeat of any attempt to win Kansas for slavery by peaceful settlement. Thereupon associations were formed in Missouri and other slave States for the purpose, avowed with brutal frankness, of expelling immigrants who came to Kansas through the efforts of these societies.

From asserting their own right to carry their slaves into the territories the slaveholders had come to deny the right of any others to settle there; after insisting that the people of each territory must decide for themselves between freedom and slavery, they now refused to allow their opponents any voice in the matter. They determined in short to win Kansas for slavery by force, and they acted promptly. Andrew H. Reeder, a pro-slavery Democrat from Pennsylvania, was made the first governor of Kansas, and entered upon the discharge of his duties in October, 1854. Upon November 29, the day named for electing a delegate to Congress, bodies of armed Missourians entered the territory and voted openly in such numbers that more than half the votes cast were illegal.

On March 30, 1855, the elections for the territorial legislature took place, and again several thousand armed Missourians invaded Kansas, drove the settlers from the polls, and voted in their places. To such open outrages even the Democratic governor could not be blind. He admitted the facts, but lacked courage to set aside the results, and issued certificates of election to most of the persons thus fraudulently chosen. The others were elected later by the legislature itself. Reeder's recognition of the election gave the President an excuse for not interfering, and thus the legislative power in Kansas became vested in representatives chosen by the invaders and not by the inhabitants.

This legislature met on July 2, 1855, and enacted the laws of Missouri bodily, together with such extreme measures in favor of slavery as to make Senator Clayton say that, under such laws, even John C. Calhoun would not be safe from the house of correction.

It was not in human nature to submit when a legislature so chosen passed such statutes; and the real inhabitants bestirred themselves in earnest. A mass meeting held at Lawrence called upon all citizens, whatever their political views, to choose delegates to a convention which should meet at Topeka on September 19, and deal with the whole situation. As a result delegates were chosen to a constitutional convention which met at Topeka on October 23, framed a constitution prohibiting slavery, but also forbidding the settlement of free colored persons, and ordered that this, afterwards called the "Topeka constitution," should be submitted to the people for ratification on December 15. A petition was presented to Congress for the admission of Kansas as a State with this constitution; so when Congress met it was confronted with the question whether it should recognize as the legislature of Kansas the body chosen by the Missouri ruffians, or should treat the Topeka convention as the real representatives of the people, or should direct the people of Kansas to begin afresh.

Before Congress could act, the situation was aggravated by something closely approaching civil war. The rescue of a prisoner from a pro-slavery sheriff led Governor Shannon, who had succeeded Reeder, to call for troops, and a force of Missourians from the border counties responded, assuming to be Kansas militia. These invaders encamped near Lawrence, and open battles were imminent when the governor, terrified at the prospect, made a treaty with the citizens of Lawrence and ordered the troops under his command to withdraw. One man was shot in these proceedings, and the escape from considerable bloodshed was very narrow. Immediately after this incident the Topeka constitution was ratified, the pro-slavery men not voting. On the same day, Atchison, whose term as senator from Missouri had just expired, and who was a leader of the pro-slavery forces, issued an appeal to the South, urging the sending of men and money to Kansas. "Twelve months," he said, "will not elapse before war — civil war of the fiercest kind — will be upon us. We are arming and preparing for it."

On January 15 the state elections were held under the Topeka constitution and were attended by much disorder and some bloodshed. This caused great excitement, and another invasion from Missouri was threatened, whereupon the leaders of the free state men telegraphed to the President for protection. On January 24 the President sent to Congress a special message on Kansas, in which he said that the Emigrant Aid Societies had attempted by colonization to prevent the free determination of the question whether Kansas should be free or slave, and had thus given excuse for the excitement in Missouri; that though the conduct of the Missourians had been " illegal and reprehensible," yet Governor Reeder's certificates of election were binding, and this legal recognition of the territorial legislature left him powerless to interfere; that he would exert the whole force at his command to suppress any resistance to the federal or territorial laws, and that he would protect the citizens of Kansas against further violence from Missourians, but only in case the territorial authorities should request his interposition. The result was that, as the Missourians had by fraud and violence created a legislature and passed atrocious laws, obedience to these would be enforced by the whole power of the government; but the President would not interfere to protect citizens against further outrage by the Missourians and their allies unless the offenders themselves requested him to do so.

In the Senate various resolutions calling upon the President for information were passed, to which he responded on February 18 by a message with documents. In the sharp debate which ensued Sumner took no part, reserving himself for the later discussion which was inevitable; but he watched the progress of the struggle in Kansas and in Washington with the keenest interest. His letters show not only his own feeling, but the general bitterness which prevailed. Thus on December 14, 1855, he wrote to Theodore Parker: "All things here indicate bad feelings. I have never seen so little intercourse and commingling among the senators of opposite opinions. Seward, Wilson, and myself are the special marks of disfavor. God willing, something more shall be done to deserve this distinction."

On March 12 two reports from the committee on territories were made to the Senate, the majority report read by Douglas, the minority report by Collamer of Vermont. The majority reported a bill for organizing a state government in Kansas when the territory should have a certain population, but provided that the steps to be taken for the purpose should be prescribed by the territorial legislature, thus recognizing as legal that fraudulent body. Douglas in his report adopted the

argument of the President's message, laying the
blame on the Emigrant Aid Societies, and Sumner, in a five-minute speech, repelled the attack.
Seward moved to substitute a bill which admitted
Kansas under the Topeka constitution.   Upon
these measures debate began on March 20, and
continued with interruptions for some months.
Douglas indulged constantly in bitter personality,
calling his colleague Trumbull a "traitor," and
suggesting that the " black Republicans " favored
amalgamation of the white and colored races.   He
charged Sumner with having obtained from him a
delay of two days in the debate on the Nebraska
bill, in order to publish "a libel " on him.   Sumner
controverted his statement, and there was a brief
colloquy in which Douglas was very offensive.   This
was Sumner's only participation in the debate until
May 19, when he made his great speech, which
is published under the title of " The Crime against
Kansas."   In the interval the lawless proceedings
in Kansas continued, and the authorities of the
territory exerted all their power to crush the free
state party.   The invasions from Missouri continued, and in May, 1856, one of his officers reported to Colonel Sumner, who commanded the
federal troops : " There are probably five to seven
hundred armed men on the pro-slavery side organized into companies. . . . For the last two or
three days these men have been stationed between
Lawrence and Lecompton, stopping and disarming
all free state men, making some prisoners, and in

many cases pressing the horses of free state settlers into service."

These outrages culminated on May 21 in an attack on Lawrence, made by the United States marshal and the sheriff with a party of Missourians which they called a posse, when the sheriff demanded the surrender of all arms, while a body of his followers broke the presses, type, and appliances of the two newspapers, burnt the Free State Hotel, broke into and plundered stores and houses, and burnt some dwellings. This attack on Lawrence was imminent when Sumner began his speech in the Senate.

This brief sketch of events has been given to remind the reader of the conditions under which he spoke, and the reasons for the fierce indignation which inspired his speech. Sumner had prepared it carefully, and, as he wrote to Theodore Parker, he meant it to be "the most thorough philippic ever uttered in a legislative body." He who reads the speech now will find it a terrible indictment of a policy which should have been impossible in a free country, and of men whose views and whose acts seem absolutely indefensible. It was an unanswerable presentation of eternal truths against the falsehoods of the hour. Its strength lies in its clear and strong statement of the whole case, from the passage of the Kansas-Nebraska bill down to the attack on Lawrence; the facts are marshaled effectively; the conduct of the administration and its representatives in Kan-

sas is described in terms which are forcible from
their naked truth; the arguments in their defense
are riddled; and civil war as the inevitable result
is clearly prophesied. Delivered as the speech
was with the earnestness of intense conviction,
when Sumner was in the full possession of his
splendid powers as an orator and was inspired by
his audience, it is very easy to understand the effect
produced alike upon friends and opponents.
Framed after classical orations, its resemblance to
his models is at times too close, and the speech
is marred by the elaborate attacks on his leading
opponents, though these were hardly written in
cold blood, for Sumner was aflame with indignation even in the solitude of his study. A man
with a keener sense of humor would not have written them, but Sumner delivered them with conscientious earnestness. The feeling which led him
to speak as he did may be gathered from his language to a friend. "There is a time for everything; and when crime and criminals are thrust
before us they are to be met by all the energies
that God has given us, — by argument, sarcasm,
scorn and denunciation. The whole arsenal of
God is ours; and I will not renounce one of the
weapons, — not one!" It is impossible by quotation here to do the speech justice, but one or two
of the most irritating passages must be quoted in
view of what followed. He compared Butler and
Douglas to Don Quixote and Sancho Panza, and
then proceeded as follows: "The senator from

South Carolina has read many books of chivalry, and believes himself a chivalrous knight, with sentiments of honor and courage. Of course he has chosen a mistress to whom he has made his vows, and who, though ugly to others, is always lovely to him; though polluted in the sight of the world, is chaste in his sight: I mean the harlot Slavery. . . . Let her be impeached in character, or any proposition be made to shut her out from the extension of her wantonness, and no extravagance of manner or hardihood of assertion is then too great for this senator. The frenzy of Don Quixote in behalf of his wench Dulcinea del Toboso is all surpassed. . . . If the slave States cannot enjoy what, in mockery of the great fathers of the Republic, he misnames Equality under the Constitution, — in other words, the full power in the national territories to compel fellow men to unpaid toil, to separate husband and wife, and to sell little children at the auction block, — then, sir, the chivalric senator will conduct the State of South Carolina out of the Union! Heroic knight! Exalted senator! A second Moses come for a second exodus! . . .

" As the senator from South Carolina is the Don Quixote, so the senator from Illinois is the squire of Slavery, its very Sancho Panza, ready to do its humiliating offices. This senator, in his labored address vindicating his labored report, — piling one mass of elaborate error upon another mass, — constrained himself, as you will remember, to unfamiliar decencies of speech. . . . Standing

on this floor, the senator issued his rescript requiring submission to the usurped power of Kansas; and this was accompanied by a manner — all
his own — befitting the tyrannical threat. . . .

"The senator dreams that he can subdue the
North. He disclaims the open threat, but his conduct implies it. How little that senator knows
himself, or the strength of the cause which he per-
secutes ! He is but mortal man ; against him is
immortal principle. With finite power he wres-
tles with the infinite, and he must fall. Against
him are stronger battalions than any marshaled by
mortal arm, — the inborn, ineradicable, invincible
sentiments of the human heart ; against him is
Nature with all her subtile forces ; against him is
God. Let him try to subdue these. . . .

"With regret I come again upon the senator
from South Carolina, who, omnipresent in this debate, overflows with rage at the simple suggestion
that Kansas has applied for admission as a State,
and, with incoherent phrase, discharges the loose
expectoration of his speech, now upon her representative and then upon her people. There was
no extravagance of the ancient parliamentary debate which he did not repeat ; nor was there any
possible deviation from truth which he did not
make, — and with so much of passion, I gladly add,
as to save him from the suspicion of intentional
aberration. But the senator touches nothing
which he does not disfigure — with error sometimes of principle, sometimes of fact. He shows

an incapacity of accuracy, whether in stating the
Constitution or in stating the law, whether in details of statistics or diversions of scholarship.   He
cannot ope his mouth, but out there flies a blun-
der. . . .

"Were the whole history of South Carolina
blotted out of existence, from its very beginning
down to the day of the last election of the senator
to his present seat on this floor, civilization might
lose — I do not say how little, but surely less than
it has already gained by the example of Kansas, in
that valiant struggle against oppression, and in the
development of a new science of emigration. . . .
Ah, sir, I tell the senator that Kansas, welcomed
as a free State, ' a ministering angel shall be ' to
the Republic when South Carolina, in the cloak
of darkness which she hugs, ' lies howling.' "

No sooner had Sumner taken his seat than the
feelings which his speech provoked found expression.   Cass first condemned his speech as " the most
un-American and unpatriotic that ever grated on
the ears of the members of this high body."
Douglas followed, attacking Sumner with great
violence, and saying: " Is it his object to provoke
some of us to kick him as we would a dog in the
streets, that he may get sympathy upon the just
chastisement ? " and again : " We have had another
dish of the classics served up, — classic allusions,
each one distinguished for its lasciviousness and
obscenity :" alluding to Sumner's description of the
policy pursued in Kansas as " the rape of a virgin

territory, compelling it to the hateful embrace of slavery." Mason came next, saying : "I am constrained to hear here depravity, vice in its most odious form uncoiled in this presence, exhibiting its loathsome deformities in accusation and vilification against the quarter of the country from which I come; and I must listen to it because it is a necessity of my position, under a common government, to recognize as an equal politically one whom to see elsewhere is to shun and despise."

Sumner replied, speaking affectionately of Cass and regretting his attitude, but dealing otherwise with Douglas. To the latter's assertion that Sumner took his seat in the Senate, and swore to support the Constitution while determined not to support a part of it, he gave a direct denial. He stated his exact position, quoted from the debates, and then, after alluding to the repeated personalities of Douglas, proceeded : —

"Sir, this is the Senate of the United States, an important body under the Constitution, with great powers. Its members are justly supposed, from years, to be above the intemperance of youth, and from character, to be above the gusts of vulgarity. They are supposed to have something of wisdom and something of that candor which is the handmaid of wisdom. Let the senator bear these things in mind, and remember hereafter that the bowie knife and bludgeon are not proper emblems of senatorial debate. . . . The senator infused into his speech the venom sweltering for months, — ay, for years; and he has alleged matters entirely without foundation, in order to heap upon me some personal obloquy. I will not descend to things which dropped so naturally from his tongue. I only brand them to his face as false. I say also to that senator, and I wish him to bear it in mind, that no person with the upright form of a man can be allowed — (*Hesitation.*)

"MR. DOUGLAS: Say it.

"MR. SUMNER: I will say it, — no person with the upright form of a man can be allowed, without violation of all decency, to switch out from his tongue the perpetual stench of offensive personality. Sir, that is not a proper weapon of debate, at least on this floor. The noisome, squat, and nameless animal to which I now refer is not the proper model for an American senator. Will the senator from Illinois take notice?"

These, the bitterest personalities ever used by Sumner in debate, were uttered in the excitement following a long speech and under extreme provocation. It is difficult after the lapse of years to reproduce the conditions and make the reader understand the feeling of the day; but a few words may be quoted from the correspondent of a Missouri newspaper, who was probably no partial critic: —

"That Sumner displayed great ability, and showed that in oratorical talent he was no unworthy successor of Adams, Webster, and Everett, no one who heard him will deny. In vigor and richness of diction, in felicity and fecundity of illustration, in breadth and completeness of view, he stands unsurpassed. . . . In his reply to Cass, Douglas, and Mason, who stung him into excitement, he was more successful than at any other time. The collision knocked fire from him; and well it might, for he was abused and insulted as grossly as any man could be; but he replied successfully to the unmeasured vituperation of Douglas, and the aristocratic and withering hauteur of Mason."

Whittier, the poet, wrote the verdict of those whom Sumner represented: "I have read and reread thy speech, and I look upon it as thy best. A grand and terrible philippic, worthy of the great occasion; the severe and awful truth which the sharp agony of the national crisis demanded. It is enough for immortality." Longfellow called it "the greatest voice on the greatest subject that has been uttered since we became a nation." The London "Times," discussing it as a "provocation" for violence, said: "The speech was elaborately strong, but not stronger than many delivered within the walls of Parliament during the discussion of the Reform and Emancipation bills."

The effect on the country was at once intensified by the events now to be narrated. On Thursday, the 22d, the Senate adjourned early, but Sumner remained writing letters. While he was thus engaged, with his legs stretched out under his desk, which was firmly screwed to the floor, Preston S.

Brooks, the son of Senator Butler's cousin, and a
representative from South Carolina, came up and
said, " Mr. Sumner." Sumner looked up and saw
a perfect stranger, who said, " I have read your
speech twice over carefully. It is a libel on South
Carolina and on Mr. Butler, who is a relative of
mine " — Then, without completing the sentence,
he struck Sumner a blow on the head with a heavy
gutta-percha cane, and followed it by a series of
blows until the cane broke. Sumner struggled to
rise, and in so doing wrenched his desk from the
floor and gained his feet, but, by the time he had
done so, his consciousness had gone, and beneath
the continuing blows he fell senseless on the floor.
Brooks was a very powerful man, over six feet tall,
and he struck with his full strength. Toombs of
Georgia, who witnessed and approved the outrage,
testified of the blows : " They were very rapid, and
as hard as he could hit. They were hard licks,
and very effective." Brooks himself, in the House
of Representatives, said : " I went to work very
deliberately, as I am charged, — and this is admitted, — and speculated somewhat as to whether
I should employ a horsewhip or a cowhide ; but
knowing that the senator was my superior in
strength, it occurred to me that he might wrest it
from my hand, and then — for I never attempt
anything I do not perform — I might have been
compelled to do that which I would have regretted
the balance of my natural life."

He had made his purpose known to Edmundson,

a representative from Virginia, and to Keitt, one
of his colleagues from South Carolina, and both
were present in the senate chamber at the time.
Edmundson had advised with Brooks on Monday
and Wednesday, and was present at his request.
Keitt, when the assault began, hurried up, flourish-
ing a cane, as if to prevent any interference with
Brooks until his purpose was accomplished.

Senators Slidell and Douglas were in the anteroom when some one rushed in and cried out that
a man was beating Sumner. Slidell said in the
Senate: " We heard the remark without any par-
ticular emotion; for my own part I confess I felt
none. I am not accustomed to participate in broils
of any kind. . . . I have no associations or relations of any kind with Mr. Sumner. . . . I did
not think it necessary to express my sympathy or
make any advances towards him." Douglas said:
" My first impression was to come into the senate
chamber and help put an end to the affray if I
could; but it occurred to my mind in an instant
that my relations to Mr. Sumner were such that, if
I came into the hall, my motives would be miscon-
strued perhaps, and I sat down again." Toombs
said: " As for rendering Mr. Sumner any assistance, I did not do it. As to what was said, some
gentleman present condemned it in Mr. Brooks; I
stated to him, or to some of my own friends probably, that I approved it. That is my opinion."

Sumner's head was bruised and gashed, and
the flow of blood was so copious as to drench his

clothes and those of the men who helped him, but
the thickness of his hair apparently prevented a
fracture of the skull and saved his life. He regained his consciousness, his wounds were sewed
up, and he was taken to his lodgings, still in a
partly stupefied condition. On reaching his rooms
he said to Wilson that he should renew the contest
with slavery so soon as he could return to his seat.

An assault, even of this cowardly and aggravated nature, was in itself a matter of compara-
tively trifling importance. There are always men
who in moments of great excitement, or for reasons
affecting them individually, will commit a crime.
The tone adopted by the pro-slavery party in
regard to the act, however, gave it the greatest
significance. The next day in the Senate Wilson
called attention to Sumner's chair, vacant for the
first time during his five years of service, and
briefly narrated the facts, stating that they showed
a grave offense not only against Sumner, but
against the rights of the Senate, which called for
prompt action. Seward moved a committee of inquiry. Mason moved as an amendment that the
committee be appointed by the Senate, and not
named by the president of that body. Seward
accepted this, and the resolution was adopted.
The committee was made up wholly of Sumner's
political opponents, not a single Republican being
chosen. Five days later it reported the facts
briefly without comment, but with the conclusion
that "the Senate, for a breach of its privileges,

cannot arrest a member of the House of Representatives, and *a fortiori* cannot try and punish him ; " that the House alone could deal with the case, and that the Senate could " not proceed further than to make complaint to the House of Representatives of the assault committed by one of its members." The only action of the Senate was an order that this report with the accompanying affidavits be sent to the House of Representatives.

In the House a committee of investigation was appointed on the day of the assault, with instructions to report the facts and such resolutions as seemed " necessary for the vindication of the character of the House." The Southern members with some Northern Democrats resisted the appointment of this committee, on the ground that there was no breach of privilege since the assault was not on a member of the House, but the resolution was passed by a vote of ninety-three to sixty-eight. The committee consisted of three Northern Republicans and two Southern Democrats. They heard witnesses, and in about a week presented a majority and a minority report. The former stated the facts and recommended resolutions expelling Brooks and censuring Edmundson and Keitt. The latter, signed by the two Democrats, concluded with a resolution that the House had no jurisdiction over the assault " alleged to have been committed," and therefore deemed " it improper to express any opinion on the subject."

These resolutions did not come before the House

for action until July 9. Meanwhile Brooks had
been tried for the assault in the Circuit Court of
the District, and sentenced to pay a fine of three
hundred dollars. After a debate lasting some
four days, the minority resolution was defeated,
yeas 66, nays 145. The resolution expelling
Brooks did not receive the necessary two thirds
of the votes cast, but a resolution censuring him
was passed. The censure of Keitt was voted by
ten majority, and the House declined to censure
Edmundson by a vote of 60 against 136. Only
one Southern vote was cast for the expulsion of
Brooks. Immediately after the vote upon the resolution of expulsion, Brooks arose and announced
his resignation. He left on July 14, returned to
South Carolina, was reëlected, receiving all the
votes cast but six, and on August 1 again took
the oath as a member of the House. Keitt also
resigned, and also was returned to the House by a
unanimous vote.

This brief statement of the facts as they appear
of record is sufficient to excite our wonder, but
the language used by the defenders of Brooks was
amazing. In October his constituents gave him
a public dinner, " in testimony of their complete
indorsement of his congressional course," and invited Senator Mason of Virginia and Jefferson
Davis, the secretary of war. Both wrote regretting their inability to accept, and in cold blood,
months after the assault, Mason said of Brooks:
" I know of none whose public career I hold more

worthy of the full and cordial approbation of his
constituents than his.   He has shown himself alike
able and prompt to sustain the rights and the interests of his constituents in debate and by vote,
or to vindicate in a different mode, and under
circumstances of painful duty, the honor of his
friend."   Davis expressed his "high regard and
esteem" for Brooks, and his "sympathy with the
feeling which prompted the sons of Carolina to
welcome the return of a brother who has been the
subject of vilification, misrepresentation, and persecution because he resented a libelous assault
upon the reputation of their mother."

In the debate members defended and applauded
the act of Brooks.   Public meetings were held in
his honor.   Students at the University of Virginia
voted to send him a cane with "a heavy gold head,
which will be suitably inscribed, and also bear upon
it a device of the human head badly cracked and
broken."   The "Richmond Enquirer," in reporting
this meeting, added, " The chivalry of the South, it
seems, has been thoroughly aroused."   Similar tes-
timonials were sent him in great numbers from all
parts of the South.   On June 12 the same newspaper said : " In the main, the press of the South
applauds the conduct of Mr. Brooks without condition or limitation.   Our approbation, at least, is
entire and unreserved ; we consider the act good in
conception, better in execution, and best of all in
consequence. . . . It was a proper act, done at the
proper time and in the proper place."

These are but specimens of numerous utterances by the recognized leaders and the public press of the South. By the open approval of many, and by the silence of others who could not applaud such a brutal and cowardly assault, the South made the act of Brooks its own, and that, which as the crime of an individual might have passed almost unheeded, became by adoption the crime of the whole pro-slavery party.

The assault and the manner in which it was received excited general and intense indignation at the North, expressed in the resolutions of public meetings, the resolves of the Massachusetts legislature, the speeches and letters of leading men in every walk of life and of all political opinions, and in the public press. The real effect of slavery, its brutalizing influence on master as well as slave, the essential barbarism of the system, and the danger to the liberty of free citizens which its continuance and extension involved, were brought home to men as by a flash of lightning. Those, who had been slow to read the lesson taught on the plains of Kansas, had their eyes opened by the strokes of Brooks. It is doubtful whether in his whole life Sumner ever struck a blow at slavery so effective as that which, through him, it received from Brooks. From that moment, on both sides of the Atlantic, the real spirit of "Southern chivalry" was revealed. Quotations might be multiplied, but the feeling and resolve of the North are perhaps epitomized best in the entry which Emerson made in his journal: "Sumner's attack is of no importance; it is only a leaf of the tree. It is not Sumner who must be avenged, but the tree must be cut down. . . . But this stroke rouses the feeling of the people, and shows every one where they are. All feel it. Those who affect not to feel it must perforce share the shame, nor will hiding their heads and pretending other tasks and a preoccupied mind deceive themselves or us."

The outrages in Kansas and this reply of slavery to the man who had characterized these outrages justly were but the first steps in the civil war, and did much to hasten it.

CHAPTER IX

THE RESULTS OF THE ASSAULT

THE result of the act, as an incident in the contest for freedom, has been stated. Its effect upon Sumner personally was serious and lasting. When he was carried to the anteroom of the Senate, it was believed that his injuries were fatal, but he revived more rapidly than was expected, and even thought of going to the Senate on the day after the assault. For several days, indeed, he seemed to be doing well; but then unfavorable symptoms appeared, — high fever, a threatening of erysipelas, and much inflammation of the scalp. The wound was opened, and for some days he remained in a very critical condition; but the immediate danger passed, and the cuts healed.

During the summer he went to various places in search of health, but without success. In August the action of his heart was weak, his gait was tottering and uncertain, the slightest exertion was followed by lassitude, his nights were wakeful, and any mental effort was followed by a sense of weight and a throbbing pain in the head. On October 9 he wrote: "My brain and whole nervous system are jangled and subject to relapse."

Within a week or two after the assault, the governor of Massachusetts recommended the legislature to pay the expenses of Sumner's illness, but when he heard of it, he telegraphed his hope that this would not be pressed, adding, " Whatever Massachusetts can give, let it be given to suffering Kansas." Some of his friends, including Josiah Quincy, Longfellow, Dana, Adams, and others, began a subscription for a testimonial; but this, likewise, he discouraged, making the same suggestion that any contributions be given to Kansas.

The campaign of 1856 was in progress, and he longed to take part in it, but this was clearly impossible. He could not refrain, however, from writing letters in support of the Republican candidates, and he wrote many in answer to requests from different parts of the country. In none of his speeches or letters, at this time or afterward, was there the least expression of indignation at the attack on himself or any personal allusion to his assailant. Years afterward, when walking with George William Curtis in the Congressional Cemetery, his attention was called to the cenotaph of Brooks, which he had not seen. Curtis asked him: " How did you feel about Brooks ? " He answered : " Only as to a brick that should fall upon my head from a chimney. He was the unconscious agent of a malign power." His hostility was directed against slavery; not against slaveholders.

He was unable to take his seat in the Senate

again in December and talked of resigning, but was persuaded to abandon this idea. Towards the end of the session, however, it became apparent that the vote on the Tariff bill of 1857 would be close, and as he wished the duties on raw material reduced, he went to Washington and entered the Senate February 26, 1857, for the first time since the assault. He found himself unable to remain and went to his lodging, but returned in the evening and stayed until an early hour in the morning, giving on two occasions the vote which saved the bill. Except on this day he was not present in the chamber during the session.

He describes his condition in a letter to Theodore Parker, March 1, 1857, as follows: "I have sat in my seat only on one day. After a short time the torment to my system became great and a cloud began to gather over my brain. I tottered out and took to my bed. I long to speak, but I cannot. . . . My own daily experience, while satisfying me of my improvement, shows a subtle and complete overthrow of my powers organically, from which I can hope to recover only slowly."

While Sumner was thus disabled the contest in Kansas and in the country had been proceeding. The sacking of Lawrence, instead of crushing the Free State party, had fired their indignation. A guerrilla warfare ensued in which many lives were lost, and it was in this that John Brown of Osawatomie first acquired prominence. The majority of the investigating committee appointed by the House reported that the elections had been carried by invaders from Missouri, that all the proceedings in Kansas had been irregular, that the conditions were such as to make fair elections impossible without further legislation, and that the Topeka convention represented the majority of the people. There followed a struggle between the two branches of Congress, the effort of the Republican House being to secure the admission of Kansas under the Topeka constitution, while the Democratic Senate proposed a new convention which should frame a constitution and so pave the way for the admission of Kansas. Congress adjourned without legislating, and left Kansas to its fate.

The country immediately plunged into the presidential election. The Republican party, for the first time a national organization, named John C. Fremont, and, relying on the indignation which the struggle in Kansas and the attack upon Sumner had aroused, confidently expected to elect him, but he lost four Northern States, and James Buchanan was chosen president. Massachusetts gave the Republicans an enormous majority, and the reëlection of Sumner was certain. He had been steadily gaining ground among his constituents during his whole term in the Senate. The assault upon him had been felt as an attack upon the State, and so soon as the legislature met he was reëlected, receiving a unanimous vote in the Senate, and all but twelve out of three hundred and forty-five votes in the House. At his first election he had been the candidate of a party which included about one fifth of the voters in the State, while now it threw about two thirds of the votes cast. Then he could expect to find only two or three senators in sympathy with his views; now his party had some twenty senators. Six years had wrought a great change in the sentiments alike of Massachusetts and of the whole country. On March 4, 1857, Sumner took the oath for the second time, and three days later he sailed for France. On the same morning the newspapers announced the decision of the Supreme Court in the case of Dred Scott. His assailant, Brooks, had died six weeks before, and Butler, in whose behalf Brooks assumed to strike, died a few weeks afterward.

Some nineteen years earlier he had made the same journey, full of enthusiasm and vigor, with the world before him and only his own personality to make good the commendations of his friends. Now, a man of forty-six, with a reputation on both sides of the ocean, but broken in health and depressed in spirit, he was to renew the friendships made on his former trip, and to extend his acquaintance among the leading men of France and England. He reached Paris on March 23, and spent a little more than seven months in Europe. A portion of this time he devoted to traveling on the continent, and the rest was divided between Paris, England, and Scotland.

In Paris he saw the best of French society, while in England his life seems to have been a round of breakfasts and dinners in the company of the most distinguished Englishmen. He met Gladstone for the first time, and as the guest of John Bright made his acquaintance, the beginning of a lifelong friendship. This visit placed him in relation with many influential men like Cobden, Palmerston, Lord John Russell, the Duke of Argyll, Dr. Lushington, Lord Cranworth, and William E. Forster, and he was thus enabled to exert a most important influence during the civil war. The Duchess of Sutherland and her daughter, the Duchess of Argyll, who were very hostile to slavery, were especially cordial, and the latter corresponded with him until his death.

What a strong man could hardly have done without fatigue, naturally did not cure a man in his condition. Yet the pleasure and excitement diverted his attention from himself, and the change from the intensity of political conflict at home to the friendly atmosphere of cultivated English society was doubtless refreshing. Gladstone, Bright, and de Tocqueville were pleasant substitutes for Douglas and Toombs, and Sumner was encouraged to believe that his recovery was at hand, though leading physicians in England strongly advised him not to return. Nevertheless, he sailed on November 7, and arrived in Boston on November 19. The next evening he attended a lecture in the Tremont Temple, where he spoke briefly, but he made no other public appearance until Congress met on December 7, 1857, when he took his seat in the Senate.

The Kansas question in its most acute stage at
once engaged the attention of Congress, and Sumner was impatient to take part in the debate; but
his physicians forbade him even to listen, and he
was obliged to leave the Senate on the third day of
the session, when Douglas began his speech against
the position of the administration. For two weeks
he attended during the morning hour, and spent
the rest of his time quietly at his rooms, in the Library of Congress, or at the Smithsonian Institution. On December 19 he wrote Theodore Parker:
" I am unhappy, and yesterday after sitting in
the Senate I felt like a man of ninety." To Dr.
Howe : " At times I feel almost well, and then after
a little writing or a little sitting in the Senate I
feel the weight spreading over my brain, but at
least for the present I shall do nothing; . . . this is
my fate. Hard! very hard! I long to speak."
The next day he left Washington, and only returned occasionally, when his vote was required on
some important question affecting Kansas.

The difficulty in walking and rising from his seat
continued, and in April he was attacked with
pressure on the brain and pain in the back, which
disabled him. After this condition had continued
for a month he listened to the advice of physicians
and friends, and decided again to visit Europe.
He sailed for Havre on May 21, two years after
he had received his injury, and on June 1 he
wrote to John Jay from the ship: " I long for
work, and especially to make myself felt again in

our cause. The ghost of two years already dead haunts me."

Before starting he addressed a short letter to his constituents, stating briefly his condition and that he left the country under the advice of his physicians. He added that had he foreseen originally the duration of his disability, he should at once have resigned his seat, and that he had not done so because he hoped to recover, and did not wish to lose the opportunity of continuing the battle against slavery.

Sumner landed June 1, 1858, and went forthwith to Paris, where he consulted Dr. Brown-Séquard, who decided that the blows on the head had produced a disturbance of the spinal cord. The remedy was "fire," and at Sumner's desire the moxa was applied the same afternoon. He declined to take chloroform lest the remedy might be less effective, and he submitted to the treatment six times in two weeks, the application lasting from five to ten minutes each time. A moxa is a burning of the skin with some very combustible substance, and the doctor said, "I have never seen a man bearing with such fortitude as Mr. Sumner has shown the extremely violent pain of this burning." Indeed Brown-Séquard never afterward used it, because he considered the pain too severe for the human system. The immediate result in Sumner's case was an inflammation which made it hard to walk or sleep, and kept him in bed for the greater part of June and July.

On July 20 he had the first attack of *angina
pectoris*, the intensely painful disease which caused
his death, and similar attacks occurred for a time
with great frequency; yet he managed to write
many letters to England, urging his friends to resist a change in the attitude of the English government towards the slave trade, which then seemed
possible.   After the middle of August he traveled
in Switzerland, Italy, and Germany, and on November 8 he wrote from Worms : —

" The last three or four weeks have shown a
palpable improvement. . . . I feel now certain of
my ultimate restoration, but know not whether it
will be in a month or a year. . . . I suppose
Charles F. Adams is now in his father's seat.
This must tell for the cause everywhere, as his
presence will tell for it incalculably on the floor of
Congress.   All alone I gave three cheers on the
night of the election, and startled the streets of
Munich."

Under the advice of his physicians, he spent the
winter at Montpellier, a pleasant city with an ancient university and a gallery, where he occupied
himself mainly with reading.   In February, 1859,
he wrote to C. F. Adams : —

" The meeting of Congress this winter presented
a question of painful embarrassment.   There were
several courses to take.   To go home in the face of
the positive counsel of eminent medical authorities,
and with a consciousness that I was still an invalid, seemed rash, and hardly to be vindicated,

but to leave my seat vacant throughout a whole session seemed inexcusable.   It only remained that I should resign.   Had I not felt that my case was exceptional, and not that of ordinary political life, of course I should have yielded to the inevitable necessity of this step.   But I could not abandon a position dearer to me now than ever, because more than ever, with returning health, I can hope to serve our cause, and because I have at heart to be heard again from the seat where my assassination was attempted."

In the spring he went to Rome, remaining there three weeks and meeting Story, Motley, Hawthorne, and others of his old friends.   " Rome now, as when I first saw it, touches me more than any other place," he wrote to Story as he left.   On the journey north from Rome he passed through bodies of soldiers gathered for the Franco-Austrian war, and the battle of Montebello was fought on the day before he left Italy.   He sympathized warmly with the Italians, and at Turin he met Cavour, with whom he had a very interesting interview.

A month was spent in Paris, and then he went to London, where he stayed till July 23.   He went into society and often attended Parliament, where the Speaker gave him a seat for a month under the gallery of the House of Commons ; but he overtaxed his strength, and was sent to Aix-les-Bains. He returned to London on October 10, and his account of his last days in England may be quoted :

" Seven days in London at the British Museum; a day with the poet-laureate Tennyson at the Isle of Wight; two days with Lord Stanhope, at Chevening Park, where I slept in the room which was occupied for three years by Lord Chatham; one day at Argyll Lodge, with the duke, where I met Gladstone; one day with Dr. Lushington at Ockham Park in Surrey; one day with my countryman, Motley, the historian of the Dutch Commonwealth, at Walton-on-Thames; one day with Lord Clarendon at the Grove; one day with Lord Spencer at Althorp; one day with Lord Belper at Kingston Hall; one day with Lord Hatherton at Teddesley Park; and here I am." He sailed from Liverpool on November 5, and reached Boston, November 21, a well man, prepared again to take his place in the Senate, and when the first session of the Thirty-sixth Congress met, on December 5, 1859, he was in his seat. His constituents had been glad to let his chair remain vacant until he himself was able to fill it.

CHAPTER X

THE TRIUMPH OF THE REPUBLICAN PARTY

DURING Sumner's absence the cause of freedom had been gaining in Kansas. Under an act of the territorial legislature the question of calling a convention to frame a state constitution was submitted to the people at the election in 1856, and as the vote was in favor of the proposition, an act was passed in 1857 for the election of delegates. This was the state of the contest when Buchanan was inaugurated and the Dred Scott decision was announced, of which Mr. Justice Curtis, who delivered an admirable dissenting opinion, once said: "If you ask me what the Supreme Court of the United States decided in the case of Dred Scott, I answer that I don't know."

From the conflicting opinions of the judges it appeared that, though the case did not call for a decision of the question, a majority meant to express the opinion that Congress had no power to prohibit slavery in any territory of the United States. This gave slavery a new weapon, and the free state men of Kansas had now to contend against the whole power of the government, sustained by the Supreme Court. When the time came for electing delegates to the constitutional convention the free state men asked for correct registration and protection at the polls, but the governor said he could do nothing. They therefore decided not to vote, and at the election in June less than seventeen hundred votes were cast, hardly more than "one tenth" of the total vote. The pro-slavery men elected their candidates and adjourned till October, when they met at Lecompton and framed a slave constitution. They directed that the question should be submitted to the people whether they would adopt the constitution with slavery or without slavery, each voter being required, if challenged, to swear that he would support the constitution "if adopted." This ingenious device was intended to prevent the rejection of the constitution as a whole, and to deter free state men from voting.

Meanwhile under the advice of Henry Wilson, the free state men voted at the election in October for members of the territorial legislature, electing a majority in both houses, and the delegate to Congress by a very large majority. Thus Kansas on a fair vote showed itself decisively for freedom, and it was clear that the new constitution would be defeated if the people were given a proper opportunity to vote. Hence the pro-slavery leaders adopted the form of submission which denied this. As the Charleston "Mercury" said: "Whether the clause in the constitution is voted out or voted in, slavery exists and has a guaranty in the constitution that it shall not be interfered with," this guaranty being a provision against interference with the right of property in slaves.

When the Thirty-fifth Congress met, December 7, 1857, Buchanan in his message approved the Lecompton constitution, and stated that the question had been " fairly and explicitly referred to the people of Kansas whether they will have a constitution with or without slavery." With a Democratic president, supported by a Democratic Congress chosen when the Kansas troubles were fresh in the public mind, and therefore ready to support the pro-slavery policy in that territory ; with a slave constitution likely to be adopted apparently under the forms of law, it seemed as if the fate of Kansas was sealed. But help came from an unexpected quarter. After the reading of the President's message, Douglas rose, — he who had been at once the author and the leading champion of the Democratic policy in Kansas, — and said : " I totally dissent from that portion of the message which may fairly be construed as approving of the proceedings of the Lecompton convention."

These few words meant freedom for Kansas — meant the final failure of the whole pro-slavery campaign. The Lecompton fraud had divided the party of slavery. On December 9 Douglas made an elaborate speech, in which he asserted that the people had been denied the right to decide whether Kansas should be free or slave, a right guarantied by the Kansas-Nebraska bill, and while, as

he said, he did not care whether they voted slavery
" up " or " down," he insisted that until the question had been fairly submitted, Kansas could not
enter the Union as a State.

On December 1 Stanton, as acting governor of
Kansas, summoned the new legislature for December 7, that it might act concerning the Lecompton
constitution, and it voted that the whole constitution be submitted to a popular vote.   On December 21 the vote on the question submitted by the
Lecompton convention was taken, and 6063 votes
were cast " for the constitution with slavery,"
against 576 votes " for the constitution without
slavery."   Of the votes for slavery an enormous
proportion was fraudulent and the free state men
generally declined to vote.   On January 4 the
vote on the constitution as a whole was taken, and
10,266 votes were cast against it.   These results
left no doubt as to the wish of the people, and
greatly strengthened the opposition to the President's position.   None the less he persevered, and
on February 2, 1858, he sent a special message
to Congress defending the proceedings by which
the Lecompton constitution was adopted, and recommending the admission of Kansas under it.   To
secure this the whole power of the administration
was exerted, but after a bitter struggle the bill
was defeated in the House of Representatives by
three votes.   Again, as at almost every important
crisis in our history, the majority for the right was
very small.

The Senate, after a heated contest, passed a bill to admit Kansas with the Lecompton constitution, and a struggle between the two Houses ensued, which ended in a compromise. This law submitted to the people of Kansas the question whether they would accept the Lecompton constitution with the provision that, upon admission, the State should receive five per cent of the sums to be realized from the sale of public lands within its borders, — a very large amount, — or reject both money and constitution. If they rejected the constitution, Kansas was to remain a territory until her population should equal the unit-quota of representation in Congress, and then a new constitutional convention was to be chosen. On August 2 the voters of Kansas repudiated the bribe by an overwhelming majority. The Democratic party had thus striven by fraud, violence, and purchase to establish slavery in Kansas. It is at once mortifying to think how nearly the monstrous attempt succeeded, and encouraging to remember that it failed.

Congress adjourned on June 14, and the congressional campaign of 1858 followed, rendered memorable by the great debate between Lincoln and Douglas in Illinois. More clearly than ever before this campaign was fought upon the question whether slavery or freedom should prevail in this country. The Kansas struggle, no longer an issue by itself, became an episode in a greater conflict. Seward put the question clearly before the

country in his speech at Rochester, in the words
so often quoted : " The two systems of free labor
and slave labor are more than incongruous, — they
are incompatible. They have never permanently
existed together in one country, and they never
can ; . . . it is an irrepressible conflict between
opposing and enduring forces, and it means that
the United States must and will, sooner or later,
become either entirely a slaveholding nation or entirely a free-labor nation." The campaign resulted
in the choice of a House in which the Republicans
had 109 members, the Democrats 101, and the
" Americans " 27.

The second session of the Thirty-fifth Congress
began on December 6, 1858, and was noteworthy
only because the debates emphasized and widened
the breach between the Douglas Democrats and the
opposing wing of the party. During this session
the Kansas legislature passed a law abolishing
slavery, and also called another constitutional convention, which met in July and adopted a free
constitution, ratified by the people in October.

Before Congress met again John Brown had
made his raid into Virginia, which resulted in his
execution for murder, on December 2, with six of
his followers, and it was amid the profound feeling
caused by this episode that the Thirty-sixth Congress — the last before the civil war — convened.
In this Sumner took his seat, well at last and
anxious again to share in the conflict. He was
now one of twenty-four Republican senators, and

was for the first time given his proper place in the formation of committees, being assigned to that on foreign relations.

Under the advice of his physicians to make haste slowly, he did not at once enter the debates. His first speech was on March 12, against a motion made by Mason of Virginia to commit Thaddeus Hyatt for refusing to testify before the committee appointed to investigate the John Brown raid. Early in March he offered a sensible resolution to substitute simple declarations for custom-house oaths, but the recommendation was not adopted. He presented some petitions against slavery, but he took no very conspicuous part in the proceedings till June. He was feeling his way back into active life.

He busied himself during the early months of the session in preparing an exhaustive speech on slavery, its nature and its effects. The Southern leaders had become more aggressive, and during the session resolutions proposed by Jefferson Davis were passed by the Senate, declaring that slave property could not be interfered with in the territories, approving the Fugitive Slave Law, and condemning the personal liberty laws of the Northern States. Sumner felt that their attitude should be rebuked and the weakness of their cause exposed. He had looked forward during his long illness to the time when he could again in the Senate tell the truth about slavery, and his hour had arrived. The House passed a bill for the admission of

Kansas with its free constitution, and when it reached the Senate many senators took the opportunity to speak on the issues of the coming campaign. On June 4 Sumner delivered his speech, published under the title " The Barbarism of Slavery." He read it from printed slips and he spoke for four hours. The temper of the Senate is indicated by the following extracts from a letter of Hammond of South Carolina to Dr. Lieber, written on April 19, 1860, just a year before the Sixth Regiment of Massachusetts was attacked by the mob at Baltimore : —

" So far as I *know*, and as I believe, every man in both Houses is armed with a revolver — some with two — and a bowie knife. It is, I fear, in the power of any Red or Black Republican to precipitate at any moment a collision in which the slaughter would be such as would shock the world and dissolve the government. . . . I tell you — knowing all about it — that unless the aggression on the slaveholder is arrested, no power short of God's can prevent a bloody fight here, and a disruption of the Union."

Sumner was aware of this condition and was urged by his friends to arm himself, but replied that it was idle, for he should be shot before he could draw his weapon, while any attempt to do so would be used as evidence that his murderer acted in self-defense. His speech showed no trace of resentment for what he had suffered, unless it was to be found in a cold indifference to the feelings of his opponents, which was apparent throughout. Hitherto he had always shown a certain sympathy with the defenders of the wrong, while he attacked the wrong itself. Now he seemed to have reached a plane whence he regarded them with no concern. It was slavery whose enormities he exposed, and the time had come when the feelings of men were not to be weighed against the duty of destroying "the sum of all the villainies."

The speech was rather an essay upon slavery than an argument. Its strength lay in the accumulation of facts rather than in the eloquence with which they were presented; and the simple recital would perhaps have been more effective without the rhetorical accompaniments. It was addressed to men who had been born under the system and who believed in it, and it exposed the wickedness and the evil effects of slavery with unsparing, almost brutal fidelity. In opening Sumner reminded his audience that his last speech in the Senate was made to urge the immediate admission of Kansas, with a constitution prohibiting slavery, and although years had intervened he took up the case precisely where he left it. After briefly recapitulating the wrongs of Kansas, he said that the most important part of his argument was untouched in his former speech; that slavery was the motive and therefore "must slavery be discussed not indirectly, timidly, and sparingly, but directly, openly, and thoroughly." "This is no time," he said, "to abandon any advantage in argument.

. . . It is a solemn battle between right and wrong, between good and evil ; such a battle cannot be fought with rose water. There is austere work to be done, and freedom cannot consent to fling away any of her weapons." He quoted from the recent statements of senators such passages as : " Slavery is a great moral, social, and political blessing, — a blessing to the slave and a blessing to the master." Its " frame of society is the best in the world." It is " ennobling to both races, the white and the black." Accepting the issue thus tendered and looking at the matter from the standpoint of a moralist, he showed the essential barbarism of slavery. He quoted from the statutes of the Southern States, from the decisions of their courts, from the advertisements in their newspapers, from the speeches of their public men, from the census, and proved that slavery blasted where it existed, and exposed the slave to every crime, while brutalizing the master. For examples he referred to a recent article in a leading Virginia newspaper, offering fifty thousand dollars for the head of William H. Seward ; another proposing to raise ten thousand dollars for the delivery at Richmond of Joshua R. Giddings, " or five thousand dollars for the production of his head." He quoted from speeches made at that same session of Congress by Southern representatives, which showed an absolute brutality now hard to imagine. The strength of his terrible picture lay in the fact that it was painted by the slave masters themselves.

Such a speech at the beginning of the campaign was intended to be and was a reservoir of facts, from which arguments could be drawn by campaign speakers for use in discussions the country over. Sumner knew that it could have no effect on the action of the Senate, but when men were more than ever considering the slavery question on moral grounds, this speech of the man who had been so conspicuous a victim of the barbarism which he denounced, and who now spoke for the first time after his return to the Senate, had a widespread influence. There was great difference of opinion even among Republicans as to its wisdom, and many felt that it would anger but not convince. A Western newspaper called it " one of the ablest, most exasperating, and most useless speeches we ever read." All admitted its truth, but many doubted whether it would aid the bill to admit Kansas or win votes at the coming election. The event proved that Sumner judged wisely. He appreciated better the state of public feeling than those who were active in the political campaign. He believed in appealing to the highest motives, and putting the evils of slavery before the people so clearly that no one with any moral sense could doubt which side was right. It was the speech which closed the discussion of slavery in Congress, and it seems more like the summing up of a merciless judge than the argument of an advocate.

The adjournment of Congress was followed by

the great campaign of 1860, which resulted in the election of Lincoln, and in this Sumner took an active interest. Requests to speak poured in upon him from all parts of the country, and after the adjournment of Congress he spoke for the Republican Union at the Cooper Institute before an enormous audience. This was an effective campaign speech in which he repeated his arguments and pointed out that by the census of 1850 there were only 347,525 slaveholders, of whom a large majority held only a very few slaves. He showed how great and how pernicious an influence this insignificant number exerted on every department of the government, and urged the vital necessity of saving the country and the age by defeating the party which upheld this abuse. As we read in the light of to-day what he said of slavery, it is difficult to realize how slaveholders believed that their institution could be preserved.

On August 29, for the first time in six years, he met the Republicans of Massachusetts in their state convention, where he discussed the candidates and pointed out that Lincoln stood for freedom, while Bell, Breckinridge, and Douglas were all for slavery. He paid especial attention to Douglas and followed him through his various changes of opinion. During the campaign he wrote many letters, and spoke often in Massachusetts. At Worcester he attacked the theory that popular sovereignty, exercised by a handful of early settlers, could determine the fate of a territory and its immense population in the future. His last speech, made in Faneuil Hall the night before the election, rings with a note of triumph. After alluding to the years that had elapsed since he last stood in that place, he said: " Could these venerable arches speak, what stories could they not tell; . . . the history of American freedom, with all its anxieties, struggles, and triumphs, commencing before national independence and continued down to the very contest now about to close, — all this might be written from the voices in this hall. But, thank God, the days of defeat, of mourning, of fear, have passed, and these walls will record only those notes of victory already beginning to sound in our ears. There are anniversaries in our history noticed by young and old with grateful emotion; but to-morrow's sun will set on a day more glorious for freedom than any anniversary since the fourth of July, 1776. . . . That power which, according to the boast of slave masters, has governed the country for more than fifty years; . . . that power which has taught us by example how much of tyranny there may be in the name of democracy, is doomed. The great clock will soon strike, sounding its knell. Every four years a new president is chosen, but rarely a new government. To-morrow we shall have not only a new president, but a new government."

CHAPTER XI

SECESSION VS. COMPROMISE

THREATS of disunion were frequent during the campaign, and Lincoln was opposed by some on the ground that his election would be followed by secession. Sumner replied to this argument, pointing out that it had been used before "at seven different stages in our history," adding: "Whatever it might have been at first it is now nothing more than 'second childishness and mere oblivion *sans* everything.' There is nothing in it which should not be treated with indignant contempt, certainly when employed here in Massachusetts to make us sacrifice our principles." He showed how little it would avail "as a remedy for the alleged grievances of the slave States," and concluded: "Remember that your first duty is to stand up straight, and not bend before absurd threats, whether uttered at the South or repeated here in Massachusetts. Let people cry 'Disunion.' We know what the cry means, and we answer back: The Union shall be preserved and made more precious by its consecration to freedom."

His view was shared by the most sagacious Republican leaders. Seward derided the cry which the slave power now uttered " with a feeble and muttering voice." Thurlow Weed wrote : "Dissolving the Union is a game for the presidency. It is nothing but a game. That it will be played desperately we admit, because Southern sportsmen play desperately." Chase took the same ground, and so did all the leading Republican newspapers. The party as a whole insisted that the threats of disunion were idle. Before Congress met, however, it had become apparent that the danger of secession was real. In South Carolina the presidential electors were chosen by the legislature, and as the law required a choice in all the States on the same day, the governor convened the legislature on November 5. His message invited them " to remain in session, and take such action as would prepare the State for any emergency that might arise," urging that, if Lincoln were elected, a convention should at once be called, and expressing the opinion that South Carolina must secede and the other slave States follow her. The news of Lincoln's election was received at Charleston with rejoicing, because it insured disunion. On November 7 the federal grand jury in that city closed its session, because the result of the election " involved the existence of the government." On the same day the district judge of the United States resigned, and his example was followed by the district attorney and the collector. Within a few days the legislature called a convention and fixed December 7 as the day for electing delegates.

The legislature of Georgia met the day after the election, heard the message of Governor Brown, who advised against secession but counseled preparation, and passed a resolution affirming the right of secession. By the middle of November the speeches of the governor, the senators, and other leading men showed that Georgia would follow South Carolina. The legislatures of Mississippi and Florida also met in November, and in the same month the governor of Alabama called a state convention, and the governor of Louisiana a meeting of the legislature, making it clear that all these States were on the brink of seceding.

When Congress met, on December 3, the country was face to face with a crisis for which no one was really prepared. Everything was uncertain. In the South a compact body of men was bent on secession, but by no means contemplated civil war. They expected to be joined by the border slave States so that the new confederation would control a large territory and present a united front. They depended on the active sympathy of Europe, believing that the manufacturing nations would exert pressure enough to prevent any war that would interrupt their supply of cotton. As Hammond said in the Senate: "What would happen if no cotton was furnished for three years? England would topple headlong and carry the whole civilized world with her. No, you dare not make war upon cotton. No power on earth dares to make war upon it." His more enthusiastic associate,

Wigfall of Texas, insisted that " Victoria's crown would not stand on her head one week if cotton was stopped, nor would her head stand on her shoulders."

They relied also on disunion at the North. Some believed that the Northwest would join them in order not to lose the control of the Mississippi. Others predicted a new union from which New England and New Jersey alone would be excluded, or to which they would be admitted only on terms to be imposed by the slave power. Nearly all believed that any attempt at coercion would lead to civil war in the free States, and fancied that the stoppage of cotton would throw millions out of employment, and create disturbances which would paralyze the aggressive force of the government. Alexander H. Stephens said, " I have but little doubt that the North will go into anarchy." With such expectations it is not singular that the Southern leaders agreed with Iverson that " there is to be no war. The Northern States are controlled by sagacious men, like the distinguished senator from New York. Where public opinion and action are thus controlled by men of common sense, who know well that they cannot succeed in a war against the Southern States, no such attempt of coercion will be made." Hence the Southern leaders were inclined to reject all proposals of compromise, believing it better to dictate terms after disunion than to negotiate while it was still doubtful. A large body of Southerners indeed opposed secession, but they were not in office, had no leaders or organization, and were in no position to make head against their aggressive opponents. In some States a majority of the voters probably were Union men, but a silent and timid majority without leading is hardly a force even in a republic.

Amid such conditions events moved rapidly from the meeting of Congress to the inauguration of Lincoln. Following the lead of South Carolina, which passed her ordinance of secession on December 20, the Southern States seceded in rapid succession. The members of the Cabinet and the senators and representatives from the seceding States successively resigned their places. On January 19 the legislature of Virginia called a convention of representatives from all the States to find a way of preventing disunion. On February 4 the Peace Conference, summoned by Virginia, met at Washington, while a convention to frame a constitution for the new confederacy met at Montgomery. On the 8th the Confederate constitution was adopted. On February 9 Jefferson Davis and Alexander H. Stephens were elected president and vice-president of the Southern Confederacy, and on February 18 they were inaugurated at Montgomery. The secessionists marched steadily on, and their plans apparently were not affected by any suggestions of compromise.

The national administration was utterly unfitted to meet the emergency. The President was old and irresolute, anxious only to reach the end of his term in peace and transfer his responsibilities to his successor. Of his Cabinet, Floyd, secretary of war, and Thompson, secretary of the interior, actively aided secession. Thompson communicated the secrets of the administration, and Floyd had long been stocking the Southern arsenals with munitions of war.

In his message to Congress, December 3, 1860, the President blamed the North and admitted that the Southern States had been wronged, but denied their right to secede, saying that the election of any citizen to the presidency was not of itself an excuse for such revolutionary action, especially since no law injurious to the interests of the South could pass both houses of Congress. He recognized his duty to enforce the laws, but suggested that where the whole machinery of the federal government had broken down, as in South Carolina, it was extremely difficult to do so. Finally, he found no power in the government to prevent secession by force, thus telling the secession leaders that they need fear nothing from the administration.

The seat of active trouble was Charleston, and the question, whether the forts in its harbor should be reinforced and held, divided the counselors of the President and was the subject of negotiation between him and commissioners from South Carolina. The President vacillated, and satisfied no one.

On December 15 Cass, the secretary of state, resigned, because the President refused to reinforce

the forts, and on the 29th Floyd resigned, because
the President would not order Major Anderson to
leave Fort Sumter. Finally the unarmed steamer
Star of the West was sent with provisions, but was
driven back by South Carolina troops advised of
her sailing by the secretary of the interior. This
was Buchanan's only attempt to assert the authority of the United States. From the first day of
the session to the last he was advising Congress to
win the seceders back by compromise, and was
trying to avoid any positive action.

What was the position of the victorious Republicans in this crisis? They owed their success to
the division of their opponents rather than to their
own strength, and their candidates had received a
minority of the popular vote even in the Northern
States. The sudden spectre of disunion, the worse
one of civil war, appalled a peace-loving community entirely unprepared to fight. Merchants were
frightened by the probable interruption of relations with half the country and the danger of enormous pecuniary loss. A veritable panic ensued.
The opponents of the Republicans loudly demanded
some compromise to relieve the situation, while
many who had voted for Lincoln joined in the
demand, regarding civil war as a far worse calamity than concession to slavery. Many of the
abolitionist leaders, Wendell Phillips, Horace
Greeley, Whittier, and others, urged that no attempt should be made to hold the seceding States.
Their view was expressed in Whittier's poem : —

"They break the links of Union; shall we light
   The fires of hell to weld anew the chain
   On that red anvil where each blow is pain?"

In the face of impending calamity every shade
of opinion found supporters, and it was not easy to
tell what course would command public approval.
A policy was needed which the North would support, which would keep the border States from
joining the South, and which would not sacrifice
what had been gained by Lincoln's election. It also
seemed to the Republicans important that any
open rupture should be avoided, until the inauguration of Lincoln should place them in control of the
government; for under Buchanan the secessionists
might gain great advantages. This alone was to
many a sufficient reason for temporizing. Some
Republicans felt it most desirable to put the South
in the wrong, in order to unite the North. Others
believed it far more essential to stand firm and
lose none of the ground which had been won with
such difficulty. A few believed adjustment possible and were willing to concede much for the sake
of peace. From whatever motive, Seward, already
known to be Lincoln's secretary of state, was active
in suggesting compromise. The existence of these
different forces must be recognized in order to
understand the confused politics of the session. It
must also be borne in mind that some resolute dis-
unionists were anxious to avoid hostilities while
Buchanan was in office, fearing that, if he were
driven to act against them, the Democrats would

rally to the support of a Democratic president and give Lincoln a united North.

The winter passed in negotiations, and there was the gravest danger that the victory so hardly won for freedom might be turned into the worst of defeats by a surrender. Such a course would not only have sacrificed the immediate fruits of the victory, but would have paralyzed future effort, by making threats of disunion more effective than a majority of the votes at a presidential election. The results of such a compromise were indicated in the following amendment to the Constitution proposed during the session : " Whenever a party shall be beaten in an election for president and vice-president, such party may rebel and take up arms, and unless the successful shall adopt as its own the principles of the defeated party and con- sent to such amendments of the Constitution as the latter party shall dictate, then in such case the Union shall be at an end."

In the House of Representatives so much of the President's message as related " to the present perilous condition of the country " was referred to a special committee of one from each State. Corwin of Ohio was chairman, and Reuben Davis of Mississippi was the most prominent representa- tive of the secessionists. On December 15 Davis offered a resolution in this committee, that it was the duty of the federal government to protect slave property like all other property on land and water. The Southern members agreed to it, and promised to recommend it as a final settlement of the slavery question. It was defeated by the casting vote of the chairman, and the Southern members left the committee room. From that moment it was apparent that this committee could not agree.

In the Senate a motion to refer so much of the message as related to the condition of the country was not adopted until the 18th, after a debate. Sumner read a letter of President Jackson, written on May 1, 1833, in which these striking words occurred: " Take care of your nullifiers; you have them among you; let them meet with the indignant frowns of every man who loves his country. The tariff, it is now known, was a mere pretext ... and disunion and a Southern Confederacy the real object. The next pretext will be the negro or slavery question." On December 18 Mr. Crittenden introduced his compromise resolutions, proposing six articles for the Constitution and many legislative acts. He spoke in support of his plan on January 7, and his resolutions were antagonized by an amendment introduced by Mr. Clark of New Hampshire, to the effect that " the provisions of the present Constitution are ample for the preservation of the Union and the protection of all the material interests of the country; that it needs to be obeyed rather than amended; ... and therefore to the maintenance of the existing Union and Constitution should be directed all the energies of all the departments of the government and the efforts of all good citizens." On January 16 this substitute was adopted, owing to the fact that the senators from the Gulf States did not vote. A motion to reconsider, however, was carried, and the resolutions of Crittenden lay upon the table until, on the last day of the session, they were called up by Mason of Virginia and defeated, most of the Southern senators having withdrawn or withholding their votes.

In the House the committee of thirty-three, after much discussion, submitted eight reports on January 14, but not one of these was fully approved by a majority of the whole committee.

The so-called majority report urged the importance of respecting the constitutional obligation to return fugitive slaves, and proposed resolutions that all state legislation obstructing the execution of the Fugitive Slave Law should be discouraged; that Congress had no right to interfere with slavery in the States; that there was no ground for the dissolution of the Union; that the States should revise their laws concerning the right of citizens of one State to travel in another; and that the States should enact proper laws against the invasion of one State by another. The report proposed an amendment to the Constitution, declaring that Congress should have no power to interfere with slavery where it existed, " until every State in the Union, by its individual state action, shall consent to its exercise." It also recommended that New Mexico be admitted as a State with its pro-slavery code. To the surprise of many, Charles

Francis Adams supported these recommendations. Into his reasons for so doing, it is unnecessary to enter. He was essentially a diplomat, and his policy was to discuss concession until the control of the government was secured.

Sumner was absolutely opposed to compromise. His object was the destruction of slavery because it was wrong, and any concession to it was to him impossible. From the time when he enlisted against it, he never saw the hour when he would have hesitated to use every legal power to free his country from its great curse. The attitude of Adams was to him inconceivable, for he believed that the offer of compromise might be accepted. The very intimacy of their previous friendship made their disagreement on this point more serious. From the difference in their tempers and modes of action, it was inevitable that their paths should diverge, and at this point they separated. The result was a coolness which terminated their cordial relations. Sumner refrained from taking part in the debates, "because," as he said in a private letter, "I could say nothing which would not be perverted by the compromisers as an attempt to widen the breach." By conversation and correspondence, however, he did much to make his political associates stand firm against any concession to slavery and disunion.

The following extracts from his correspondence show his position. On January 1, 1861, he wrote to William Claflin, president of the Massachusetts

Senate and chairman of the Republican state committee : " Massachusetts has now an important
post. Her most difficult duty is to be true to
herself and her own noble history. In the name
of Liberty, I supplicate you not to let her take
any backward step, — *not an inch, not a hair's
breadth.*"

January 8 he wrote : " Sunday evening I had
a visit from Thurlow Weed and Seward. . . .
They urge that we cannot have a united North
unless we make an effort for adjustment ; to which
I reply : ' We have the verdict of the people last
November : that is enough.' The slave States are
mad. They will all move. Nothing now but abject humiliation on the part of the North can stay
them. Nobody can foresee precisely all that is in
the future, but I do not doubt that any conflict
will precipitate the doom of slavery. It will probably go down in blood."

He hastened to deny his alleged adherence to
the Virginia " Peace Conference," and said : " I
am against sending commissioners to treat for the
surrender of the North. Stand firm."

On February 2, after an interview with the
President, he wrote to Governor Andrew : " I said
to him, ' Mr. President, what else can we do in
Massachusetts for the good of the country ? ' A
pause. ' Much, Mr. Sumner.' ' What ? ' said I.
' Adopt the Crittenden propositions,' said he. ' Is
that necessary ? ' said I. ' Yes,' said he. To which
I replied, ' Massachusetts has not yet spoken di-

rectly; but I feel authorized to say that, such are the unalterable convictions of her people, they would see their State sunk below the sea, and turned into a sandbank, before they would adopt propositions acknowledging *property in men*, and disfranchising a portion of her population.' I think I was right."

When the legislature of Massachusetts was urged to repeal her personal liberty laws, Sumner wrote to members strongly opposing such action, and his influence prevailed. Seward urged compromise, though he offered no definite propositions. He seemed to think that a solution might be found if a rupture could be avoided until the new administration came into power. On January 12, in a great speech, he recognized the constitutional obligation to return fugitive slaves, expressed his willingness by constitutional amendment to provide that Congress should never be given power to deal with slavery in the States, and to pass acts for the admission of future States without special prohibition of slavery. Of this speech, Sumner wrote to Andrew on January 17: " Our friends are all tranquil, except so far as disturbed by Seward's speech. If his propositions were pressed, I think they would split the party. . . . He read me his speech four days in advance of its delivery. I pleaded with him for the sake of the cause, the country, and his own good name to abandon all his propositions, and simply to declare that Mr. Lincoln would be inaugurated on the 4th of March President of the United States, and rally the country to his support. I do not think we should allow this opportunity to pass without trying the question whether a single State can break up the Union. What is it worth, if held by any such tenure ? I have no concession or compromise of any kind to propose or favor."

On the 21st : " Pray keep our beloved commonwealth firm; yet a little longer and the crisis will be passed. Save her from surrender. Nothing she can do will stay secession. *Impossible*. Let her not write a shameful page in the history of human freedom." On the 26th : " The mistake of many persons comes from this, — they do not see that we are in the midst of a revolution, where reason is dethroned, and passion rules instead. . . . I have but one prayer, — stand firm, keep every safeguard of human rights on our statute-book."

When the rest of the Massachusetts delegation urged Governor Andrew to appoint delegates to the Peace Conference, Sumner declined to sign. The governor thought it better to send delegates in order that volunteers might not go who would misrepresent Massachusetts.

February 10, after the conference had assembled : " Every word of concession thus far has done infinite mischief, — first, by encouraging the slave masters ; and, secondly, by demoralizing our own friends, and filling them with doubt and distrust."

On February 12 Crittenden presented in the

Senate in support of his proposals a petition from more than twenty thousand citizens of Massachusetts, who alleged that " their sentiments towards the Union and towards their common country have been misrepresented and misunderstood." This brought Sumner to his feet. He pointed out how enormously the proposed compromise increased the power of slavery, and how it discredited our whole system of government, and he took the distinct ground that " there is but one thing now for the North to do : it is to stand firm." Of this speech Emerson wrote to him : " Peace and prosperity adhere to your truth and firmness as they ought. I am always consoled in the bad times by your fidelity."

It is interesting to compare the words of Sumner with the counsels of Lincoln at the same time, who, on January 11, 1861, wrote : " We have just carried an election on principles fairly stated to the people. Now we are told in advance the government shall be broken up, unless we surrender to those we have beaten before we take the offices. In this they are either attempting to play upon us, or they are in dead earnest. Either way, if we surrender, it is the end of us and of the government."

And on February 1 to Seward : " On the territorial question — that is, the question of extending slavery under the national auspices — I am inflexible. I am for no compromise which assists or permits the extension of the institution on soil owned by the nation. And any trick by which the nation is to acquire territory, and then allow some local authority to spread slavery over it, is as obnoxious as any other. I take it that to effect some such result as this, and to put us again on the high road to a slave empire, is the object of all these proposed compromises. I am against it."

Chase was equally inflexible, and these views prevailed. The compromise propositions were defeated. The Peace Conference and the committees of House and Senate alike failed. The seceding States were unwilling to accept any concession that the North was prepared to make. On the last day of the session the Senate concurred with the House in adopting a hastily drawn amendment to the Constitution, intended to prevent any amendment which should give Congress the power to interfere with slavery in the States, but this abortive result of the attempt to stay a revolution was soon forgotten in civil war.

On March 4, 1861, Lincoln was inaugurated, and the withdrawal of the Southern senators left the Republicans in control of the Senate, which remained to act upon the appointments of the new President. The committees were at once reorganized, and Sumner was made chairman of the committee on foreign relations in place of his opponent Mason. He had been suggested for the English mission, but he preferred to remain in the Senate. His tastes, his training, and his European acquaintance fitted him well for his new position. It was thoroughly agreeable to him, and the selection was approved at home and abroad.

He was at once interested in the choice of our diplomatic representatives. As he wrote : " There is chaos in our foreign system. But it is of incalculable importance that our cause should be represented at every European government with all the character, skill, and persuasion which we can command." It was urged then, as it has been ever since, that these great positions should be used to reward political service and should be distributed geographically. To such views Sumner was absolutely opposed, though somewhat inclined to favor men conspicuous for anti-slavery zeal. He felt that a minister should speak the language of the country to which he was sent, and that fitness was essential. His advice was influential but not always controlling, and to some changes he was strongly opposed. In one case where an incompetent politician was appointed against his urgent counsel, Mr. Lincoln came to agree with him, for he afterwards said : " When I think of —— as minister to ——, I wish the earth would open and take me in."

The only important subject referred to his committee during the short session of the Senate was the message of the President, asking advice upon the question whether the proposition of Great Britain to refer the San Juan boundary question to arbitration should be accepted. Mr. Sumner promptly reported in favor of acceptance and the selection of Switzerland as arbiter.

The Senate adjourned on March 28, 1861, but Sumner remained in Washington until after Sum-

ter was fired upon and the administration called
for troops.   Leaving on April 18, he spent the
night in Baltimore, where he narrowly escaped
being mobbed.   He left there on the morning of
the day when the Sixth Regiment of Massachusetts
was fired upon while passing through the city, and
three days later he addressed the third battalion of
Massachusetts Rifles in New York on its way to the
front.   His speech was brief but inspiring, and it
was clear, as his biographer Mr. Pierce says, that
"at last a war had come which the author of ' The
True Grandeur of Nations ' thought honorable and
worthy of every patriot's blessing."

CHAPTER XII

EMANCIPATION

So soon as the true nature of the conflict was recognized the question of its effect upon slavery was presented. This was of vital importance, especially in the border States, where men were divided between love of the Union and fear of losing property. Even in the free States many were ready to support the government in restoring the Union who were not yet opposed to slavery, and the administration justly felt that it could not alienate these men or strengthen the secessionists in the border States. Its first duty was to stop the spread of the conflagration and to retain in the Union the States which had not seceded. Could this be done and the North remain united, the defeat of the South became only a question of time. The administration therefore was supported by public opinion, when in the early stages of the conflict it declared that its purpose was simply to restore the authority of the government in the seceded States, and that slavery would not be interfered with. This was stated by Seward in his instructions to our foreign representatives.

In pursuance of this policy the army was instructed not to interfere with slaves, and the attorney-general instructed the marshals of the United States in Missouri that the Fugitive Slave Law must be executed. The secretary of war met General Butler's famous suggestion that slaves were " contraband of war " with the statement: " It is the desire of the President that all existing rights in all the States be fully respected and maintained; " and the President annulled General Fremont's order of August 30, 1861, emancipating the slaves of those Missourians who should take arms against the government. The policy thus proclaimed and carried out was doubtless wise. It won for the President the confidence of many who had not been his supporters, it strengthened the Union cause in the border States and perhaps prevented their secession, and when in the fullness of time the President decided that slavery must perish to save the Union, he had behind him a support which he could not have commanded earlier, and without which his blow might have been futile.

Sumner recognized the wisdom of not attacking slavery too soon, but he never believed that the Union and slavery could both be preserved. He had seen in slavery the root of all our trouble too long not to feel that the government should use every power to destroy it, and that no real union was possible until this was done. His never varying purpose from the moment when the Republicans came into power was to end slavery, and strike from the statute-book every recognition of its exıstence, and every denial to colored men of their equal rights as citizens. He saw with the eye of a statesman that there could be only one real end to the conflict, and he sought that end with a directness which more politic men could not imitate. He was a force constantly pushing for freedom, and trying to carry his fellow countrymen with him. It was necessary, perhaps, that others should hold back, that the army might be kept together, — that men might gradually outgrow the prejudices with which they began the struggle. The war was a process of education, and Sumner was a teacher constantly inculcating its lesson. Without him and those who shared his views progress would have been slower; without others it might have been less sure.

The President and he were in thorough accord as to the end, but Sumner felt that the time to strike had arrived before the President was ready to act. He thought that foreign intervention, on which the Confederate leaders relied, would be made impossible by emancipation, since we should have the sympathy of Europe in a contest for freedom, while we should not have it in a contest for empire. He believed also that there was no weapon so effective against the armies in the field. At the end of May, 1861, in conversation with the President he admitted that the time had not yet come, but he urged him to be ready for action at the first favorable moment. Two days after the defeat of Bull Run, when the news showed

that the country was thoroughly aroused, he told
the President that the time had come. The President thought not, and recalling their earlier conversation said : " Did you not then approve my
course ? "   " Certainly," was the reply, " at that
time ; but I said also that you must be ready to
strike at slavery, and now the moment has come.
Of this I have no doubt." But though this was
his private advice, he betrayed no impatience in
public.

Congress met in extra session on July 4, 1861,
and Mr. Crittenden, now a member of the House,
introduced a resolution to declare the object of the
war, which was passed with only two opposing
votes.   Andrew Johnson introduced almost the
same resolution in the Senate, and in it was this
statement : " That this war is not prosecuted on our
part in any spirit of oppression ; . . . nor for the
purpose of overthrowing or interfering with the
rights or established institutions of those States ;
but to defend and maintain the supremacy of the
Constitution and all laws made in pursuance thereof,
and to preserve the Union." This general language was evidently intended to protect slavery
and the Fugitive Slave Law, but it received the
support of all the senators except Trumbull, who
voted against it, and Sumner, who did not vote
because, though opposed to the resolution, he was
" unwilling to separate openly from political associates." For the same reason, in two bills which
he introduced during this session for punishing

treason and confiscating the property of traitors,
he made no reference to slaves, though he used
language broad enough to cover all property.

There was some evidence during the session that
Sumner's view was gaining ground in the passage
by the House, on July 9, of a resolution " that it is
no part of the duty of the soldiers of the United
States to capture and return fugitive slaves," and
the passage of a law that the slaves of rebels used
by them for military purposes should be freed.
Nevertheless, the policy of protecting slavery
against the natural consequences of war still continued, and the attitude of the President was made
apparent by the various military orders above mentioned.

Sumner felt that it was not safe to delay until
the course of the war had educated the country up
to emancipation, and that something should be
done to create a public opinion upon which the
President could lean.   His opportunity came in an
invitation to address the State Republican Convention of Massachusetts, and his speech on October 1,
1861, was the first public demand for emancipation
made by any responsible statesman.   After dwelling on the suffering and disasters caused by the
civil war, and pointing out that all these were
borne to preserve slavery, he proceeded : —

" It is often said that war will make an end of
slavery. This is probable. But it is surer still
that the overthrow of slavery will make an end of
the war.

" If I am correct in this averment, which I be-lieve beyond question, then do reason, justice, and policy unite, each and all, in declaring that the war must be brought to bear directly on the grand conspirator and omnipresent enemy. Not to do so is to take upon ourselves all the weak-ness of slavery, while we leave to the rebels its boasted resources of military strength. . . . It is not necessary even, borrowing a familiar phrase, to carry the war into Africa. It will be enough if we carry Africa into the war."

To sustain his position, he quoted John Quincy Adams, who always held that the government had power to destroy slavery in the event of war; and having established the power to strike he said: " I calmly deliver the whole question to those on whom the responsibility rests, contenting myself with reminding you that there are times when *not to act* carries with it greater responsibility than *to act*. It is enough for us to review the unquestioned pow-ers of government, to handle for a moment its mighty weapons, yet allowed to slumber, without assuming to declare that the hour has come when they shall flash against the sky." In conclusion he recognized the duty of compensating loyal owners for their losses. Outside the convention and on both sides of the ocean opinion was sharply divided as to the wisdom of the speech. Conservatives re-garded it as unfortunate, and its author as im-practicable, perverse, and almost insane. They thought that it would divide the North, embarrass the administration, and render more difficult the prosecution of the war. On the other hand, it was warmly applauded by large numbers, including some of those very border state men, whose sensibilities the North was so anxious to consult. It stirred men's minds, and awakened in many a fresh enthusiasm, especially among the rank and file of the Republican party.

Sumner followed it up by a more carefully prepared address, delivered during October and November in various cities, and finally at the Cooper Institute in New York on November 27, 1861, where a singularly brilliant audience adopted by acclamation a resolution approving his position.

His line of argument was essentially the same as in his speech to the Worcester convention, and the reasons for striking slavery directly were presented with great force. He dwelt especially upon the fact that it was the labor of slaves at home which kept their masters in the field, saying, "Thus by singular fatality is this doomed race, without taking up arms, actually engaged in feeding, supporting, succoring, invigorating those battling for their enslavement." This speech, like the preceding, was attacked as unwise, but it did much to change public opinion.

When the session of Congress opened, on December 2, 1861, Sumner was in his seat. He found the President in sympathy with the policy which he had advocated, but not ready to act. "He tells me," wrote Sumner to Andrew, "that I

am ahead of him only a month or six weeks." The
President in his message suggested his favorite
plan of colonization, but took no decided stand as
to freeing the slaves of rebel owners. The tendency of his mind was indicated by his declaration :
" The Union must be preserved, and hence all
indispensable means must be employed ; " but his
doubts found expression in the qualifying clause :
" We should not be in haste to determine that radical and extreme measures, which may reach the
loyal as well as the disloyal, are indispensable.'
He was feeling his way, knowing the danger of
hasty action, and in justification of his policy he
was able to adduce the fact that from Maryland,
Kentucky, and Missouri, which at first would not
offer a soldier, at least forty thousand men were
then in the Union army.

Sumner at once addressed himself to the work
of educating the people to demand emancipation.
On December 4 he offered a resolution calling
for General Halleck's orders in Missouri, which directed that fugitive slaves be not received within
the lines, and that those already there should be
expelled. In a brief speech he criticised these orders as " disheartening to our soldiers," " irrational
and inhuman." There was some hesitancy on the
part of our generals in regard to escaped slaves,
and Sumner again spoke on the subject in May,
urging the folly of protecting slavery while it was
attempting to destroy the government. He followed his first speech by a resolution directing the

committee on military affairs to consider the expediency of legislation against the surrender of fugitive slaves by our armies. The subject received prompt attention in both Houses, and, after much discussion as to form, a bill was passed by the House adding a new article of war prohibiting the use of the United States forces for the return of fugitive slaves. This passed the Senate, and became a law on March 13, 1862.

On December 4 he took advantage of a debate over the condition of the courts and prisons in the District of Columbia to suggest that the evils of which senators complained were due to the black code, and that the remedy was to be found in the abolition of slavery in the District. He had long urged the abolition of slavery wherever the United States had exclusive jurisdiction, but this was the first public word on the subject since the Republican party came into power.

On December 16 his colleague, Mr. Wilson, introduced a bill to abolish slavery in the District of Columbia with compensation to loyal owners, which was amended by adding an appropriation of one hundred thousand dollars for colonizing in Hayti or Liberia slaves who desired to migrate. While this was pending in the Senate the President sent for Mr. Sumner, and showed him the draft of a message recommending the following resolution: "That the United States ought to co-operate with any State which may adopt gradual abolishment of slavery, giving to such State pecuniary aid, to be used by such State, in its discretion, to compensate for the inconveniences, public and private, produced by such change of system." Sumner did not believe the plan practicable, but he welcomed the evidence of the President's tendency towards the course which he so strongly urged. He made some suggestions as to the language, which the President adopted, and the message was sent in. The resolution was passed, and soon afterwards the bill for compensated abolition in the District of Columbia came up for discussion. Sumner spoke in favor of the bill on March 31, addressing himself especially to the doubt of anti-slavery men whether it was right to acknowledge property in man by paying the owners for their slaves. To many it seemed that the payment should be made to the slaves. Sumner urged compensation: *first*, because Congress had recognized and supported slavery in the District, thus making the whole country responsible for the wrong, and therefore properly chargeable with the expense of righting it; *second*, because it was the most practical way of removing slavery. To meet the scruples of friends, he called the payment ransom, and compared it with our payments to the Dey of Algiers. The speech was not especially noteworthy; for he was speaking to a body which agreed with him, and was only waiting for the end of the debate to pass the bill. This was done in the House on April 11, but the President withheld his signature till the 15th. Sumner could not understand the delay, and called upon Mr. Lincoln to urge action. "Do you know," he said, "who at this moment is the largest slave-holder in this country? It is Abraham Lincoln, for he holds all the three thousand slaves of the District, which is more than any other person in the country holds."

The President, in a message approving the bill, explained his delay by pointing out that certain classes, such as minors, married women, and others, were not sufficiently protected by it, and suggested additional legislation, which was passed. He was, however, pleased that it recognized the two principles of compensation and colonization. Thus was paid, in the words of Sumner, "a small installment of that great debt to an enslaved race which we all owe."

CHAPTER XIII

THE TRENT AFFAIR

DURING this autumn occurred an event which gave Sumner the opportunity to render his country perhaps the greatest single service of his life. The state of our foreign relations was far from satisfactory, and Mr. Seward had created the impression that he was hostile to England and not averse to war with that country. The people of the North had expected English sympathy, and were irritated by the hostile tone of many prominent Englishmen. The early recognition of belligerency by England and France had seemed unfriendly, and on both sides misunderstanding and ill feeling existed. The course of the war also had been unfavorable to the government.

In this condition of affairs, on November 8, 1861, Captain Wilkes, in command of the United States ship San Jacinto, stopped the British mail steamer Trent on the high seas, while on a voyage from Havana to Nassau, and took from her Mason and Slidell, envoys from the Confederate States to England and France. The Trent was allowed to proceed, while the prisoners were brought to the United States. This action of Captain Wilkes was received

throughout the North with warm approval, perhaps
the more cordial because Mason and Slidell had
been especially arrogant and offensive champions
of slavery. On November 30 the secretary of the
Navy sent to Captain Wilkes the "emphatic approval" of the department, and two days later the
House of Representatives passed a joint resolution
giving him the thanks of Congress. The press and
leading men of all parties, like Edward Everett,
Governor Andrew, Chief Justice Bigelow, and Caleb
Cushing in Massachusetts, united in applauding the
act.

Sumner was in Boston when the news came, and
at once said, "We shall have to give them up."
He went to Washington and found the President
doubtful and anxious, but his Cabinet, except Postmaster-General Blair, in sympathy with the feeling
of the country. On November 30 Mr. Seward
wrote to Mr. Adams that Captain Wilkes had acted
without instructions, and expressed the desire of
the government so to deal with the case as to avoid
conflict. While waiting dispatches from the British
government the administration did nothing to anticipate the discussion. The news of the capture
reached London on the night of November 27.
Earl Russell, after consulting the law officers of the
Crown, sent a dispatch to Lord Lyons at Washington on November 30, instructing him to demand the surrender of Mason and Slidell and a
suitable apology. In a letter accompanying the
dispatch, Earl Russell authorized Lord Lyons to

permit a delay not exceeding seven days. If a favorable answer were not then given, he was instructed to leave Washington with the whole legation, and to repair immediately to London. At the same time preparations were made for war, troops were dispatched to Canada, and ships were hastily fitted for sea. The English press was bitter and Parliament was hostile. "Three fourths of the House of Commons," wrote Cobden, "will be glad to find an excuse for voting for the dismemberment of the great republic." The Southern press was jubilant, and the situation was critical in the extreme.

Sumner exerted all his influence to promote a peaceful adjustment. He strongly urged that the envoys be given up, and showed the President that according to the doctrines always maintained by the United States the capture was unjustifiable. He insisted that England, on the other hand, in demanding their release abandoned claims on which she had always insisted, and it was thus in our power to win a diplomatic victory by surrendering the prisoners and accepting England's surrender of rights which she had always asserted, and we had as constantly denied.

But the peremptory tone of the English demand and the strong feeling in this country made such a course very difficult, and for a time it was doubtful what the answer would be. Sumner persistently urged his views on Mr. Lincoln, and on December 25 he read to him and the Cabinet private letters

from Cobden and Bright, which sustained him.
Cobden wrote: "I am sure that the President
and the people of the United States would be but
too happy to let these men go free, unnatural and
unpardonable as their offenses have been, if by it
they could emancipate the commerce of the world.
. . . If I were in the position of your government, I would act upon their traditional policy,
and thus by a great strategic movement turn the
flank of the European powers, *especially of the
governing classes of England*. I would propose
to let Mason and Slidell go, and stipulate, at the
same time, for a complete abandonment of the old
code of maritime law as upheld by England and
the European powers."

Sumner's anxiety and his appreciation of the
crisis appear in numerous letters. Thus he wrote
to Dr. Lieber on December 24: "War with England involves: (1.) Instant acknowledgment of
rebel States by England, followed by France. (2.)
Breaking of the present blockade with capture of
our fleet. (3.) The blockade of our coast from
Chesapeake to Eastport. (4.) The sponging of
our ships from the ocean. (5.) The establishment
of the independence of rebel States. (6.) Opening
of these States by free trade to English manufacturers, which would be introduced by contraband
into our States, making the whole North American
continent a manufacturing dependency of England.
All this I have put to the President. . . . But my
anxious desire is to associate with our decision

about Mason and Slidell some triumph of our traditional policy with regard to maritime rights."
He labored with his English friends to prevent
war. .To Cobden he wrote December 31, 1861:
" On reaching Washington for the opening of
Congress I learned from the President and from
Mr. Seward that neither had committed himself
on the Trent affair, and that it was absolutely an
unauthorized act. Seward told me that he was reserving himself in order to see what view England
would take. It would have been better to act on
the case at once, and to make the surrender in conformity with our best precedents; but next to that
was the course pursued. . . . The question was not
touched in the Cabinet. It was also kept out of
the Senate. . . . These circumstances will let you
see how little there was of study or effort against
England. . . . Telling the President a few days
ago that it was now important to drive out from
the British government their distrust of his administration, and to plant confidence instead, he said
at once with perfect simplicity, ' I never see Lord
Lyons. If it were proper I should like to talk with
him, that he might hear from my lips how much I
desire peace. If we could talk together, he would
believe me.' "

In the same letter he says : —

" Last evening, at a dinner by the secretary of
war, where were Seward, Chase, and two or three
senators, while we were seated the President entered and took a seat at the table. . . . The con-

versation was much of it on the Trent case. Speaking of the course of England, Seward said he had no memory for injuries, and that in surrendering Mason and Slidell he did it in good faith, — laying up nothing for future account or recollection. I mention this conversation and the surrounding circumstances that you may know the inner sentiments of our Cabinet, and especially of the man who is most suspected by Englishmen. Seward may be careless or hasty ; he is not vindictive. The President is naturally and instinctively for peace, besides being slow to conclusions. He covets kindly relations with all the world, especially with England. I say this confidentially, for I have seen him almost daily and most intimately, ever since the Trent question has been under discussion."

He pressed upon both Bright and Cobden the idea that interference by England in behalf of slavery would be a crime against civilization, and pointed out clearly the danger that such conduct would leave behind it "an ineradicable, undying sting."

Pending the settlement, Sumner was very anxious to prevent any discussion in Congress which would embarrass the administration. When the resolution of the House approving the action of Wilkes was sent to the Senate, he moved its reference to the committee on foreign relations. But Hale of New Hampshire moved that it be sent to the committee on naval affairs, and to avoid debate Sumner yielded. On December 26, the last of the seven days allowed by Earl Russell, Senator Hale made an occasion in the Senate to assail vehemently the suggested surrender of national honor. Sumner spoke briefly in reply, urging that the matter be left with the administration unembarrassed by any action in Congress.

The administration decided to surrender the prisoners, and Mr. Seward, in announcing the decision, wrote that it was made " upon principles confessedly American." But he took the narrow ground that the error of Captain Wilkes lay in not seizing the Trent herself and bringing her before a prize court for condemnation. This view was indeed sustained by the opinion of the Crown lawyers, but it was not sound. He added in his letter that, " if the safety of the Union required the detention of the captured persons, it would be the right and duty of this government to detain them," thus substantially asserting the right to disregard international law whenever it seemed expedient. This contention naturally was rejected by Earl Russell, and it was felt that the subject was left in an unsatisfactory position. The government was attacked for its course, and the country felt sore over what seemed a humiliation.

The President sent to the Senate the correspondence relating to the Trent case, and Sumner moved its reference to his committee, making a speech on January 7, in which he stated fully the history of the case and discussed the principles involved, the historical precedents, and the position of the two governments. By this review he established his main proposition which he stated thus : —

"The seizure of the rebel emissaries on board a neutral ship cannot be justified, according to declared American principles and practice. There is no single point where the seizure is not questionable, unless we invoke British precedents and practice, which, beyond doubt, led Captain Wilkes into his mistake. . . . In this surrender, if such it may be called, the national government does not even 'stoop to conquer.' It simply lifts itself to the height of its own original principles. The early efforts of its best negotiators, the patriot trials of its soldiers in an unequal war at length prevail, and Great Britain, usually so haughty, invites us to practice upon principles which she has so strenuously opposed. There are victories of force; here is a victory of truth. If Great Britain has gained the custody of two rebels, the United States have secured the triumph of their principles."

This speech was generally approved by men of all parties on this side of the ocean. It smoothed ruffled sensibilities and turned apparent humiliation into triumph. It converted many who had defended the capture. It strengthened Sumner's personal influence greatly by letting men see that he was a conservative statesman, and an international lawyer in whose hands the foreign relations of the United States were safe. It also produced

an excellent impression upon the continent.   In
England, however, the speech was regarded very
differently. The " Times " gave it sneers and
abuse, but did not print it, while Mr. William
Vernon Harcourt, as " Historicus," thus concluded
a vituperative article : —

" Whether we turn to the puerile absurdities of
President Lincoln's message, or to the confused
and transparent sophistry of Mr. Seward's dispatch, or to the feeble and illogical malice of Mr.
Sumner's oration, we see nothing on every side but
a melancholy spectacle of impotent violence and
furious incapacity."

More reasonable Englishmen received it in a
very different spirit, and the wrath of " The Times "
was taken as evidence that the speech was effective.
The whole result was favorable to Sumner alike
at home and abroad, and his speech gave him a
position as an authority on international law, both
in the Senate and in the country, which was never
shaken.

CHAPTER XIV

THE END OF SLAVERY

DURING the second session of the Thirty-seventh Congress, Sumner was constantly active. Reconstruction was hardly imminent, but feeling certain that the relations between the government and the seceded States should be settled, and foreseeing that this could not be done without prolonged discussion, he offered on February 11, 1862, a series of resolutions with a view of bringing the difficulties to the attention of the country, and at the same time presenting his own solution afterwards known as the theory of " state suicide." The recitals which preceded the resolutions declared that the seceding States, " through their respective governments," had undertaken to renounce their allegiance to the United States and to levy war upon them ; that the territory " thus usurped by these pretended governments . . . belonged to the United States as an inseparable part thereof under the sanction of the Constitution, to be held in trust for the inhabitants in the present and future," and that the Constitution could not be displaced by any " pretended government." Upon these statements was based the proposition that the or-

dinances of secession and other acts " by a State "
hostile to the Constitution were void ; and, " when
sustained by force," were " a practical abdication
of all rights under the Constitution," while the
treason involved worked " instant forfeiture of all
functions and powers essential to the continued
existence of the State as a body politic, so that
from such time forward the territory falls under
the exclusive jurisdiction of Congress, as other territory, and the State becomes *felo de se.*"

From this were deduced as conclusions that the
termination of the State ended all " peculiar local
institutions," and that therefore slavery in the
seceded States, being " without any origin in the
Constitution or in natural right," must fall with
the State whose creature it was ; that Congress
must provide for the termination of slavery in fact
throughout the whole seceded territory ; that as
allegiance to the government and protection by it
are corresponding obligations, the slaves were
entitled to its protection ; and that Congress must
" assume complete jurisdiction " of the " vacated
territory," and proceed to establish therein governments republican in form with due regard to
the equal rights of all the inhabitants.

These resolutions were in aid of Sumner's fixed
purpose that the war should end slavery, and suggested another way of accomplishing this object ; but
such radical propositions naturally encountered bitter opposition. That the void acts of men assuming to be the government of a State were ineffec-

tual to displace the authority of the United States
over the territory of the State, yet were effectual
to terminate the legal existence of the State and
to destroy rights of property created lawfully
by the State and recognized by the Constitution,
was a proposition open to destructive attack. Yet
though the premises were unsound, the conclusion
was ultimately adopted.   Stripped of the argu-
mentative propositions which were questionable,
the resolutions declared the purpose of the United
States to reconstruct the Union without slavery,
and to establish in each of the seceded States a
government which should be republican in reality.
It was harder to justify this result on Sumner's
theories of law than to sustain it by practical considerations of justice and expediency.

Upon Sumner's motion the resolutions were laid
upon the table, and were never taken up.   His
purpose was accomplished by presenting them.
Leading Republicans like Fessenden, Sherman,
and Dixon of Connecticut, hastened to declare
dissent from his theories, and to make it clear that
he spoke only for himself and not for the Republican party, Sherman saying that "candid men
must know that they [the resolutions] are but the
emanation of a single individual, who has decided
convictions on the subject and who is far in
advance of any political organization in this country." Yet Sumner was not without influential
supporters, and it will be interesting hereafter to
compare the final legislation of the Republican

party on reconstruction with this early statement
of his theory.

His attention, however, was not confined to
slavery. On February 13 he made an elaborate
argument upon the proposition to make treasury
notes a legal tender in payment of all debts, con-
cluding that Congress had the power to do so, but
expressing grave doubts as to the wisdom of exercising it. He found ample reason for these doubts
in the history of previous experiments, and they
have been justified fully by the results.

Grave questions besides those growing out of the
Trent case came before the committee on foreign
relations. Prominent among them was that of
our duty towards Mexico, then threatened with
intervention by England, France, and Spain, for
the alleged purpose of securing redress for their
citizens who held bonds, upon which Mexico had
suspended the payment of interest. The object
of our diplomacy was to keep Mexico from falling into hands likely to aid the Southern Confederacy, and also, in accordance with the Monroe
Doctrine, to prevent the establishment on this continent of a new foreign monarchy. Our minister
to Mexico, Mr. Corwin, sent to Washington the
project of a treaty by which the United States
should lend Mexico a sum sufficient to meet the undoubted claims of her creditors, taking as security
mining property or other resources. The President
submitted this to the Senate for its advice, and Mr.
Sumner reported in favor of assuming the interest

on the Mexican debt for a limited time, and of paying certain claims, provided the allied powers would accept this and withdraw from Mexico; and provided further that the advance should "be secured by such mortgage or pledge as is most practicable without any territorial acquisition or dismemberment of Mexico." Political leaders at this time were willing to help a neighboring nation and to preserve its freedom, but were careful that no portion, even of contiguous territory, should be taken in payment for this country's help. Our hands were too full, however, and the Senate declined to follow the committee. Instead, a resolution was adopted, "that it is not advisable to negotiate a treaty that will require the United States to assume any portion of the principal or interest of the debt of Mexico, or that will require the concurrence of European powers." The result was the tragedy of Maximilian.

Through his committee Sumner was able also to serve the cause which he had most at heart. While slavery dominated the government the "colored republics," Hayti and Liberia, had never been accorded diplomatic recognition. As Mr. Benton put it: "The peace of eleven States in this Union will not permit the fruits of a successful negro insurrection to be exhibited among them." In his annual message of December, 1861, President Lincoln stated that he saw no reason for longer withholding our recognition, and Mr. Sumner reported a bill, which was passed, authorizing the President to send diplomatic representatives. He supported it by a speech suggesting commercial and business considerations, but not alluding to the reason which had prevented earlier recognition, or even to the fact that the population of the two countries was colored. Senator Davis of Kentucky moved an amendment, and attacked the policy of establishing diplomatic relations with negroes, excusing his opposition on the ground that such a step was distasteful to the people of the slave States. Sumner replied : —

"I made no appeal on account of color. I did not allude to the unhappy circumstance in their history that they had once been slaves. It is the senator from Kentucky who introduces this topic. . . . In presenting this measure, I make no appeal on account of an oppressed race. I urge it simply as an act for our own good. . . . Thus far we have stood aloof from two important opportunities of extending and strengthening our influence. It is time to change."

Though not presented to the Senate as a step in the contest with slavery, this measure was so regarded in the country, as was abundantly shown by the letters which Sumner received from Governor Andrew and others. The people of Liberia and Hayti were especially grateful to him, and for this and his later service a medal was presented to him in the name of the Haytien people, which, however, he felt obliged to decline, and it is now in the State Library.

A more signal triumph was won when the treaty
with England for the more effectual suppression
of the slave trade, negotiated in the spring of
1862 and signed in Sumner's presence, was ratified by the Senate without a dissenting voice.
It was sent to the Senate on April 11; it was
reported by Sumner on the 15th, and ratified on
the 24th after a brief speech by him, in which
he pointed out its especial features, the granting
of a mutual and restricted right of search, and
the establishment of mixed courts with authority
to condemn ships. The President announced the
ratification of the treaty on June 7, and on the
13th Sumner reported a bill to carry it into effect,
which was passed at once. The effect was immediate. The infamous traffic ceased when it was
found that Great Britain and the United States
were united and in earnest. No business ever came
before the mixed courts, for no ship was ever captured, and they were abolished by mutual consent
in 1869. The promptitude with which Congress
acted was largely due to Sumner, and he wasted
no time in speech, though the occasion must have
been tempting.

In pursuance of his purpose to remove from the
statute-book every discrimination on account of
color, he introduced a bill to amend the law which
provided " that no other than a free white person "
should be employed to carry the mail. This law,
passed in 1825, was first suggested in 1802 by the
postmaster-general, who, speaking of the negroes,

said: "Everything which tends to increase their knowledge of natural rights, of men and things, or that affords them an opportunity of associating, acquiring, and communicating sentiments, and of establishing a chain or line of intelligence, must increase your hazard because it increases their means of effecting their object. The most active and intelligent are employed as post-riders. These are the most ready to learn and the most able to execute. By traveling from day to day, and hourly mixing with people, they must, they will, acquire information. *They will learn that a man's rights do not depend on his color. They will in time become teachers to their brethren.* They become acquainted with each other on the line. Whenever the body, or a portion of them, wish to act, they are an organized corps, circulating our intelligence openly, their own privately."

Sumner's bill provided that no person should be disqualified, by reason of color, to carry the mails. It passed the Senate without amendment or dispute, but was reported adversely by Mr. Colfax in the House, and was defeated on his motion, — a singular fate for such a measure. Mr. Sumner again introduced it in the next Congress, and eventually it was passed.

He proposed and carried legislation preventing the exclusion of witnesses in the District of Columbia on account of color, and made repeated attempts to extend the same rule to the federal courts, but without success at this session. Only thirteen other senators supported Sumner, but in this, as in many cases, his views soon prevailed.

Unable to convince the President that immediate emancipation was wise, but sure that it was the most effective weapon against the Confederates, Sumner neglected no opportunity to urge measures tending to accomplish it. We see now that he grasped the situation with the instinct of a statesman; but many of his associates were confused by legal and constitutional doubts as to the rights of slaveholders. It was a singular survival of the tenderness for slavery, which had been fostered by the Whig and Democratic parties during years of agitation. In May, 1862, Sumner attacked these scruples in a powerful speech delivered in support of an amendment to the confiscation bill. This proposed that any person, who after the passage of the act should engage in or abet the rebellion, should forfeit all claim to his slaves, and that these should thereafter be free; further, that any claimant of a slave must establish his loyalty as a condition of recovery. Sumner dwelt upon the distinction between a law intended to punish treason, which must be passed in the exercise of sovereignty and must not violate constitutional limitations, and a law exercising those rights of war which international law gives to every belligerent. It was a legal argument, founded on the decisions of courts, the principles laid down by recognized authorities, and the well-established practice of all nations. The common sense of his position is shown by the following extracts from his speeches made in the debate on this proposition : —

"The rebel in arms is an enemy, and something more. . . . In appealing to war, he has voluntarily renounced all safeguards of the Constitution, and put himself beyond its pale. . . . And yet, sir, the Constitution is cited as a limitation upon these rights. As well cite the Constitution on the field of battle to check the bayonet charge of our armies. . . . The Constitution is entirely inapplicable. Sacred and inviolable, the Constitution is made for friends who acknowledge it, and not for enemies. . . .

"If it be constitutional to make war, to set armies in the field, to launch navies, to occupy fields and houses, to bombard cities, to kill in battle, — all without trial by jury, or any process of law, or judicial proceeding of any kind, — it is equally constitutional, as a war measure, to confiscate the property of the enemy and to liberate his slaves. . . . You may condemn confiscation and liberation as impolitic, but you cannot condemn them as unconstitutional unless, in the same breath, you condemn all other agencies of war, and resolve our present proceeding into the process of a criminal court, guarded at each step by the technicalities of the common law. . . . I confess frankly that I look with more hope and confidence to liberation than to confiscation. To give freedom is nobler than to take property, and on this occasion it cannot fail to be more efficacious."

Mr. Sumner's amendment, altered so as to affect only slaves coming actually under the control of the federal armies, became a part of the law as enacted. It doubtless helped to familiarize the public with the idea of emancipation as a war measure.

At this session Sumner voted against the bill to admit West Virginia, because the Senate refused to amend it by providing that, after July 4, 1863, slavery should cease in the State; though it inserted the provision that slaves in the State on July 4, 1863, and under twenty-one years of age, should be free at certain ages. He successfully opposed a bill to establish temporary governments in the seceded States because it provided that the laws and institutions which existed in each State at the time of its secession should not be interfered with. He pointed out that "institutions" meant "slavery," and read some of the laws which would thus be enforced. By various resolutions from time to time he sought to prevent the surrender of fugitive slaves, and to make the public see how much the slaves could help us, and the importance of encouraging them to do so.

At this time Sumner asserted the right of Congress to control reconstruction. The President had appointed Edward Stanly as military governor of North Carolina, with absolute power, including even the right to suspend the writ of *habeas corpus*. Stanly undertook to act despotically and showed a disposition to protect slavery. Andrew Johnson was made governor of Tennessee, and it seemed probable that, if this policy were to be countenanced, the Executive would dictate the terms of reconstruction, at least so far as to tie the hands of Congress. Sumner, therefore, on June 6, 1862, introduced a resolution reciting Stanly's acts, and asking the President to revoke the appointment. A second resolution declared that such an appointment was without sanction in the Constitution and laws, and subordinated the civil to the military authority, " contrary to the spirit of our institutions and in derogation of the powers of Congress." This resolution, though never acted upon, accomplished its purpose, and no more military governors were appointed.

Sumner also introduced a resolution : " That in the efforts now making for the restoration of the Union and the establishment of peace throughout the country, it is inexpedient that the names of victories obtained over our fellow citizens should be placed on the regimental colors of the United States." No action was taken upon it, and it provoked no noticeable opposition. On the contrary it was cordially approved by many, including General Winfield Scott, who afterwards said : " This was noble and from the right quarter." A very different reception was accorded later to a similar proposition.

Sumner was constantly in his seat, and nothing escaped his attention. He opposed adjournment on July 16, because much important business demanded attention. Unduly shortened as the session seemed to him, yet Congress accomplished much upon which he looked back with profound satisfaction. He thus recapitulated its legislative achievements : ". . . Emancipation in the national capital ; freedom in all the national territories ; the offer of ransom to help emancipation in the States ; the recognition of Hayti and Liberia ; the treaty with Great Britain for the suppression of the slave trade ; the prohibition of the return of fugitive slaves by military officers ; homesteads for actual settlers on the public lands ; a Pacific railroad ; endowments of agricultural colleges out of the public lands ; — such are some of the achievements by which the present Congress is already historic. . . . Besides these measures of unmixed beneficence, the present Congress has created an immense army and a considerable navy, and has provided the means for all our gigantic expenditures by a tax which in itself is an epoch."

No one had been more responsible for the actions of Congress against slavery than had Sumner, and he might well rejoice in the record. Through it all he never lost sight of his great object nor neglected an opportunity to press emancipation on the President. He urged him to commemorate the Fourth of July by proclaiming freedom and calling the slaves to our assistance ; but Lincoln was not ready. Even after Congress adjourned Sumner remained to press his views. Lincoln was more than six weeks behind him, though not very much more. On July 13 he

said to Seward and Welles that emancipation was
a military necessity, and on July 22 he submitted to his Cabinet the draft of a proclamation declaring that slaves should be free on January 1,
1863, in States then in rebellion. He waited for
a victory, and then he acted. On September 22,
five days after Antietam, the preliminary proclamation of emancipation was issued, and the Republican party became, what Sumner had been denounced for trying to make it a year before, an
emancipation party. To this result no one had
contributed so much as he. The President was
doubtless right in waiting, but that he was able to
strike when he did was largely due to Sumner and
those who, with him, had educated the people to
approve the blow.

Though Sumner sometimes differed with the
President on questions of policy, and was impatient with his deliberation, they were in essential
harmony, and Sumner never lost his confidence in
Lincoln. His feelings appear clearly in private
letters written early in June, 1862, from which
some passages may be quoted : —

" Your criticism of the President is hasty. I am
confident, if you knew him as I do, you would not
make it. Could you — as has been my privilege
often — have seen the President while considering
the great questions on which he has already acted,
. . . even your zeal would be satisfied ; for you
would feel the sincerity of his purpose to do what
he can to carry forward the principles of the Declaration of Independence."

In the interest of harmony he urged the passage of a resolution construing the confiscation bill so as to limit the forfeiture of real estate to the life of the offender. This was introduced while the bill was in the President's hands, to meet certain doubts on his part. Without sharing these doubts Sumner was willing to adopt the President's view in order that the bill might be signed.

During this session Sumner was the most conspicuous senator. He was in full vigor of mind and body, and there was no one among his associates who had been so prominent as he in the contest which had ended in the rebellion. He was the recognized political leader of those who sought the destruction of slavery through the war. An English traveler thus described him : "That great, sturdy, English-looking figure, with the broad, massive forehead, over which the rich mass of nut-brown hair, streaked here and there with a line of gray, hangs loosely ; with the deep blue eyes and the strangely winning smile, half bright, half full of sadness. He is a man whom you would notice amongst other men, and whom, not knowing, you would turn round and look at as he passed by you. . . . A child would ask him the time in the streets, and a woman would come to him unbidden for protection." Judge Hoar described "his commanding presence, his stalwart frame (six feet and four inches in height), the vigor and grace of his motions, the charm of his manners, the polish of his rhetoric, the abundance of his learning, the fervor

and impressiveness of his oratory;" and said,
" he was every inch a senator."

Yet it was a question whether he would again
be sent to the Senate. His second term expired on
March 4, 1863, and the autumn campaign of 1862
in Massachusetts was especially important on this
account. The reasons for his reëlection may be
taken from the answer of John Bigelow to one of
Sumner's critics : —

" First, he was the most accomplished man in
public life in America ; second, the ablest senator
in Congress ; third, of unblemished private character ; fourth, of unblemished public character,
which no breath of calumny had ever reached, and
whom no one had ever dared to approach with a
dishonorable proposition ; fifth, a man whose zeal
and talents had been expended, not upon selfish
schemes, but upon measures and policies looking
to the improvement of the condition of society —
such ends as, whatever difference of opinion may
prevail as to the adaptation of his means to secure
them, must possess the sympathy and respect of
all good citizens ; sixth, he is very amiable ; and
seventh, a man whose decorum of character and
whose talents have done and are doing more than
those of any other man in the Senate to avert the
gradual decline of that body in the estimation of
the country."

Against such arguments his opponents urged his
radical views on slavery, and his determination to
force a policy of emancipation ; that he was so

absorbed in this that he could not give the necessary attention to the other interests of his constituents; that his relations with the President
were not sufficiently cordial, and that he embarrassed the administration. It was a period of reaction and depression all over the country. Some
of Sumner's friends had grown conservative, and
were inclined to the opposition, which actually received the powerful support of the "Springfield
Republican." But the suggestion that his reëlection was in doubt aroused to enthusiastic action
the moral forces of Massachusetts. Ministers,
teachers, editors, anti-slavery veterans, all over the
State, rallied to his support. His life had given
him a hold upon his constituents not easily shaken,
and the attempt to unseat him was defeated as
soon as it was known. His friends in the Republican convention were resolved that the party should
be committed to his support, and a complimen-
tary resolution nominating him for reëlection was
adopted with enthusiasm. The Emancipation Proclamation of September 22, issued some two weeks
later, completely answered the suggestion that
Sumner's policy of emancipation was not approved
by the President. The administration had taken
his advice and was thus his strongest supporter.
To vote against him on this ground was to vote
against Lincoln.

In the campaign Sumner made several speeches,
in which he planted himself upon the proclamation
and urged his constituents to support the policy of

the government as both necessary and right.   He
referred briefly to the charges against himself, saying : —

"There are two accusations, . . . to which I reply on the spot ; and I do so with less hesitation
because the topics are germane to this debate.
The first is, that from my place in the Senate I
early proclaimed slavery to be barbarism.   Never
shall the cause of freedom go by default if I can
help it ; and I rejoice that, on that occasion, in
presence of the slaveholding conspirators vaunting
the ennobling character of slavery, I used no soft
words. . . . Was I not right?

"The other accusation is similar in character.
It is said that I have too often introduced the slavery question.   At this moment, seeing what slavery
has done, I doubt if you will not rather say that I
have introduced it too seldom. . . . The slave is
the humblest and the grandest figure of our times.
. . . In his presence all other questions are so
petty that for a public man to be wrong with regard to him is to be wholly wrong.   How, then,
did I err?   The cause would have justified a better
pertinacity than I can boast."

Phillips, Whittier, Greeley, all the anti-slavery
leaders came to his support, and while other States
deserted the Republican party, Massachusetts stood
firm, and reëlected him by an overwhelming majority in both houses of the legislature.   He returned
to the Senate with increased influence, to complete
the work which he had carried on so long and well.

CHAPTER XV

THE CRITICAL PERIOD OF THE CIVIL WAR

THE second session of the Thirty-seventh Congress began in December, 1862, and ended March 3, 1863. It was a period of anxious waiting. The death of slavery had been decreed by the Emancipation Proclamation, but it remained to execute the decree. The United States was to be free in fact as in name, but it was still doubtful what would constitute the United States. It was indeed true that the year just closing had seen a distinct advance of the Union arms. The border States had been saved ; the Mississippi, at its mouth and for the larger part of its course, had been brought under the control of the government, and with it the largest part of Tennessee. The desperate battle of Stone River had destroyed the Confederate hope of recovering Kentucky. An invasion of Maryland had ended in disaster to the invaders, and important points had been won upon the coast. The area of the rebellion was materially reduced, and its resources were greatly impaired. On the other hand, however, the year ended ingloriously with the defeat at Fredericksburg. The main army of the Confederates under Lee still menaced Washington, while Grant was besieging Vicksburg with doubtful prospect. Our enemies in England and France took courage and threatened intervention. Cruisers, fitted out in England, were destroying our commerce. The elections had indicated dissatisfaction at home, and the falling off in voluntary enlistments had compelled the resort to conscription. The Republican senators asked the dismissal of Mr. Seward, on the ground that he lacked earnest convictions, and that his influence in the councils of the administration was unfortunate. Both Seward and Chase offered their resignations, and though Mr. Lincoln refused to accept them, the discussion left bitter feeling behind, and to our other difficulties was added this lack of harmony among Republican leaders. It was for a statesman, in this time of doubt and despondency, to sustain the courage of his countrymen, to keep Congress and the Executive united in a vigorous prosecution of the war, and to prevent any backward steps. Sumner never shared the prevailing discouragement. To him it was morally impossible that a war waged to establish human slavery could succeed, and he did his part in persistently urging on the work.

It is not surprising that in these circumstances, and after the great legislative activity of the preceding session, the last session of the Thirty-seventh Congress was uneventful. Its work lay rather in prevention than in action. Sumner's action may be stated in a few words. His first resolution was in favor of establishing a hospital and ambulance corps. He moved to amend a bill regulating the appointment of midshipmen, by providing that candidates should be selected "on the ground of merit and qualification, to be ascertained by an examination" under regulations to be prescribed by the secretary of the navy. The spoils system was then too well intrenched, and his amendment commanded only six votes. He introduced a bill for enlisting all negroes freed by the confiscation act or any other lawful authority "exercised in suppressing the present rebellion," also for receiving colored volunteers, but the bill was not reported, and fell with the session. By a resolution offered in May, 1862, he had urged the enlistment of colored men, and in July of that year laws had been passed which authorized their employment in the army and navy. His present bill went a step further, but the policy of using the negroes was now fully adopted by the Executive.

At the recommendation of the President the House of Representatives passed a bill to aid Missouri in abolishing slavery by a gift of ten million dollars in bonds, to be used in compensating the owners. The senate committee on the judiciary amended by providing for "gradual or immediate emancipation," offering twenty millions if there was "full and perfect manumission" before July 4, 1865, and half as much if it was at a later day before July 4, 1876. Sumner opposed gradual emancipation, both because the expenditure could

only be justified as a war measure, and it was
absurd to order a blow at the enemy to be delivered ten or twenty years later, and because slavery
was an evil of such a character that it should
not be permitted to exist for any period. He considered it a new compromise, and after pointing
out the disastrous consequences of former compromises, used words of more than temporary application : " Alas, that men should forget that God
is bound by no compromise, and that sooner or
later He will insist that justice shall be done."
In those days of procrastination his words struck a
different note : " What is done in war must be
done promptly, except perhaps under the policy of
defense. . . . If you would be triumphant, strike
quickly, let your blows be felt at once, without
notice or premonition, especially without time for
resistance or debate. Time deserts all who do not
appreciate its value. Strike promptly, and time
becomes your invaluable ally. Strike slowly,
gradually, prospectively, and time goes over to
the enemy."

The greatest danger of the moment was the
danger of foreign intervention, and while pressing
action against the enemy, Sumner was solicitous
to prevent anything which might precipitate this
calamity. His associates were not all equally
conservative. On January 19, 1863, Senator
McDougall of California introduced resolutions
condemning the intervention of the French in
Mexico, describing it as " an act not merely un-

friendly to this republic, but to free institutions everywhere, and . . . regarded by this republic as not only unfriendly, but as hostile; " and declaring it our duty to require the immediate withdrawal of the French forces, and to aid Mexico in resisting them. On February 3 he moved to take them up, and Sumner opposed, saying that if the resolutions " mean anything, they mean war," and asking : " Have we not war enough already on our hands without needlessly and wantonly provoking another ? "

The Senate took up the resolutions that McDougall might have an opportunity to speak, and Sumner replied that the way to drive the French from Mexico and to prevent any other attempt by foreign nations on this hemisphere was to crush the rebellion ; " after which," he said, " this whole continent will fall naturally, peacefully, and tranquilly under the irresistible influence of American institutions." The Senate followed his lead and tabled the resolutions.

The sharpest struggle during this session arose over a proposition to issue letters of marque. Seward had favored this early in the war, and a bill to authorize it in this and in any future war was reported from the committee on naval affairs. It came up in February, 1863, and Mr. Grimes, the chairman, supported it. Sumner opposed it pertinaciously in a series of direct and simple speeches. He pointed out that privateers were vessels employed to prey upon the commerce of an enemy, and that the Confederacy had no commerce. He contended that if more ships were needed they should be made a part of the navy, for the reason that every privateer is entitled to the right of search, saying: "By virtue of this right, he and every licensed sea rover is entitled on the ocean to stop and overhaul all merchant vessels under whatever flag. If he cannot capture, he can at least annoy. . . . Every exercise upon neutral commerce of this terrible right of search will be the fruitful occasion of misunderstanding, bickering, and controversy at a moment when, if my voice could prevail, there should be nothing to interfere with that accord, harmony, and sympathy which are due from civilized states to our republic in its great battle with barbarism. . . .

"The speaking trumpet of a reckless privateer may contribute to that discord which is the herald of bloodshed itself."

Failing to defeat the bill he tried to modify it, but in vain. The bill, limited to three years, became a law, and Mr. Seward at once sought to have it carried into effect. Mr. Sumner, however, was so convinced that it was futile against the Confederacy, and effective only to embroil us with foreign nations, that he remained in Washington and used all his influence to prevent action under it. He pressed his views upon the President, and showed him confirmatory letters from John Bright and Joshua Bates, the well known American banker in London. He wrote a letter for publication, reiterating his objections. Mr. Adams, from England, opposed the step, and the Cabinet was divided, Mr. Welles agreeing with Sumner, while Chase supported Seward. Eventually Sumner prevailed, and no letters of marque were issued. The struggle excited much attention in England, and Mr. Bates wrote afterward : " I am convinced that their issue would have led to a war, and would have given those who in this country wish for war an opportunity through the press to make a war popular. . . . It is the last card the Confederates have to play." This judgment of an able witness may help to show the value of Sumner's service to his country in this matter.

On the other hand, while anxious not to provoke war, he desired equally to avoid inviting it by an appearance of fear. Offers of mediation had been made by Russia in 1861, and in 1862 the French Emperor tried to secure the coöperation of Russia and England in obtaining a suspension of hostilities for six months or longer. Failing in this, he tendered his good offices to facilitate negotiations, but his offer was declined. In England, intervention in various forms was from time to time suggested in the press and in Parliament. In consequence of all this, on February 28, 1863, Sumner reported a series of resolutions drawn by him. These recited the offer of the Emperor and the danger that " the idea of mediation or intervention in some shape may be regarded by foreign governments as practicable," and then declared that " any further proposition from a foreign power, intended to arrest the efforts of the United States to crush the rebellion, was calculated to prolong and embitter the conflict," and would be regarded by Congress as " an unfriendly act."

The resolutions were passed promptly, and, being communicated through our ministers to foreign governments, did much to end a course of action which had excited the hopes of the Confederate States, and had created irritations which might at any time have led to war with new enemies. It was a bold and dignified step which was justified by the event.

After the Senate adjourned Sumner remained in Washington till July. Though the Emancipation Proclamation had aroused the anti-slavery sentiment in England and had led to manifestations of sympathy with the North, our relations with England and France were never more critical than between March and October, 1863. Influential Englishmen like Gladstone openly declared that the South would succeed, and so thought many of Sumner's closest personal friends. The tone of Earl Russell was most irritating; the escape of the Alabama and Florida, the building and equipping of ships of war for Confederate use in English shipyards, and the depredations of the privateers created intense feeling in this country, well expressed in Lowell's " Jonathan to John." The climax was reached when, in September, Earl Russell at first refused to stop the Confederate iron-

clads, nearly ready at Birkenhead, and Mr. Adams
sent his famous note, in which he said : " This is
war."

During this period Sumner constantly corresponded with his English friends, impressing them
with the fixed resolution of the North to restore
the Union, no matter at what cost of civil or foreign
war ; insisting that England could not, upon moral
grounds, throw her weight for slavery, and in every
way endeavoring to prevent war. In Washington
he was in constant consultation with the President
and Seward, in touch with each difficulty as it
arose, and while his efforts were not known to the
public they were of the greatest value.

Some extracts from his correspondence will show
the nature of his labors, and his unfailing confidence during the darkest hours.

To Cobden, on March 16, 1863 : —

" I am anxious, very anxious, on account of the
ships building in England to cruise against our
commerce. Cannot something be done to stop
them ? Our people are becoming more and more
excited, and there are many who insist upon war.
A very important person said to me yesterday : ' We
are now at war with England, but the hostilities
are all on her side.' . . . To-day the Cabinet consider whether to issue letters of marque under the
new statute. I have seen the President twice upon
this question, which I regard as grave, for it is
intended as a counter movement to what is done
in England. . . . I found myself powerless against

it in the Senate, for there was a 'war fever,' and
you know how irresistible and diabolical that becomes."

To the Duchess of Argyll, on April 13 : —

"Let me say frankly and most kindly where I
think England has erred. It is twice. First, she
declared neutrality between the two parties, —
fatal mistake, from which Lord Russell's speech is
the beginning of extrication. There can be no
just neutrality between the two parties. . . . Such
a government, founded on such a pretension, seeking admission into the fellowship of Christian
States, should have been told at the beginning that
there was no place for it. . . . The next mistake
of England is that, having declared neutrality, she
has not been true to it. I do not allude now to
the ships, though to us that case is flagrant; but
I allude to the declarations of at least two of her
ministers, made long ago, that separation was inevitable. The direct tendency of their declarations
was twofold : first, to encourage the slavemongers,
and to give hope and confidence to slavery wherever it was; and, secondly, by an infirmity of
human nature, to bind these ministers, who had
thus made themselves prophets, to desire the verifi-
cation of their prophecy."

Again, on April 21 : —

"It has seemed to us an obvious duty of the
English government to take the responsibility of
enforcing its own statute of neutrality, which is little more than the requirement of international law,

and that it was enough for us to direct attention to the reported fact. Some of our Cabinet were so strongly of this opinion that they were unwilling that our minister or agents should take any further steps, . . . it being generally understood that the sailing of the ships would be a declaration of war. I insisted most earnestly that, while I did not differ from others as to the obvious duty of the English government, yet, as it had become a question of peace or war, I would not stand upon any form ; that I would employ agents, attorneys, and counsel ; institute law proceedings, — do all that we thought the British government ought to do, so far as we might be able to do, whether in courts or out of courts. The President at last adopted this view, and Mr. Evarts, who is a very eminent lawyer, without a superior in the country, has been dispatched to do all that he can, in consultation if possible with your law officers or with others, to arrest the guilty vessels."

To Bright, on July 21 : —

" I have read the debate of the 30th of June. . . . My friend Mr. Gladstone dealt with the whole question as if there were no God. Englishmen may doubt. I tell you, there can be but one end to this war. I care not for any temporary success of the slavemongers, they must fail ; but English sympathy is a mighty encouragement. . . . We are too victorious ; I fear more from our victories than our defeats. If the rebellion should suddenly collapse, Democrats, Copperheads, and

Seward would insist upon amnesty and the Union, and 'no question asked about slavery.' God save us from any such calamity."

Again, on August 4 : —

" There are two things which make me anxious. First, I fear that devil of compromise. I do not think the danger is great, but any such danger is terrible. The longer our triumph is postponed, the more impossible this becomes. Our present policy is, therefore, (1) two hundred thousand negroes under arms ; (2) the admission of a Gulf State with an altered constitution abolishing slavery ; . . . (3) to insist that there can be no talk of admission into the Union except on the basis of the actual condition at the moment, with slavery abolished by the Proclamation.

" The second cause of anxiety is in our relations with England. Your government recklessly and heartlessly seems bent on war. You know how the Democracy, which it now courts, will turn and rend it, while the Irish have at last their long-sought opportunity. A leading merchant said to me this morning that he would give fifty thousand dollars for a war between England and Russia, that he might turn English doctrines against England. The feeling is very bitter."

To Cobden, on September 4 : —

" I do not differ from you when you say that you never would have counseled a war for emancipation. Nor I; indeed, I have done nothing but accept the conditions imposed by the other side. Of course, I would not surrender to slavery. There was a moment when, perhaps, it was possible to let the States go; but I doubt. Since then the thing has been morally impossible; the war must be fought out. This is sad enough to me! It costs me a pang to give up early visions, and to see my country filled with armies, while the military spirit prevails everywhere. Everywhere soldiers come forward for offices of all kinds, from the presidency to the post of constable; and this will be the case from this time during my life."

To Bright, on October 6: —

"At this moment I am more solicitous about France and England than about our military affairs. In the latter there is a temporary check, and you know I said long ago that I was prepared for further disaster; but this can only delay, not change the result. Foreign intervention will introduce a new, vast, and incalculable element; it would probably provoke a universal war. You will observe the hobnobbing at New York with the Russian admiral. Why is that fleet gathered there? My theory is that when it left the Baltic war with France was regarded as quite possible, and it was determined not to be sealed up at Cronstadt; if at New York, they could take the French expedition at Vera Cruz."

The replies of Bright and Cobden kept Sumner advised of English feeling and English difficulties, and they were at once shown to the President. This familiar and frank correspondence helped our

government and strengthened the hands of those
Englishmen who favored the North, of whom from
first to last John Bright was the bravest and most
unfaltering. He never deserted nor doubted the
success of the government.

Sumner felt that the position of the United
States should be stated so that the people of England and France might understand our feelings and
the dangers of the situation, and that the American people might be instructed as to their rights.
He therefore prepared a speech during the spring
and summer, which he delivered in New York on
September 10, at the very crisis of our troubles
with England. It was a long oration, with the faults
of Sumner's elaborate addresses, and we miss the
spontaneity and directness of his letters. There
are passages which seem intemperate; but, coming
from Sumner, the indignation which they expressed
made the greater impression in England. None
the less, it was a strong statement of the American
case.

He enumerated the unfriendly acts of England,
dwelling first on the proclamation of neutrality,
"foremost in time, foremost also in the magnitude
of its consequences;" issued with indecent haste,
it gave the Southern cruisers equal rights with our
own on the seas and in British ports, and enabled
Englishmen to sell munitions of war to the Confederates. He alluded next to the captious tone of
England when the Trent was stopped, when ships
were sunk at the entrance of Charleston harbor,

and on other occasions, when she complained of action justified by her own precedents.

He spoke of unfriendly speeches in Parliament, and of official declarations by members of the Cabinet, quoting the statement that our war was "a contest for empire on one side and for independence on the other;" and he dwelt upon their constant prophecies of disaster and the assertion that Jefferson Davis had "created a *nation*."

Passing to acts, he said : " I am sorry to add that there are acts, also, with which the British government is too closely associated. I do not refer to the unlimited supply of 'munitions of war,' so that our army everywhere, whether at Vicksburg or Charleston, is compelled to encounter Armstrong guns and Blakely guns, with all proper ammunition, from England. . . . Nor do I refer to the swarms of swift steamers, always under the British flag, with contributions to rebel slavery. . . . Of course no royal proclamation can change wrong into right, or make such business otherwise than immoral; but the proclamation may take from it the character of felony.

" Even the royal manifesto gives no sanction to the fitting out in England of a *naval expedition* against the commerce of the United States. And yet . . . powerful ships are launched, equipped, fitted out, and manned in England, with arms supplied at sea from another English vessel, and then . . . proceed at once to rob and destroy the commerce of the United States. *England is the naval base* from which are derived the original forces and supplies enabling them to sail the sea. . . . Of these incendiaries, the most famous is the Alabama, with a picked crew of British seamen, with 'trained gunners out of Her Majesty's naval reserve,' all, like those of Queen Elizabeth, described as 'good sailors and better pirates,' and with everything else from keel to truck British, which, after more than a year of unlawful havoc, is still firing the property of our citizens, *without once entering a rebel slavemonger port*, . . . and never losing the original nationality stamped upon her by origin. . . . It is difficult to see how the British government can avoid the consequences of complicity with the pirate ships in all their lawless devastation. I forbear to dwell on all the accumulating liability, amounting already to millions of dollars, with accumulating exasperation also."

Thus early was England warned of the Alabama claims.

Passing from England to France, he stated our grievances against Louis Napoleon, dwelling on the invasion of Mexico, and on the Emperor's attempt to procure a joint mediation in our affairs with "an armistice for six months, during which every act of war, direct or indirect, should provisionally cease." Of this he said: "Any such offer, whatever its motive, must be an encouragement to the rebellion." and he spoke of the Emperor thus: "Trampler upon the republic in France, trampler upon the republic in Mexico, it remains to be seen if the French Emperor can prevail as trampler upon this republic."

Having framed his indictment, he proceeded to discuss the rights of intervention and mediation, prefacing his argument by a significant warning: —

"Nations are equal in the eye of international law, so that what is right for one is right for all. . . . Therefore, should our cases be reversed, there is nothing England and France now propose, or may hereafter propose, which it will not be our equal right to propose when Ireland or India once more rebels, or when France is in the throes of its next revolution. . . . We may reject the precedents they furnish; but it will be difficult for them to complain if we follow their steps."

He reviewed at great length the subject of intervention, quoting Canning's statement that the "British government disclaimed for itself, and denied for other powers, the right of requiring any changes in the internal institutions of independent states with the menace of hostile attack in case of refusal;" and that "a menace of direct and imminent danger could alone, in exception to the general rule, justify foreign interference."

Dilating on England's long "intervention against slavery," he asked: "And can it be that now . . . a rebellion inspired by slavery turns to England with hope?" He discussed the law of recognition and the precedents, showing how impossible it would be to recognize the Southern Confederacy "when, *in fact*, nothing is established, nothing

untroubled, nothing secure, not even a single boundary line, . . . when, *in fact*, the conflict is still
waged on numerous battlefields, and these pretend-
ers to independence have been driven from State
to State, driven away from the Mississippi which
parts them, driven back from the sea which sur-
rounds them, and shut up in the interior or in
blockaded ports, so that only by stealth can they
communicate with the outward world."

In conclusion he dwelt upon the fact that the
new confederacy was founded to maintain slavery,
and enforced by a wealth of quotation and argument his contention that no civilized nation, and
England least of all, could help to establish such a
government.

At home the speech was received with the warmest approval by press and public, and by leaders
like Seward and Chase. In England it excited
much indignation, and was criticised as unjust and
unduly bitter. None the less it commanded attention, and made England appreciate as never before
the real feeling of the United States and the grav-
ity of the situation. From this time foreign powers gave us no serious anxiety, and their attitude
was doubtless due in part to the enlightenment
conveyed by this speech, reënforced by the success
of our arms. The Argylls, Cobden, and others of
Sumner's friends regretted the speech, and Cobden
wrote : —

" I was, I confess, rather beset with the feeling
of *cui bono* after reading your powerful indictments

against England and France together; it should have been your policy to have kept them asunder."

Sumner answered thus : —

"Not for controversy, but for statement, I reply to your *cui bono:* (1.) As regards my own country. People here had a right to expect from me a statement of the case. There was a feverish and indignant feeling against Great Britain, without much knowledge. The facts which I set forth, none of which can be questioned, are now accepted as an exhibition of what your government has done. The effect has been excellent; for the people now understand the points in discussion. Instead of exciting them, I think that speech allayed existing excitement, followed as it was by a change in England. (2.) As regards England. It was important that your government and people should know how those in our country most friendly felt with regard to their conduct. For months we have done all that could be done, and Lord Russell down to the 9th of September (I spoke on the 10th of September) gave no hint that we should not have war. . . . For weeks before I spoke bankers and leading business men had revealed to me their anxieties, and the agent of a great English house had told me he could not venture to open credits. It was time that something was said openly and plainly. I knew too well the prejudices of country and of party not to see that such an exposition would draw down upon me abuse and misrepresentation. But it seemed clearly my duty, and I am

glad I did it. I know England well, and I know
my own country; being somewhat behind the
scenes, too, I felt that I could judge what was
needed, not to soothe for the moment, not to grat-
ify personal feelings, but to secure the great object
of my heart, — solid peace between our two countries."

The death of his brother George, on October 6,
led him to decline all invitations to speak during
the autumn campaign, and he made no other public address before the meeting of Congress.

CHAPTER XVI

PRESIDENT LINCOLN regarded reconstruction from the standpoint of the Executive. His policy was to suppress the insurrection and then to permit the loyal citizens of each State to organize its government, giving them military protection during the process. He was in a hurry to see reconstruction accomplished, and distrusted the tedious methods of Congress. He perhaps did not sufficiently appreciate that the people were yet in doubt upon the questions involved, and that debates in Congress were the best way of educating leaders and people alike, until was formed that public opinion upon which any enduring reconstruction must rest. He seems also to have underestimated the danger of allowing a state government to be formed by a minority, especially where the persons allowed to act were determined by military order, and were bitterly hated by the majority.

Sumner felt that the conditions of reconstruction must be fixed by Congress and the President together, that the new governments must rest upon the consent of substantially the whole community, and that the freedom and rights of the colored race must be insured. Hence delay was necessary. He wished to build upon sound foundations an enduring structure, and this was not possible until the passions of war had cooled. While Lincoln lived harmony was preserved ; but when Andrew Johnson succeeded, inheriting Lincoln's opinions but not fully understanding them, and his violent, ill-regulated nature was substituted for Lincoln's "perfect steel," the conflict between the executive and the legislative policies became acute. Sumner was perhaps the first to appreciate the dangers of Lincoln's plan, and from the outset he led the opposition to any reconstruction without the consent of Congress. This controversy in its various phases occupied many years, and none more important ever engaged the attention of our people. The results of the war, the whole future of the country, were at stake, and at every stage in the struggle Sumner's influence was predominant.

Sumner contributed to the " Atlantic Monthly" for October, 1863, an article upon reconstruction, originally prepared as a speech on his resolution of February 11, 1862, but withheld because the military situation was unfavorable. In tone and style it differed much from his speech on our foreign relations. It is temperate, simple, and direct, and is a strong argument for the policy ultimately adopted by Congress. He began by pointing out that the President, without consulting Congress, had appointed military governors in four States, giving them practically absolute power, and that if this precedent were to be followed, eleven States and more than nine millions of people would be governed arbitrarily by one man, in a way not recognized by the Constitution nor regulated by law.

He reviewed the history of the confederation and the reasons which led to the adoption of the Constitution, reaching the conclusion that " this government is not established *by the States*, nor is it established *for the States;* but it is established *by the people*, for themselves and their posterity." He discussed the various theories as to the effect of secession on the relations of the States to the Union, and then stated an impregnable position : " For the time being, *and in the absence of a loyal government*, they can take no part and perform no function in the Union, *so that they cannot be recognized by the national government.* . . . Therefore to all pretensions in behalf of state governments in the rebel States I oppose the simple *fact*, that for the time being no such governments exist."

To the suggestion that loyal men might reorganize the governments, he replied : " Assuming that all this is practicable, as it clearly is not, it attributes to the loyal citizens of a rebel State, however few in numbers, — it may be an insignificant minority, — a power clearly inconsistent with the received principle of popular government, that the majority must rule." He found abundant authority for congressional action in the necessity of the case, in the rights of war, and in the obligation imposed upon the United States "to guarantee to every State in this Union a republican form of government," which clearly conferred upon the national government "jurisdiction above all pretended state rights." He urged that this view must be adopted, because threats were openly made that the States would restore slavery, and because of the danger to loyal men involved in the recognition of the existing governments. In a word, he dealt with a condition to which all theories must bend, and argued that since military government was not permanent and no trustworthy civil government existed, Congress must deal with the situation, and pass laws to secure reconstruction with safety to the loyal and freedom to all. This plan was attacked by Montgomery Blair and others as revolutionary, but it is difficult to see what other course was possible. The article shows Sumner at his best.

The first session of the Thirty-eighth Congress began in December, 1863, and adjourned the following July. It was a busy session, but not marked by any exciting issue. As Sumner wrote to Gladstone on January 1, 1864: "Our politics seem to have something of the tranquillity of our neighboring army. Never since I have been in public life has there been so little excitement in Congress. The way seems at last open. Nobody doubts the result. The assurance of the future gives calmness." There was, however, much to do in legislation and in education. Early in February, 1864, Sumner offered a series of resolutions in order to bring his theory of reconstruction to public attention. In substance these declared that slavery was the cause of the rebellion; that to crush the rebellion it was necessary to destroy it; that in order to eradicate every germ of rebellion, any scheme of reconstruction must be rejected which did not provide " by irreversible guaranties against the continued existence or possible revival of slavery," and that these guaranties could be had only through the national government; that it was therefore the duty of Congress to let no State resume its functions until within its borders proper safeguards were established, " so that loyal citizens, including the new-made freedmen, cannot at any time be molested by evil-disposed persons, and especially that no man there may be made a slave;" that slavery must be destroyed in the loyal as well as the seceded States, so that it should " no longer exist anywhere to menace the general harmony," and that to this end the Constitution must be amended so as to prohibit slavery everywhere within the jurisdiction of the United States. On the next day he presented the petition of one hundred thousand persons praying Congress to pass an act of universal emancipation, and supported it briefly. Though Sumner did not disclose it, he inspired the movement which led to this petition; but the time was ripe, and before Sumner moved his resolutions, two amendments abolishing slavery had been introduced in the House and one in the Senate. On the day when he introduced his resolutions he also proposed the amendment in this form: "Everywhere within the limits of the United States and of each State or Territory thereof, all persons are equal before the law, so that no person can hold another as slave."

When the amendment, in the form ultimately adopted, came before the Senate, Sumner proposed some changes in the phraseology, not liking the possible implication that men might be enslaved as a punishment for crime; but finding his suggestions not acceptable, he withdrew them and supported the amendment. In his speech upon it he insisted that Congress could abolish slavery by statute, and urged that the power should be exercised without waiting for the slow process of constitutional amendment; but he apparently asserted the existence of this power with reference to possible future exigencies, rather than with any hope of present action. He might have been pardoned some personal exultation over the change in public sentiment since he entered the Senate, to which his own efforts had so largely contributed, but none appears in his speech. The cause for which he had sacrificed so much was about to win the final victory, but he is not exultant, only devoutly thankful. "For myself, let me confess," he said, "that in the presence of the mighty events now thronging, I feel how insignificant is any individual, whether citizen or senator." The amendment failed to receive the necessary two thirds vote in the House of Representatives until January 31, 1865, after Mr. Lincoln's reëlection, and being subsequently ratified, it became a part of the Constitution on December 18 in the same year.

Sumner's first great speech in the Senate was made on August 26, 1852, in support of a motion to repeal the Fugitive Slave Law. Twice afterward he had renewed the attack in vain. This session was to witness his final victory. On February 8, 1864, he introduced a bill to repeal all fugitive slave laws, and had it referred to a committee of which he was the chairman. On February 29 he reported it with an elaborate report, but when it was taken up in the Senate, Sherman proposed to amend it so as to repeal only the act of 1850, leaving the act of 1793 in force. Against Sumner's opposition the amendment was adopted, and therefore he decided not to press the bill, but to wait the action of the House of Representatives, which on June 13 passed a bill repealing all fugitive slave laws. Sumner took charge of this in the Senate, and pressed it vigorously till it passed, the Senate rejecting the amendment to preserve the act of 1793, which it had previously adopted. On June 28 this bill was approved, and thus all laws for the rendition of fugitive slaves were wiped from the statute-book. Sumner's report was a thorough historical and legal discussion of these acts and of the provision in the Constitution upon which they rested. His speech against Sherman's amendment expressed almost indignant surprise that senators should at that late day be trying to protect slavery.

He proceeded to attack and destroy the buttresses of slavery one by one. On the day when he introduced his amendment to the Constitution he introduced also a bill to prevent the exclusion of witnesses on account of color in the courts of the United States. One would suppose that at so late a period in the civil war the bill would have passed at once, but Sumner could not get the Senate to consider it. He therefore moved it as an amendment to the civil appropriation bill, and though Sherman begged him not to press it because the weather was very hot and the amendment would provoke discussion, he insisted, and his proposition, with immaterial amendments, became the law. He had an almost identical experience with a bill to prohibit commerce in slaves among the States, but could not get it before the Senate until he moved it as an amendment to an appropriation bill. The amendment, at first lost, was renewed later, and carried.

It was in the debate upon this amendment that Mr. Hendricks of Indiana made a suggestion, half a taunt but wholly true, when he said : " I am surprised that any senator should oppose the proposition of the senator from Massachusetts, for we all know that eventually it will be adopted. The objection as to its suitability, or proper connection with the measure, is but an objection of time. No gentleman can question that the senator from Massachusetts will eventually carry his proposition." During the last ten years of his life the opponents of his proposals repeatedly attributed to Sumner such control over his Republican associates that, no matter how distasteful to them his ideas might be at the outset, they always finally adopted them; or as Mr. Doolittle said in 1868, " he had not only educated, but had Sumnerized the Senate."

During this session also he began the contest for negro suffrage. The first battle occurred upon a bill to provide a temporary government for the territory of Montana, amended in the Senate by giving the suffrage to every " free male citizen." Reverdy Johnson insisted that under the Dred Scott decision " black men " were not citizens. Sumner in reply asserted the right of Congress " to interpret the Constitution without constraint from the Supreme Court," and denounced the Dred Scott decision. The House of Representatives refused to concur, and the Senate yielded, perhaps for the reason suggested by Mr. Morrill of Maine, that there were no negroes in Montana to whom the amendment could possibly apply. Sumner, however, insisted that this made no difference, saying: " It is something to declare a principle, and I cannot hesitate to say that at this moment the principle is much more important than the bill. The bill may be postponed, but the principle must not be postponed."

The contest was renewed on a bill to regulate

elections in the District of Columbia, which did
not confine the suffrage to white citizens. Mr.
Cowan of Pennsylvania moved to amend by inserting the word " white," and Sumner opposed
him. The bill was never again considered, but a
resolution relating to the registration of voters was
reported later, which in effect excluded colored
men. Sumner moved to amend by a proviso that
no person should be excluded on account of color,
insisting that his opponents were defending slavery. Many friends of negro suffrage, however,
considered the resolution a temporary arrangement, and refused to imperil its passage by voting
for the amendment, which was lost. Thus ended
the contest for that session of Congress.

Sumner's persistency in battling against all discrimination founded on color was conspicuously
exhibited at this time in his efforts to prevent the
exclusion of colored persons from street cars in the
District of Columbia. The struggle lasted through
several sessions with varying fortunes, but in the
end he accomplished his object. He also actively
supported the attempt of his colleague, Mr. Wilson, to secure for colored soldiers equal pay with
white, a result finally achieved by leaving the question to the attorney-general, who sustained the
equality.

The condition of the recently emancipated slaves
was deplorable. Without property or education
and with no knowledge of their rights, they were
largely at the mercy of their white neighbors. The

social system of the South was destroyed and the result was general demoralization.

At this session the first steps were taken to deal with this situation by establishing the Freedmen's Bureau, which Sumner called " a bridge from slavery to freedom." The measure, originating in the House of Representatives, reached the Senate in March, 1864, and was referred to Mr. Sumner's committee on slavery and freedmen, which on May 25 reported it, with a substitute drawn by him and adopted by the committee. This substantially established a bureau in the Treasury Department to take charge of freedmen, to secure for them an opportunity to work, and to protect them against any enforced labor, by requiring the submission to local officers of their contracts with their employers. The officers of the bureau were to see that the freedmen did not suffer from ill treatment or breach of contract; to do what was possible as arbitrators in disputes, and " to appear as next friends of the freedmen in trials before any court." In short, the bill undertook to supply the lately emancipated negroes with official friends to watch over them, advise them, and protect their interests, exercising, however, no real authority, since they were dealing with free men. This was made perfectly clear by an amendment which Mr. Sumner himself offered: " And every such freedman shall be treated in every respect as a freeman with all proper remedies in courts of justice; and no power or control shall be exercised with regard to him except in conformity with law."

Mr. Sumner's substitute was adopted in the Senate, but the House postponed the measure until the next session, when, amended so as to place the new bureau in the War Department, it became a law. The burden of supporting this bill at every stage fell upon Sumner as the senator in charge. It was vigorously opposed, especially by Mr. Grimes of Iowa, whose opposition seemed to Sumner almost personal. Sumner made the importance of the measure clear in describing the condition of the freedmen : —

" They look about and find no home. They seek occupation, but it is not within their reach. They ask for protection, sometimes against former taskmasters and sometimes against other selfish men. If these are not supplied in some way by the government, I know not where to look for them. . . . To this end a central agency is proposed at Washington, with subordinate agencies where the freedmen are to be found, devoted to this work of watching over emancipation, so that it may be surrounded with a congenial atmosphere."

Such were the steps in the extirpation of slavery which Sumner urged during this session of Congress, and at its close he could look back upon substantial victories. Slavery was dead. Henceforth his work was to remove from the statute-book all traces of its existence, and to secure for the new freedmen all their rights as citizens.

Sumner did not neglect the work of the committee on foreign relations, but at this session made an exhaustive report upon the "French Spoliation Claims," in which their whole history was given, and the obligation of the United States was made apparent. Though Congress was not willing then to satisfy these claims, their justice was established, and with a fuller treasury provision has since been made for their payment. He supported the proposition to appoint consular pupils, dwelling upon the character of our service, and saying : "It is a shame that our offices abroad, whether consular or diplomatic, are served in this inferior way."

On April 30, 1864, he introduced the first bill to reform the civil service, which he "matured alone without consultation," and which contained all the essential features of the present system. It gave the preference to the first on the list, and provided against removals except for cause, and for promotions according to seniority ; but it allowed one fifth of the promotions to be made for merit "irrespective of seniority." The bill was cordially approved by the press, and the comments showed that the spoils system had begun to attract public disapproval ; but the time was not ripe for its passage and no actual legislation was had until March, 1871, when the appointment of the first Civil Service Commission was authorized by an amendment to an appropriation bill.

In the debates upon the bill to establish national banks, Sumner persistently opposed subjecting the shares to state taxation. He offered an amendment which imposed a national tax on their circulation, deposits, and capital, in lieu of all other taxes. He argued that the instruments by which the new national currency was created should not be exposed to attack from the States, and he saw in the attempt to make them liable another assertion of state rights. Secretary Chase and other prominent men agreed with Sumner; but Fessenden, for the finance committee, opposed his amendment with some bitterness, and the Senate followed the committee. Fessenden's acrimony in the debate disturbed for some years his relations with Sumner, but the bitterness disappeared before they died. Sumner also advocated the establishment of a branch mint in Oregon, his speech showing a remarkable knowledge of foreign experience as well as our own, and containing an excellent discussion of coinage and the true function of government in regard to it. He prevailed, and the branch mint was established. At this session, as always, he opposed imposts on books and on philosophical apparatus and instruments imported for schools, colleges, and like institutions, as taxes on knowledge never to be imposed in a land where education was free; but Congress would not follow him. He proposed a bill to incorporate a national academy of literature and art, but in the contest between different measures this bill was not considered. He took part also in the discussion of the tariff, saying that he regarded the taxes imposed " as temporary or provisional," and levied merely to carry on the war.

The reconstruction problem came up again in June upon a resolution recognizing the free state government of Arkansas. The Union forces having occupied a part of Arkansas, a government had been organized within their lines, and members of Congress as well as state officers had been chosen. Sumner opposed recognition because the government represented only a minority of the people; and to let this minority elect representatives and two senators, and cast the vote of the State in the electoral college, was to give it a wholly disproportionate influence in the government. He opposed also because civil order was not sufficiently restored in Arkansas, and the new government rested in fact upon a military edict, and not upon that peaceful action of the people which is the proper foundation of civil government. He asserted the necessity of congressional sanction to any permanent government, and insisted that this must not be given until freedom had been secured by "irreversible guaranties." The resolution of recognition was referred to the committee on the judiciary, which reported adversely. A few days later, when a bill postponing elections in the seceded States was pending, Mr. Sumner offered an amendment abolishing slavery in these States by act of Congress, but it was lost.

With characteristic pertinacity he opposed the final adjournment of Congress, because increased taxes were necessary, and Congress ought not to adjourn without laying them. He acted invariably as if "thinking naught done while aught remains to do," and his catalogue of unfinished work often irritated his less diligent or enduring associates.

During this session our foreign relations were not troublesome, but Sumner kept up his correspondence with leading Englishmen, and on the day of adjournment, July 4, 1864, he wrote this summary to the Duchess of Argyll : —

"Congress will disperse to-day, having done several good things : (1) all fugitive slave acts have been repealed ; (2) all acts sustaining the traffic in slaves on the coast from one domestic port to another have been repealed, so that now there is no support of slavery in our statute-book ; (3) the railroads here in Washington have been required to admit colored persons into their carriages ; (4) greatest of all in practical importance, the rule of evidence excluding colored testimony in the United States courts has been abolished. All these measures are now the law of the land. They were all introduced and pressed by myself. I feel happy in the result, but I shrink from saying that anything can make me happy now."

To Gladstone, Bright, and Bishop Wilberforce among others, he urged action by England which would range her clearly on the side of freedom in the struggle to extirpate slavery.

CHAPTER XVII

THE LAST YEAR OF THE WAR

DURING the summer of 1864 occurred the contest over the renomination of Mr. Lincoln. Many leading Republicans had lost confidence in him, and an attempt to secure some other candidate was made, in which men like Wade, Henry Winter Davis, Horace Greeley, Governor Andrew, and many leading journalists were active. Mr. Chase had many supporters, and Grant and Sherman were suggested. Lincoln was renominated in June, but it was still felt by many that defeat was certain unless he withdrew, and steps were taken to secure his withdrawal and the substitution of another candidate. In these movements Sumner took no part; he shared to some extent the doubts of his associates as to Lincoln's entire fitness, but his correspondence and conversation showed no strong feeling. A conference of leading men was held in New York on August 14, 1864, which resolved that a committee should request Mr. Lincoln to retire, and Dr. Lieber, who was present, informed Sumner of it. In reply Sumner stated his position, and in this letter to an intimate friend he spoke with absolute frankness. He said : —

"Your letter about the meeting was very interesting. I do not see how anything can be done
except through Mr. Lincoln and with his good-will.
If he could see that patriotism required his withdrawal and would sincerely give his countenance
and support to a new candidate, I am sure that the
candidate of that convention, whoever he might
be, could be chosen. . . . If Mr. Lincoln does not
withdraw, then all who now disincline to him must
come to his support. I have declined to sign any
paper or take any action, because I was satisfied
that nothing could be done except through Mr.
Lincoln and with his good-will. To him the appeal must be made and on him must be the final
responsibility. But the Chicago platform will
make it possible to elect him, if not easy. Indeed,
I am prepared for an uprising against it."

This platform described the war as " four years
of failure " and demanded that it cease. Sumner
was right in his anticipation, and under such a
banner the Democrats marched to overwhelming
and deserved defeat.

Andrew Johnson was substituted for Hannibal
Hamlin as the Republican candidate for the vice-
presidency, not from any loss of confidence in Mr.
Hamlin, but because it was felt that a Southern loy-
alist would strengthen the ticket, and at that crisis
nothing could be neglected which tended to insure
success. The Massachusetts delegation supported
the change, and one of them is quoted by Mr.
Hamlin's son as saying that " Mr. Sumner and

the Massachusetts delegation desired another candidate," and that "Mr. Sumner appealed to the Massachusetts delegates and insisted that they should advocate the nomination of a war Democrat for vice-president, in order to bring more Democrats to the support of the Republican ticket." Mr. Dawes, then a representative in Washington, also is quoted as saying that this was the understanding at the time. But neither speaks of any interview with Mr. Sumner, or seems to know personally of any action by him. Mr. Dawes could readily have seen him, and if much interested in the controversy would doubtless have done so, but he does not speak of any conversation. On the other hand, Senator Morrill, who attended the convention and on the day after its adjournment wrote Mr. Hamlin the history of Mr. Johnson's nomination, does not allude to Mr. Sumner; nor has any one ever shown any word or act of his before the nomination. He was in the Senate during the convention, his correspondence is silent on the subject, and it was not his habit to interest himself in such contests. The whole evidence sustains the conclusion that he took no part in bringing about the change of candidates.

Writing to Cobden after the campaign had begun, he summed up the political situation thus:—

"The hesitation in the support of Mr. Lincoln disappears at the promulgation of the Chicago treason. There was a meeting in New York of persons from different parts of the country to bring

about a new convention to nominate a Union candidate. The 'Tribune,' 'Evening Post,' 'Independent,' and Cincinnati 'Gazette,' were all represented in it, but as soon as they read the platform,
they ranged in support of Mr. Lincoln. I declined
to take any part in the meeting, for I could not
but see that nothing could be done except with
Mr. Lincoln's good-will. . . . You understand that
there is a strong feeling among those who have
seen Mr. Lincoln in the way of business, that he
lacks practical talent for his important place. It
is thought that there should be more readiness,
and also more capacity for government. But these
doubts are now abandoned, and all are united to
prevent the election of McClellan. To my mind
the election is already decided."

In the campaign of 1864 Sumner took an active
part, speaking in a number of cities. Two of his
speeches are preserved in his works and are excellent specimens of his most effective oratory. They
are simple and direct, and present the issues of the
campaign with great grasp and power. A single
warning against party spirit may be quoted : —

"Local prejudice, personal antipathy, and selfish interest obscure the vision. And far beyond
all these is the disturbing influence of 'party,' with
all the power of discipline and organization added
to numbers. Men attach themselves to political
party as to a religion, and yield blindly to its be-
hests. By error of judgment, rather than of heart,
they give up to party what was meant for country

or mankind. I do not condemn political parties,
but warn against their tyranny. . . . It is, unhappily, an evil of party always, even in its best estate,
that it tends to dominate over its members. . . .
This influence becomes disastrous beyond measure,
when bad men obtain control or bad ideas prevail."

In this speech he made his famous comparison
between the Mayflower and the slave-ship : —

"Go back to the earliest days of colonial history, and you will find the conflict already preparing. It was in 1620 that twenty slaves were
landed at Jamestown, in Virginia, — the first that
ever pressed the soil of our country. In that same
year the Pilgrims landed at Plymouth. Those
two cargoes contained the hostile germs which have
ripened in our time. They fitly symbolize our
gigantic strife. On one side is the slave-ship, and
on the other is the Mayflower. . . . Each had ven-
tured upon an untried and perilous ocean to find
an unknown and distant coast. In this they were
alike, but in all else how unlike! One was
freighted with human beings forcibly torn from
their own country, and hurried away in chains to
be sold as slaves ; the other was filled with good
men, who had voluntarily turned their backs upon
their own country, to seek other homes, where at
least they might be free. One was heavy with
curses and with sorrow ; the other was lifted with
anthem and with prayer. And thus, at the same
time, beneath the same sun, over the same waves,
each found its solitary way. By no effort of

imagination do we see on one Slavery and on the other Liberty, traversing the ocean to continue here, on this broad continent, their perpetual, immitigable war." This warfare thus begun could be ended, however, only by the destruction of slavery.

To the demand of the Democratic party that hostilities should cease he replied : —

" If you agree to abandon patriots and slaves in the rebel States, you will only begin your infinite difficulties. How determine the boundary line to cleave this continent in twain? Where shall the god Terminus plant his stone? What States shall be left at the North in the light of Liberty? What States shall be consigned to the gloom of Slavery? . . .

" Suppose the shameful sacrifice consummated, the impossible boundaries adjusted, and the illusive terms and conditions stipulated, do you imagine that you have obtained peace? Alas, no! Nothing of the sort. You may call it peace, but it will be war in disguise, ready to break forth in perpetual, chronic, bloody battle. Such an extended inland border, over which Slavery and Liberty scowl at each other, will be a constant temptation, not only to enterprises of smuggling, but to hostile incursions, so that our country will be obliged to sleep on its arms, ready to spring forward in self-defense. . . . Military preparations, absorbing the resources of the people, will become permanent instead of temporary, and the arts of peace will yield to the arts of war.   Have we not war enough now?"

A few words at Faneuil Hall after the election may well be given as a contrast with those which he uttered when he first spoke in that venerable building at the beginning of his political career: —

"The voice of the people at the ballot box has echoed back that great letter of the President, 'To whom it may concern,' declaring the integrity of the Union and the abandonment of slavery the two essential conditions of peace. Let the glad tidings go forth, 'to whom it may concern,' — to all the people of the United States, at length now made wholly free, — to foreign countries, — to the whole family of man, — to posterity, — to the martyred band who have fallen in battle for their country, — to the angels above, — ay, and to the devils below, — that this Republic shall live, for slavery is dead. This is the great joy we now announce to the world."

It was during the campaign, on October 7, 1864, that the Wachusett captured the rebel privateer Florida in the harbor of Bahia, and carried her off from under the guns of the Brazilian fleet and forts. This daring breach of our obligations to Brazil naturally created some excitement, and the English press denounced it as an outrage. In a letter to the " Advertiser " Mr. Sumner replied that the act accorded with too many British precedents for England to complain; and contended that, while Brazil might demand reparation, the precedents did not require a return of the ship. In January, after the incident was closed, he wrote another letter. Both were written to put English critics on the defensive, and the first to strengthen the hands of the government in its negotiations with Brazil, rather than to justify the seizure under international law.

During the recess of Congress Chief Justice Taney died, and Sumner urged the appointment of Chase to the vacant chair. Mr. Lincoln had lost much of his confidence in Chase and hesitated to appoint him, believing that, though chief justice, he would still aspire to the presidency; but he yielded to the general opinion, and made the appointment. A few weeks later Sumner moved the admission of a colored man, J. S. Rock of Boston, to the bar of the Supreme Court, and the chief justice granted the motion, thus ignoring the Dred Scott decision and holding that a negro was a citizen, since none but a citizen could be admitted. This result was reached after a correspondence between Sumner and Chase and a consultation, in which the other judges apparently decided not to depart from the usage by which the chief justice acts upon admissions to the bar without consulting his associates. Thus quietly was the equality of colored men before the law recognized by the highest tribunal in the country, and for so brief a time did the Dred Scott decision survive its author.

Not content with this, Sumner opposed a bill to place a bust of Taney in the Supreme Court room, speaking twice against it, and severely criticising his opinion in the Dred Scott case. His opposition defeated the bill, and it was not till two months before his death, and when illness kept him from the Senate, that a resolution providing for busts both of Taney and Chase passed Congress.

The last session of the Thirty-eighth Congress began in December, 1864. The rebellion was tottering to its fall, and the session was uneventful. A raid from Canada into Vermont was made in the interest of the rebellion by a party of men who broke open banks and plundered citizens in St. Albans, and caused a brief excitement. A bill was introduced authorizing the President to spend ten million dollars in fortifications and floating batteries to protect our northern border, but in a few temperate remarks Sumner pointed out the danger of letting the rebels succeed in disturbing our relations with England, and the bill was sent to the committee on foreign relations, where it died.

The treatment of our soldiers in Southern prisons had produced deep indignation throughout the North, and naturally retaliation in kind was demanded. The public feeling found expression in a resolution reported from the committee on military affairs in January, 1865, which provided that the prisoners in our hands should receive the treatment " practiced towards our officers or soldiers in the hands of the insurgents, in respect to quantity and quality of food, clothing, fuel, medicine, medical attendance, personal exposure, or other method of dealing with them; that with a view to the same ends the insurgent prisoners in our hands ought to be placed under the control and in the keeping of officers and men who have themselves been prisoners in the hands of the insurgents and have thus acquired a knowledge of their mode of treating Union prisoners." A few days later Sumner moved as a substitute a series of resolutions, which declared that retaliation, always harsh, was allowable only where it was likely to effect its object and within narrow limits, and that, while the treatment of our officers and soldiers in rebel prisons was cruel, "any attempted imitation of rebel barbarism in the treatment of prisoners" was impracticable, useless, and immoral; "that it could have no other result than to degrade the national character and the national name, and to bring down upon our country the reprobation of history." His final resolution declared the determination of the United States to end the barbarous treatment of prisoners by ending the rebellion.

He expanded his argument in a speech, and a long debate ensued in which many leading Republicans — Wade, Howard, Chandler, Howe, Gratz Brown, Harlan, and others — favored the original resolutions, while the Democrats with some Republicans opposed. Sumner spoke again, saying: —

"The committee . . . propose that Congress shall instruct the President to enter upon a system of retaliation, where we shall imitate as precisely as possible rebel barbarism, and make our prisons the scenes of torments we here denounce. Why, sir, to state the case is to answer it. . . . What civilization forbids cannot be done. Your enemy may be barbarous and cruel, but you cannot be barbarous and cruel. The rule is clear and un- questionable. . . . Even if you make up your minds to do this thing, you cannot. The whole idea is impracticable. The attempt must fail be- cause human nature is against you."

The opposition was effective, and upon Sumner's motion the resolution was so modified as to sug- gest only retaliation " in conformity with the laws and usages of war among civilized nations." Thus amended it passed the Senate, but was never acted upon by the House. In thus opposing the indig- nation of the country Sumner showed the moral courage and the enlightened humanity which never failed him. Of these he gave another proof when he moved to amend a joint resolution authorizing a contract with the artist Powell for a picture to be placed in the Capitol, by adding: " *Provided*, That in the national Capitol, dedicated to the na- tional Union, there shall be no picture of a victory in battle with our fellow citizens."

This found little or no support, and was rejected without division, but his action on these two mat- ters helped to teach many that his course towards slavery was dictated by hatred of the crime and not by personal bitterness against slaveholders.

CHAPTER XVIII

RECONSTRUCTION AGAIN

THE question of reconstruction, heretofore discussed as a question of the future, now became pressing, and the struggle, which had begun at the last session in the case of Arkansas, was renewed over a resolution to recognize a state government in Louisiana. The first issue was, whether the President by military order, or Congress by law, should control reconstruction; the second was, whether the right of suffrage should be given to the colored men in the seceded States. Everything else was really matter of detail. The issue between Congress and the President had first to be fought out, and it was in effect settled at this session of Congress. To John Bright Sumner wrote, on January 1, 1865: —

" The President is exerting every force to bring Congress to receive Louisiana under the Banks government. I do not believe Louisiana is strong enough in loyalty and freedom for an independent State. . . . I have discussed it with the President, and have tried to impress on him the necessity of having no break between him and Congress on such questions."

That the reader may understand the discussions, the history of reconstruction in Louisiana may be sketched briefly. In December, 1863, President Lincoln had issued a proclamation proposing a plan of reconstruction. He offered all persons in the seceded States, with certain exceptions, pardon and restoration of property, except slaves, upon their taking an oath to support the Constitution of the United States, and the laws and proclamations with reference to slaves. He declared that whenever persons who had taken this oath, equal in number to one tenth of the votes cast at the presidential election of 1860, and qualified to vote by the laws of the State in force at the time of secession, should establish a state government republican in form and recognizing the freedom of the negroes, this government would be recognized as that of the State. This proclamation was discussed in the President's annual message of December, 1863. In accordance with it, and under orders issued by General Banks, which in effect allowed only male white citizens to vote, elections were held in Louisiana early in 1864, at which state officers and delegates to a constitutional convention were chosen. Only some eleven thousand voters, including soldiers, took part in the elections, and a much smaller number voted when the constitution was submitted to the people in September, 1864. The orders of Banks were not to be reconciled with constitutional principles, and while the State was the scene of hostile operations any fair and free expression of

the popular will was impossible. The government thus established rested on military force and
did not really represent the people of Louisiana.
Meanwhile, Congress took up the subject, and
after long deliberation passed an act in July, 1864,
providing for conventions in the seceded States and
for reconstruction by a majority of the voters; but
the President withheld his signature, and it failed
to become a law. He refused his approval, partly
because he did not wish to set aside the governments which had been organized in Arkansas
and Louisiana under his proclamation, "thereby
repelling and discouraging the loyal citizens, who
have set up the same, as to further effort." The
result was to leave him in control of reconstruction.

This bill, as it passed the House, made the perpetual prohibition of slavery in the constitution of
each reconstructed State an essential condition,
but it gave the suffrage only to "white male citizens." The Senate committee reported it with an
amendment striking out the word "white," but
subsequently abandoned the amendment as endangering the bill. Sumner and four others voted for
the amendment, and he then tried to amend the
bill so as to give the Emancipation Proclamation
the force of a statute. Defeated in this he voted
for the bill, because it asserted the power of Congress over the terms of reconstruction and assured
the freedom of the slaves, waiving for the last
time his objection to any reconstruction without

equal suffrage.   Soon afterward he took his final
position, that there could be no just and lasting
reconstruction unless the negroes were given the
vote, and thereafter he never wavered.

The refusal of the President to sign the act
passed by Congress, and his attempt to effect reconstruction by proclamation and military order
upon terms fixed by himself without the consent
of Congress, had irritated some of the Republican
leaders, and there were many who, like Sumner,
felt that his plan was objectionable in itself.   An
issue was thus created between the President and
many of his own supporters, which made the struggle in Congress especially interesting.   The contest
of the session began on February 18, 1865, with
the introduction of a resolution from the committee
on the judiciary, recognizing the government of
Louisiana as the legitimate government of the
State.   Sumner opposed it, because the government
thus established was " not republican in origin
or form," and because it furnished "no security for the rights of colored persons."   When it
was taken up on February 23, he moved a substitute, which declared that neither the people nor
the legislature of any seceded State should elect
senators or representatives in Congress, until the
President should declare by proclamation that
armed hostility to the government had ceased
therein, nor until the people had adopted a constitution in harmony with the Constitution and laws
of the United States, and Congress had by law

declared the State entitled to representation. This substitute was defeated, but Sumner continued to antagonize the resolution, and in the press of business at the close of the session his determination to discuss the subject fully, and his refusal to permit a vote, prevented action upon it. He was charged with making obstructive motions, and replied that he thought the measure dangerous, and was justified in opposing it with all the weapons in the arsenal of parliamentary warfare.

In the course of the discussion Sumner offered an amendment to the resolution, providing that it should not take effect " except upon the fundamental condition that within the State there shall be no denial of the electoral franchise, or of any other rights, on account of color or race, but all persons shall be equal before the law," and requiring the assent of the legislature to this fundamental condition. He made no extended speech, but he took the same ground in regard to the origin of the government that he had taken in discussing the similar organization in Arkansas.

For the same reasons he opposed the admission of Mr. Segar as senator from Virginia, saying: " It is in vain that senators say that Virginia, now in war against the Union, is entitled to representation on this floor, when you have before you the inexorable fact that the greater part of the State is at this moment in the possession of an armed rebellion, and that other fact, repeated by the newspapers of the land, that the body of men who have undertaken to send a senator to Congress are little more than the common council of Alexandria."

In support of his theories as to the position of the States in rebellion and the true method of reconstruction, he offered two sets of resolutions during the session. The first in substance declared that the seceded States were not to be regarded as States in determining whether the constitutional amendment prohibiting slavery had been ratified. The other asserted that it was the duty of the United States by act of Congress to reëstablish republican governments in the States whose governments had been vacated; that the governments, to be republican, must rest on the consent of the governed, and that all persons must be equal before the law; that no government " founded on military power or having its origin in military orders " could be republican.

The defeat of the attempt to secure recognition for the governments of Arkansas and Louisiana established the control of Congress over the whole subject of reconstruction. In this contest Sumner opposed the President, and when we consider what the governments favored by Lincoln really repre sented and upon what a slender foundation they rested, whether of numbers or character, it is clear that Sumner was not only right as a matter of principle, but practically wise in refusing to support them. If the power of the President to prescribe the conditions of reconstruction had been conceded, it is hard to say what evil might not have been

done by President Johnson. Sumner's attitude in
this debate was supported by the anti-slavery sentiment of the country, and it doubtless secured the
establishment of equal suffrage without regard to
color. His course was fiercely attacked, and the
President criticised it freely. Indeed many believed that the difference would lead to a breach
of their friendly relations. Mr. Lincoln, however,
was too magnanimous not to respect Mr. Sumner's
right to differ with him on a public question, and
he invited him to join the President's party at the
inauguration ball. Sumner accepted, and his appearance with the President on this occasion effectually silenced all doubts as to their friendship.
Until Lincoln's death their intercourse continued
to be constant and cordial. In the Senate Sumner
had avoided making any extended speech, for he
recognized the difficulty of speaking without saying
something that might be misinterpreted by the
President; but in a letter to John Bright, written
just after the session closed, he spoke freely : —

"I insist that the rebel States shall not come
back except on the footing of the Declaration of
Independence, with all persons equal before the
law and government founded on the consent of
the governed. In other words, there shall be no
discrimination on account of color. If all whites
vote, then must all blacks; but there shall be no
limitation of suffrage for one more than the other.
It is sometimes said, 'What; let the freedman,
yesterday a slave, vote?' I am inclined to think

that there is more harm in refusing than in conceding the franchise. . . . Without their votes we cannot establish stable governments in the rebel States. Their votes are as necessary as their muskets; of this I am satisfied. Without them the old enemy will reappear, and under the form of law take possession of the governments, choose magistrates and officers, and, in alliance with the Northern democracy, put us all in peril again, postpone the day of tranquillity, and menace the national credit by assailing the national debt. To my mind the nation is now bound by self-interest — ay, self-defense — to be thoroughly just."

At the special session of the Senate, which began on March 4, 1865, Sumner offered again substantially the same resolutions, which he had offered as a substitute for the resolution recognizing the government of Louisiana, and his policy, though at the time attacked by many leading Republicans, became, before another session, the accepted policy of the Republican party.

This special session terminated on March 11, 1865, but Sumner as usual remained in Washington, seeing much of the President. When Mr. Lincoln was at the headquarters of the army, whither he went on March 23, Sumner by his invitation joined the party, and remained with it for several days, returning with it to Washington on April 9. During a part of the time Mr. Johnson, the Vice-President, was in the neighborhood, and Mr. Sumner learned how much Mr. Lincoln

disliked him, — a feeling which he was at little
pains to conceal.

Lee's surrender was announced to Sumner by a
message from the White House; but after a day
or two of rejoicing the assassination of the President came like a thunderbolt to change joy into
profound grief, and to work a revolution in the
political situation. Sumner heard the news shortly
after the assassination occurred, and he went at
once to the bedside of the President, where he remained till the end. One witness, who described
the scene shortly after midnight, said : " Senator
Sumner was seated on the right of the President's
couch, near the head, holding the right hand of
the President in his own. He was sobbing like a
woman, with his head bowed down almost on the
pillow of the bed on which the President was
lying." He attended the meeting of senators and
representatives in Washington, and drew the resolutions which they adopted. He did what was
possible for Mrs. Lincoln, and on leaving Washington she sent him her husband's cane, with a
note in which she said : " Your unwavering kindness to my idolized husband and the great regard
he entertained for you prompt me to offer for your
acceptance this simple relic." These reminiscences
show his relations with President Lincoln, and that
differences upon questions of policy never impaired
their mutual confidence and respect.

Sumner did not realize the consequences which
were to flow from Mr. Johnson's accession. Writ-

ing to Mr. Bright on April 18, he said : " Our government will continue tranquilly according to the requirements of fundamental law. It is probable that the policy towards leading rebels will be modified. President Lincoln was so essentially humane and gentle that he could not make up his mind to any severity, even to Jefferson Davis. . . . President Johnson is in a different mood." In a letter of April 25, he said : " I have seen a good deal of the new President, and have conversed on questions of business and of general policy. . . . On Saturday the chief justice and myself visited him in the evening, especially with the view of conversing on negro suffrage. Suffice it to say that he is well disposed, and sees the rights and necessities of the case, all of which I urged earnestly. Both of us left him light-hearted." A week later he writes, after another interview : " Last evening I had a long conversation with him mainly on the rebel States, and how they shall be tranquillized. Of course my theme is justice to the colored race. He accepted this idea completely, and indeed went so far as to say, " There is no difference between us.". . . He deprecates haste ; is unwilling that States should be precipitated back ; thinks there must be a period of probation, but that meanwhile all loyal people without distinction of color must be treated as citizens, and must take part in any proceedings for reorganization."

In repeated interviews Sumner presented his

views, and he left Washington well assured that
Johnson agreed with him, and that the battle for
equal rights was won.

On June 1 he delivered in Boston a eulogy upon
President Lincoln, and, possessed with the importance of persuading the country that negro suffrage
was essential to lasting reconstruction, he availed
himself of this opportunity to urge his views. The
speech did full justice to Lincoln's great character-
istics, and dwelt especially upon the consecration of
his life to the principles embodied in the Declaration of Independence, of which the orator said:
" The inevitable topic to which he returned with
most frequency, and to which he clung with all the
grasp of his soul, was the practical character of the
Declaration of Independence in announcing the liberty and equality of all men. No idle words were
there, but substantial truth, binding on the conscience of mankind."

His entire harmony with Lincoln in devotion to
human rights, is made absolutely clear by the tone
in which he quoted from Lincoln's speeches and
the admiration which he expressed. He firmly
believed in the words of Lincoln: " This is a
world of compensations; and he who would be
no slave must consent to have no slave. Those
who deny freedom to others deserve it not for themselves, and, under a just God, cannot long retain
it." Their fellow countrymen will do well to burn
these words upon their hearts.

Three days earlier, the President had disap

pointed the country by his proclamation of May 29 in regard to North Carolina, and this act may have added something to Mr. Sumner's speech. It certainly changed the whole political horizon. Johnson, in accepting the nomination for the vice-presidency, had denounced treason as "worthy of the punishment of death," and after he succeeded to the presidency he frequently repeated: "Treason is a crime and must be punished as a crime." His treatment of the South seemed sure to be more vigorous than that which Mr. Lincoln proposed, and the impression which he conveyed to Sumner and Chase as to his views upon negro suffrage was confirmed by his public statements to various delegations. Therefore, when on May 29 he issued a proclamation of amnesty, and another providing for reconstruction in North Carolina by a convention to be chosen only by persons qualified to vote before secession, thus excluding all colored men from the electorate, he astonished and greatly disappointed the loyal States. By some his change of position has been attributed to the persuasion of Southern men, for whom he had the instinctive respect of one who had held an inferior social position among them ; by others to the influence of Seward and the Blairs. It is possible also that his public declarations were intended to assure his hearers of his general sympathy with their purposes and of his honest intention, rather than to announce a fixed policy. He was not a master of accurate statement, and his speeches can be explained consistently with his subsequent action. He may have thought that in following substantially the policy of Lincoln he was pursuing a safe course, which the country would approve, and in that case it is easy to understand how the attacks upon him might seem to him unjust, and operating upon a man of strong will, violent temper, and little education might drive him to the indefensible line of action which he afterwards adopted. President Johnson will probably be regarded by the historian as a patriotic man of pure intentions, but who could brook no opposition and was entirely unfitted for his great office. But whatever the verdict upon him *in foro conscientiæ*, his course endangered the whole results of the war. He had the will and it was not yet certain that he had not also the power to adopt a policy which would have left the negroes only the name of freedom and have given reconstruction into the hands of disloyal men.

Sumner felt that unless this policy was defeated, the battles which had been won for equal rights must be fought again. So soon, therefore, as the proclamation of May 29 disclosed the President's purpose, he strove at once by letter and speech to kindle an opposition. He wrote to members of the Cabinet, members of Congress, and other men of influence, urging the importance of arresting the President's course and the necessity of giving the freedmen suffrage. A petition from colored men of Savannah was sent to him for presentation to the President, and in a published letter he said : " It

is impossible to suppose that Congress will sanction governments in the rebel States which are not
founded on 'the consent of the governed.' This
is the corner-stone of republican institutions. Of
course by the 'governed' is meant all the loyal citizens without distinction of color. Anything else
is mockery."

For a few months Sumner found little support.
There was, indeed, a meeting in Boston to demand
equal suffrage; but the Cabinet expressed no sympathy with Sumner's views, some members, like
Seward, being in active sympathy with the President, while others, like Stanton, were disinclined to
make an issue with him. Sumner wrote of them
on August 11: "The attorney-general [Speed] is
the best of the Cabinet; but they are all courtiers,
unhappily, as if they were the counselors of a
king."

Among the Republican leaders in Congress some
doubted the power of prescribing the conditions of
suffrage in the Southern States; others, like Fessenden and Wilson, felt it wiser to persuade than
to oppose the President; others again, like Stevens
and Wade, thought opposition hopeless. Outside
of Congress there was the same division of opinion.
Governor Morton of Indiana, Governor Andrew of
Massachusetts, and several of the leading newspapers opposed Sumner's attitude. Some of the old abolitionists, and Horace Greeley, in the "Tribune,"
threw their weight for equal suffrage, but among
prominent Republicans, Sumner, almost alone, in-

sisted that there should be no reconstruction unless impartial suffrage was allowed; that until the colored men were secured not only their freedom, but also absolute political equality before the law, the seceded States should not reënter the Union.

To Mr. Schleiden, on June 27, he wrote: "On the suffrage question the President has changed. Shortly after I left Washington Southern influences proved too strong. The ascendency is with the Blairs. I have a letter from a member of the Cabinet, telling me of a strong pressure on the President to enforce the Monroe Doctrine as a safety valve now, and to divert attention from domestic questions." Then, as always, a "vigorous foreign policy" was the favorite resort of those whose domestic policy had failed, and whose power was therefore threatened.

To Dr. Lieber, on August 14, he said: "All my first impressions were for the writing and reading qualification; but on reflection it seemed to me impracticable. Of course any rule must apply to the whites as well as to the blacks. Now you cannot get votes of Congress to disfranchise, which you must do in imposing this qualification. Providence has so arranged it that the work shall be done completely, because it must be done. Besides, there are very intelligent persons, especially among the freedmen, who cannot read or write. But we need the votes of all, and cannot afford to wait."

Again, on August 21: "The true policy of the

administration is as plain as noonday. No path
was ever clearer, and how they could get away
from it is astonishing. (1.) Refer the whole question of reconstruction to Congress where it belongs.
What right has the President to reorganize States?
(2.) Meanwhile, by good government through military officers, to lead public opinion in the right
direction. (3.) To obey the existing laws of Congress, which expressly exclude from public service
any person who has sustained the rebellion. (4.)
To obey the Constitution, which refuses to make
any distinction of color. (5.) To redeem the promises of the Declaration of Independence instead
of openly setting them at defiance. Why the Cabinet have not insisted upon these plain rules is very
strange. I have been invited to preside at the
coming Republican State Convention for Massachusetts. At any other time I should not do it;
but I shall now, in order to speak the voice of
Massachusetts."

He carried out this purpose, and on September
14 made a speech to the convention, which Massachusetts received with cordial approval. It was
a discussion of the conditions to be observed in reconstruction, with no criticism of the President
or of those who agreed with him, — a statement of
what could and ought to be done. At the outset
he said : —

" When last I addressed my fellow citizens, at
the close of the late presidential canvass, . . . I
said to friends near me, ' This is my last anti-

slavery speech.' I so thought at the time; for I anticipated the speedy downfall of the rebellion, carrying with it slavery. I was mistaken. Neither the rebellion nor slavery is yet ended. The rebellion has been disarmed ; but that is all. Slavery has been abolished in name ; but that is all. . . . The work of liberation is not yet completed. Nor can it be, until the equal rights of every person once claimed as a slave are placed under the safeguard of irreversible guaranties.

"It is essential . . . that all men should be hailed as equal before the law; and this enfranchisement must be both civil and political. Unless this is done, the condition of the freedman will be deplorable. Exposed to every brutality, he will not be heard as a witness against his oppressor. Compelled to pay taxes, he will be excluded from all representation in the government. Without this security, emancipation is illusory. . . . It is *impartial suffrage* that I claim, without distinction of color, so that there shall be one equal rule for all men. And this, too, must be placed under the safeguard of constitutional law."

He counseled against any reliance on oaths or pardons and against the too prompt removal of political disabilities, saying of the Confederates : —

"I would not be harsh. There is nothing humane that I would reject. Nothing in hate. Nothing in vengeance. Nothing in passion. I am for gentleness. I am for a velvet glove ; but for a while I wish the hand of iron." But it was not yet time to trust them: "Therefore, we turn from recent rebels to *constant loyalists*. This is only ordinary prudence. As those who fought against us should be for the present disfranchised, so those who fought for us should be at once enfranchised. . . .

"All these guaranties should be completed and crowned by an *amendment of the Constitution of the United States*, especially providing that hereafter there shall be no denial of the electoral franchise or any exclusion of any kind on account of race or color, but all persons shall be equal before the law."

These quotations indicate his position, but give no idea of his speech, which was very effective. The Massachusetts convention applauded and indorsed it, and by contrast we may note the position of Pennsylvania, as it appeared to Thaddeus Stevens, whose views were not less radical than those of Sumner, and whose courage was undoubted: —

"I am glad you are laboring to avert the President's fatal policy. I wish the prospect of success were better. I have twice written him, urging him to stay his hand till Congress meets. Of course he pays no attention to it. Our editors are generally cowardly sycophants. I would make a speech, as you suggest, if a fair occasion offered. Our views (Reconstruction and Confiscation) were embodied in our resolutions [in the Republican State Convention, recently held] at Harrisburg, amidst much chaff. Negro suffrage was passed over, as heavy and premature. Get the rebel States into a territorial condition, and it can be easily dealt with. That, I think, should be our great aim. Then Congress can manage it."

The President's plan of reconstruction was simple. In each State he appointed a provisional governor, and provided for a constitutional convention to frame a state government under which there should be held elections for state officers and for members of Congress. Under the proclamation of amnesty all white men in the Southern States might vote and hold office on taking an oath to support the Constitution, except those belonging to certain specified classes who could be pardoned and restored to their rights on special application to the President. On the other hand colored men were denied all right to vote or hold office. Men who had shown their sympathy with secession by their acts were appointed provisional governors, and thus given the power to direct the course of reconstruction. It was not to be expected that those who had held slaves for years and had lost them suddenly by what seemed to them an arbitrary and unjust act should be ready at once to treat them as citizens. The passions which had brought on the war had not been quenched by the bitter struggle of four years, and it was not in human nature that the defeated should at once become loyal. The radical vice of the President's plan was that it placed the freedmen and the loyal minority of whites absolutely in the power of the disloyal majority. It opened to men but lately in rebellion the pathway to power in the national government through an alliance with the Democratic party in the North, while it assured them control of their own section.

The conventions and legislatures organized under the President's proclamation annulled the ordinances of secession, ratified the Thirteenth Amendment, and declared the Confederate debt invalid, but uniformly excluded negroes from all rights as citizens, and passed statutes designed to keep them in subjection to the whites, restoring slavery in fact, if not in name. Assured of the President's support and of their own restoration to power, they took little pains to conceal their feelings, and as a result the Southern Unionists found themselves in danger, while the colored people were exposed to outrages of every kind.

CHAPTER XIX

SUCH were the conditions which confronted the Thirty-ninth Congress on December 4, 1865. Sumner reached Washington two days earlier, and at once called on the President. Some weeks before this he had sent him a telegram, which began : "As a faithful friend and supporter of your administration, I most respectfully petition you to suspend for the present your policy towards the rebel States," and gave with necessary brevity his reasons, which were those of his speech to the Republican convention. He had not criticised Mr. Johnson personally, and he called upon him as a leader of the party which had made him president. He thus described his interview and his relations with the administration : —

"I found him changed in temper and purpose. How unlike that president who only a few days after arrival at power made me feel so happy in the assurance of agreement on the great question. No longer sympathetic, or even kindly, he was harsh, petulant, and unreasonable. Plainly his heart was with ex-rebels. For the Unionist, white or black, who had borne the burden of the day, he had little feeling. He would not see the bad spirit of the rebel States, and insisted that the outrages there were insufficient to justify exclusion from Congress. . . . I left the President that night with the painful conviction that his whole soul was set as flint against the good cause, and that by the assassination of Abraham Lincoln the Rebellion had vaulted into the presidential chair. Jefferson Davis was then in the casemates at Fortress Monroe, but Andrew Johnson was doing his work."

On the first day of the session Sumner opened his campaign by introducing six bills and a number of resolutions. The bills were: to secure equal suffrage in the District of Columbia; to secure the presence of colored jurors upon the panel at the trial of cases in which the rights of colored persons were involved ; to prescribe a form of oath which should be required of every voter or officer in the seceded States ; to forbid the denial in those States of rights, civil or political, on account of race or color, and to make all persons " equal before the law, whether in the court room or at the ballot box ; " to enforce the Thirteenth Amendment by making it a crime to " claim any right to control the services " of any person in contravention of its provisions. This last bill gave the federal courts jurisdiction of offenses committed by or against persons of African descent, and of all suits to which such persons should be parties, and it annulled all state laws or customs making any distinction of rights on account of race or color.

Another bill contained a complete scheme of reconstruction. It was carefully drawn, but its exact provisions are not material. In effect it gave Congress the control of reconstruction, insured equal suffrage, prevented all distinctions of race or color, and disfranchised the leaders of the rebellion.

A set of resolutions presented the same ideas in a different form. Another resolution proposed the amendment to the Constitution which he had previously offered, apportioning representatives according to the number of voters in each State, while a third declared the Thirteenth Amendment ratified by the action of the loyal States. Thus Sumner placed before Congress and the country his method of dealing with the existing situation.

On December 19, in answer to a resolution of the Senate, the President sent the reports of Generals Grant and Schurz as to the condition of the seceded States, and accompanied them by a message in which he expressed his belief "that sectional animosity is surely and rapidly merging itself into a spirit of nationality, and that representation, connected with a properly adjusted system of taxation, will result in a harmonious restoration of the relations of the States to the national Union."

The report of General Grant, made after a brief tour, expressed the belief that the Southern States were in good faith accepting the results of the war, and were anxious to resume their relations with the Union, and said nothing to indicate that the

colored race was in any way ill treated. General
Schurz, whom the President had sent to examine
into the conditions at the South, had reached
exactly opposite conclusions. After the President's
message and General Grant's report had been read,
Mr. Sumner called for the reading of General
Schurz's report. Some senators objecting on account of its length, Sumner said : —

"It is a very important document. . . . We
have a message from the President which is like
the whitewashing message of Franklin Pierce with
regard to the enormities in Kansas. Such is its
parallel. I think the Senate had better at least
listen to the opening of Major-General Schurz's
report."

The phrase "whitewashing" provoked some of
the President's supporters, and Mr. Doolittle of
Wisconsin urged Sumner to withdraw or at least
to qualify it, but he refused, disclaiming any "reflection on the patriotism or the truth of the President," but insisting that the adjective properly
described the message. The remark was the first
shot in the impending war, and caused an extended
discussion in the press and elsewhere. Sumner's
attitude was strongly criticised by some as injudi-
cious and as likely to provoke unhappy dissension,
but the more positive men recognized and rejoiced
in the justice of the phrase, and applauded it. On
the following day Sumner spoke upon Mr. Wilson's
bill to establish the civil rights of the negroes in
the rebel States, beginning thus : —

" When I think of what occurred yesterday in this chamber, when I call to mind the attempt to whitewash the unhappy condition of the rebel States, and to throw the mantle of official oblivion over sickening and heart-rending outrages, . . . I feel that I ought to speak of nothing else."

He then showed the real condition of the South by many quotations from letters written by officers, travelers, and citizens, from speeches of Southern men, and from official documents. The testimony was overwhelming. The case thus presented may be judged from one or two quotations, which are specimens of the whole : —

" This is precisely what ninety-nine in every hundred of the men, women, and children believe sincerely as to the situation to-day : first, that the South of right possesses, and always possessed, the right of secession; secondly, that the war only proved that the North was the strongest.; thirdly, that negro slavery was and is right, but has been abolished by the war.

" All expect the negro will be killed in one way or another by emancipation. The policy of those who will eventually become the leaders here at the South is, for the present, to accept the best they can get, to acquiesce in anything and everything, but to strain every nerve to regain the political power and ascendency they held under Buchanan. This, they believe, cannot be postponed longer than up to the next presidential election. They will do all in their power to resist negro suffrage, to reduce taxation and expenditures, and would attack the national debt if they saw any reason to believe repudiation possible. They will continue to assert the inferiority of the African, and they would to-day, if possible, precipitate the United States into a foreign war, believing they could then reassert and obtain their independence. . . . On the whole, looking at the affair from all sides, it amounts to just this: If the Northern people are content to be ruled over by the Southerners, they will continue in the Union, if not, the first chance they get they will rise again."

"The former masters exhibit a most cruel, remorseless, and vindictive spirit toward the colored people. In parts where there are no Union soldiers I saw colored women treated in the most outrageous manner. They have no rights that are respected. They are killed, and their bodies thrown into ponds or mud holes. They are mutilated by having ears and noses cut off."

The evidence collected in this speech and the report of General Schurz justified Sumner's description of the President's message, and from that time the President steadily lost ground in public opinion. It was a process of education, and Sumner's position was sustained by evidence of Southern feeling daily brought to the North by the press and private correspondence. Men were reluctant to realize that a conflict with their own President must be won before the results of the war were finally assured, and they would gladly have closed their eyes to the facts, fearing disturbance of business, loss of office and political power, — in a word, trouble, of which they had had enough. But the facts were too strong and the unsettled question of the day, as always, had "no respect" for their "repose." The rapid change in public opinion is perhaps shown by the history of the very bill upon which Mr. Sumner made his speech.

In the debate which followed Mr. Trumbull and other leading Republicans expressed the hope that the measure was unnecessary, that the South would change its laws in good faith so as to secure the rights of the freedmen, and that the conditions were exaggerated by Mr. Sumner. By general consent Mr. Wilson's bill was laid aside; but on January 5, 1866, only some two weeks later, Mr. Trumbull himself introduced a bill to prevent any discrimination in civil rights on account of race, color, or previous condition of slavery. On the same day he introduced a bill giving to the Freedmen's Bureau jurisdiction wherever there were freedmen or refugees, and empowering it to protect freedmen against hostile discrimination on account of race or color. This was fiercely opposed by the congressmen from the slave States which had not seceded, and by some Republicans, but it passed both Houses by large majorities. The President vetoed it on February 19, and the Senate failed to pass it over his veto, though his veto message contained no argument which had not been presented when the bill was under consideration.

The first vote in the Senate was thirty-seven to ten; on the question of passing it over the veto it was thirty to eighteen. Congress was not yet fully enlisted in the struggle with the President.

Opinion was forming rapidly, however, as is shown by the fate of Mr. Trumbull's Civil Rights bill, introduced on the same day with his Freedmen's Bureau bill. This was a bill to prevent any discrimination in civil rights on account of race or color; and it was reported by the committee on the judiciary, with an amendment declaring "all persons born in the United States and not subject to any foreign power " " to be citizens of the United States, without distinction of color." After a full debate, in which the measure was supported upon the grounds already urged by Sumner, the bill passed both Houses. On March 27 the President refused his approval, but Congress passed the bill over his veto on April 9, and thus made apparent the position which the Republican party would take as to the state governments erected under the President's proclamation. Later in the session another bill enlarging the powers of the Freedmen's Bureau, and extending the period of its existence, was passed over the President's veto. In the excited debate over these measures Sumner took no part, content with the arguments of his associates. After his speech of December 20, he made no further attacks on the President's policy.

The state legislature of Florida, chosen under the President's proclamation, had elected Mr. Marvin senator, but when his credentials were presented Sumner objected, calling attention to the composition of the legislature in which Confederate officers largely predominated, and to the state constitution which disfranchised negroes. The credentials were laid on the table, and the case was never moved again. In this case, as in Mr. Segar's, Sumner's objections settled the case against the state government organized by executive action.

On February 5 the Senate took up a resolution, which had passed the House, in favor of an amendment to the Constitution providing that representatives should be apportioned among the States according to the population, " excluding Indians not taxed," with the proviso : " That whenever the elective franchise shall be denied or abridged in any State on account of race or color, all persons therein of such race or color shall be excluded from the basis of representation." This was strongly supported by many Republican leaders, including Thaddeus Stevens, who usually sympathized with Sumner but was a more practical politician. Sumner was absolutely opposed to this proposition and put forth all his energies to defeat it. He spoke against it on February 5 and 6, 1866, very elaborately and effectively. This speech and the others which he made during the debate are upon a high plane, discussing the question with earnestness and dignity, but without personal feeling. The elevation of tone is made more striking by comparison with the speeches of other senators, notably Mr. Fessenden, who was in charge of the measure, and spoke at times with acrimony.

The real nature of the proposition which Sumner was combating was well stated by Mr. Cowan of Pennsylvania, who sympathized with the President, and opposed the amendment. He said: "This committee proposes in this amendment to sell out four million (radical count) negroes to the bad people of those States for ever and ever. In consideration of what? . . . For about sixteen members of Congress. Has there ever been before, sir, in the history of this or any other country, such a stupendous sale of negroes as that?" Sumner opposed it on various grounds. He said that after Congress had been "carefully expunging from the statute-book the word 'white,'" it was proposed to insert in the Constitution itself a distinction of color, and to make another of those fatal compromises with human rights which had fastened slavery upon the country. His demand was for enfranchisement as the necessary complement of emancipation, without which it must fail, and he added: "By enfranchisement I mean the establishment of the equal rights of all, so that there shall be no exclusion of any kind, civil or political, founded on color, and the promises of the fathers shall be fulfilled."

He proved from historical sources what was meant by "a republican form of government" as used in the Constitution, and that its essence was expressed by James Otis in his famous "Taxation without representation is tyranny." In reply to Fessenden he showed that representation did not mean representation of communities, but of individuals. Upon these points his speeches are a magazine of learning. His postulate was thus stated:

" A state which, in the foundation of its government, sets aside 'the consent of the governed,' which imposes taxation without representation, which discards the principle of equal rights, and lodges power exclusively with an oligarchy, aristocracy, caste, or monopoly, cannot be recognized as a 'republican form of government,' according to the requirement of American institutions."

His principal speech is unnecessarily long, yet it is stimulating and refreshing. The quotations with which he seemed to overload this and other elaborate speeches served at least one purpose: they created an atmosphere removed from the political struggles of the day, and placed the reader in association with the great men of successive ages, so that it was easier to recognize as eternal the principles which such even united in accepting, and to see the baser arguments of the moment in their true relation.

He gave the figures which showed the proportion of negroes in the total population of the South, and argued that no government could be called republican where political rights were denied to so large a portion of the people. He met the argument drawn from laws which impose educational and other qualifications as follows : " Let me be understood. What I ask especially is impartial suffrage, which is, of course, embraced in universal suffrage. What is universal is necessarily impartial. For the present, I simply insist that all shall be equal before the law, so that in the enjoyment of this right there shall be no restriction not equally applicable to all."

He dwelt upon the value of the ballot as assuring peace and reconciliation, as an educational influence, as a means of defense to the negro; and he claimed also that it was necessary for the safety of the country. He said : " It is idle to expect any true peace while the freedman is robbed of this transcendent right, and left a prey to a vengeance too ready to wreak upon him the disappointment of defeat. The country, sympathetic with him, will be in perpetual unrest. With him it will suffer; with him alone can it cease to suffer. . . . He is our best guaranty. Use him. If he votes now, there will be peace. Without this you must have a standing army, which is a sorry substitute for justice. Before you is the plain alternative of the ballot box or the cartridge box : choose ye between them."

The whole speech, with its array of authority, had, perhaps, as much effect on public opinion as any that Mr. Sumner ever made. Its temperate and earnest statements carried conviction to many who hesitated, and educated the public to accept negro suffrage. The resolution which he opposed did not receive the necessary votes in the Senate, and the proposed amendment failed. During the debate Sumner explained the difference between this proposition and his own proposal for apportioning representatives according to voters and not according to population. His proposition in no way prevented Congress from securing impartial suffrage, or brought into the Constitution any recognition of color as a reason for inequality of rights, and he offered simultaneously a series of resolutions declaring the duty of Congress to secure equal rights for the freedmen. He proposed the rule adopted in Massachusetts and urged by him in the constitutional convention of 1853. There was nothing inconsistent, therefore, in Sumner's opposition to the amendment.

The defeat of the resolution left the question unsettled, and paved the way for the Fourteenth and Fifteenth amendments. The result was received with much regret by many of Sumner's associates, who held him responsible. The President also was excited, and on the day after Sumner's speech, speaking to a delegation of colored men, he criticised it with some feeling, dwelling upon his own service to their cause, and expressing his unwillingness to adopt a policy likely to result in race conflicts. He was more violent in a speech from the steps of the White House on February 22, when he classed Stevens, Sumner, and Wendell Phillips with Davis, Toombs, and Slidell, as opposed to the Union and anxious to destroy our institutions.

This was the first attack by the President on Republicans by name, and it increased the growing hostility.

The amendment to the Constitution was defeated on March 9, and three days later a bill for the admission of Colorado was taken up. Sumner opposed it, partly because the population was small and decreasing, and it seemed to him unfair that so small a body should be given an equal voice with New York in the Senate. But chiefly he urged that the Constitution of the State allowed only white citizens to vote. He took an active part in the discussion of the bill and offered an amendment providing that the State should not be admitted except upon the condition, accepted by a majority of the voters, that there should be no denial of suffrage or of any other right on account of race or color. This was finally defeated and the bill was passed. The President vetoed it, and on a motion to assign it for further consideration Sumner announced his purpose to sustain the veto; but the bill was never taken up and fell with the session.

The desire to increase the Republican vote in the Senate caused the pressure for the admission of the State, and this probably explains the President's opposition. Sumner met this argument characteristically, saying : —

" Tell me not that it is expedient to create two more votes in this chamber. Nothing can be expedient that is not right. If I were now about to pronounce the last words that I could ever utter in this chamber, I would say to you, Senators, do not forget that right is always the highest expediency. You can never sacrifice the right without suffering for it."

Later in the session the question was raised again on a bill to admit Nebraska. Mr. Sumner moved the same condition as in the case of Colorado, but the motion was lost. The bill passed, but was not signed by the President, and the session closed with the question still open. Upon a resolution declaring Tennessee entitled to representation, Sumner made the same point and undertook to attach the same condition; but his amendment was defeated, and the resolution passed and was signed by the President.

The Republican leaders were not satisfied to leave the question of suffrage as it was left by the defeat of the proposed constitutional amendment, and on April 30, 1866, Mr. Stevens reported a new resolution, proposing the first form of what, after many changes of language and some of substance, was afterwards adopted as the Fourteenth Amendment. Wilson, in his " Rise and Fall of the Slave Power," says that the committee on reconstruction had adopted a much more sweeping amendment, which forbade any discrimination as to civil rights, and, after July 4, 1876, as to suffrage, on account of race, color, or previous condition of servitude, but that this failed because the Republican representatives from New York, Illinois, and

Indiana were afraid that the adoption of negro suffrage by the Republicans might defeat the party
at the next election in those States. This shows
that Sumner's associates were themselves in agreement with him, but feared their constituents, so
that the differences which appeared in the debate
were more apparent than real. The amendment
as finally drawn avoided the objection made by
Mr. Sumner to the earlier one, in that it did not
recognize the right of a State to deny the suffrage
to any citizen on account of color. On this point
it conformed more nearly to his idea of apportioning representatives according to voters, while it
left Congress at liberty to prevent any discrimination inconsistent with a republican form of government. It also contained two other things which
he had proposed and considered vital: the declaration that the national debt should not be questioned,
nor any debt incurred in aid of the rebellion paid;
and the exclusion from office of all persons who,
having as federal or state officers sworn to support the Constitution of the United States, had
afterwards taken part in or aided the rebellion.
Satisfied on these points, he did not speak, but
voted for the amendment. It was one step towards the goal which he had in view, and it left the
way open. He would have preferred to take the
final step at once, but did not decline to make
the advance for which his associates were ready.
So far as it provided for reducing the representation of a State the amendment has thus far been
of no effect.

The net result of the session was that the question of equal suffrage had been thoroughly discussed, that the doubts as to the power of Congress to impose it upon the States were gradually disappearing, that the necessity of requiring it was becoming clearer, that nothing had been done affecting the control of Congress over the question, and that an amendment had been defeated, which would have placed in the Constitution a recognition of the power to deny political rights on account of color. The session also made it clear that Congress would control reconstruction, that the freedmen would be protected by law against oppression, and that no state governments organized and controlled by disloyal men would be recognized. The President's plan had failed, and the situation which confronted Congress at the beginning of the session had been changed for the better. To John Bright, on May 21, Sumner wrote: "I am sure there can be no tranquillity or security here until complete justice is rendered to the negro. . . . I confess I can see nothing but 'agitate and convert' until the franchise is extended."

Besides these matters, other things also engaged Sumner's attention during this session. When the trial of Jefferson Davis was impending, a bill was introduced to remove the disqualification of jurors who had formed an opinion founded on common notoriety, public rumor, or newspaper statements. Sumner doubted the wisdom of this, saying: "I shrink from any change in the law to meet an indi-

vidual case, even though of transcendent importance." The bill was not passed. On the legal
question whether a senator could be elected by a
plurality of the votes cast in the joint assembly of
a state legislature, he argued that a majority was
necessary ; and he contended that on this question
the senator whose title to a seat was involved could
not vote. In these positions Fessenden supported
him.

He spoke on the subject of relieving the Supreme
Court from the undue accumulation of cases; he
discussed the power of Congress to establish quaran-
tine regulations ; he urged with success an amendment to the consular and diplomatic appropriation
bills giving a higher rank to our foreign ministers ;
he reported from a special committee bills to authorize the metric system of weights and measures,
and supported them with a careful and instructive
speech ; and he did his best to prevent the contract
with Vinnie Ream for a statue of Mr. Lincoln.
His speeches on this question were sensible and
direct, and the statue, which he failed to prevent,
stands a monumental proof of his wisdom. As he
said, the artist might as well have contracted " to
furnish an epic poem or the draft of a bankrupt
bill."

At the very end of the session the House passed,
unanimously, a bill amending our neutrality laws.
It was dictated by hostility to England, and it repealed the provisions against the fitting out in this
country of military expeditions against nations

with which the United States was at peace. In the Senate Sumner had it sent to his committee, resolved to let it sleep there. Some of its friends decided to move that the committee be discharged, whereupon Sumner armed himself with books and kept his seat from seven at night till seven in the morning on the last night of the session, that no advantage might be taken of his absence. At eleven in the morning the motion to take up the bill was made, but Sumner announced that he should speak for the rest of the session, and the motion was not pressed. He was determined that no provocation should induce this nation to abandon the true position of a neutral; and in the same spirit he carried a bill through the Senate to pay an award made to a British subject, saying that " our own country should be kept firm and constant in the attitude of justice." While Sumner was at the head of the committee on foreign relations our peace was not to be disturbed by any hasty or ill-considered legislation, and his countrymen had come to rely upon him.

It is not strange that we find him writing to Mr. Bright in May: " Curiously, I too have fallen into the doctor's hands. He finds my brain and nervous system overtaxed; and, suffering from my original injuries as a predisposing cause, I long for rest, and yet every day I grind in my mill." When we consider all that he did, it is only wonderful that he did not suffer more.

As Sumner was afterward charged with allowing his personal feeling to interfere with the conduct of public business, it is interesting to note that, though he thought Seward largely responsible for the President's course, his personal relations with his old associate remained undisturbed during the whole struggle between Congress and the President, and until Sumner's death. This enabled him quietly to stifle some rather extraordinary propositions of Seward's, such as an attack on Ecuador for failing to pay an award promptly.

The feeling at this time upon the tariff, since a great issue, is thus stated in a letter to Mr. Bright on May 21, 1866 : " On protection and free trade there does not seem to be any general feeling. The question will be settled for some time by the necessities of our position without much reference to principles. My own people, originally strong protectionists, are silent now. It is Pennsylvania which is clamorous, and the balance of parties in this important State makes the question one of political power." This is a succinct statement of a great historical truth.

After the adjournment the President, in a series of absurd and intemperate speeches made apparently in the hope of securing popular support at the autumn elections, violently attacked Congress and its policy, and charged it with endeavoring " to prevent the restoration of peace, harmony, and union," calling it a body " hanging on the verge of the government, as it were, a body called, or which assumes to be, the Congress of the United States, while in fact it is a congress of only a part of the States." Then followed his extraordinary electioneering tour, described in the political slang of the day as "swinging round the circle," from a phrase used in one of his speeches. His conduct and language were so indecent and so unworthy of his high office that later they were made one of the grounds for his impeachment.

Thus the issue was made very clear. On the one hand the policy of the President was to admit the Southern States, with the leaders of secession in control, and with loyal men, white and black, substantially at their mercy, — the whites because they were in a hopeless minority among a bitterly hostile population, the blacks because they were entirely without political power. To sustain his policy the President exerted all his prerogatives; by pardons he restored prominent Confederates to power, and by removals and appointments he used the whole patronage of the government to build up a party which should support him. Thus encouraged, the governments established by him in the South made no concealment of their bitter feeling toward the North, nor of their determination to keep the colored race, deprived of civil and political rights, in a state of vassalage hardly distinguishable from slavery. Their legislation as to the negroes was barbarous, and their spirit was proved by a series of outrages which kept this unhappy race in abject terror. On the other hand Congress and the party of which Sumner

was the most prominent leader were determined
that there should be no reconstruction, unless the
civil and political rights of loyal men in the South
were established beyond possible doubt, and that
the supporters of secession should not be admitted
to office or power until they had become loyal in
fact as well as in name. The whole result of the
civil war, the whole future of the country were
at stake, and upon the question between the opposing policies the autumn campaign was fought.

During this campaign Sumner spoke in Boston.
He stated the issue clearly, pointing out that the
President denied to Congress and claimed for himself the whole power to legislate upon the question
of reconstruction. He dwelt upon the vices of the
President's policy, showed its deplorable results in
the actual condition of the South, repeated the
arguments in favor of a reconstruction which should
be real and permanent, and insisted that the fundamental conditions of reunion were "emancipation, enfranchisement, equality, and education,"
which it was the duty of Congress to impose, thus
insuring the results of the war and proper security
for the future. He spoke of the President's weakness, held him responsible for the death of colored
men recently slain at Memphis, New Orleans, and
elsewhere, and placed him next to Jefferson Davis
as the country's " worst enemy."

Some two weeks later Mr. Sumner was married
to Mrs. Hooper, a lady then twenty-eight years of
age, and a daughter-in-law of Samuel Hooper, a

representative in Congress from Boston. His marriage prevented his taking any further part in the campaign, and opened to him a prospect of great happiness. These hopes were disappointed, and his brief married life ended in a separation, followed later by a divorce procured by him. In a biography which deals only with Mr. Sumner as a statesman it is not necessary to do more than mention these facts.

The second session of the Thirty-ninth Congress met on December 3, 1866. The elections had resulted in Republican victories, and the policy of the President had been condemned. His opponents returned fully assured of popular support, and with ample power to adopt any measure which their judgment approved. On the third day of the session Sumner, according to his practice, presented his views on reconstruction in the form of resolutions. These asserted the power and duty of Congress to control reconstruction, and insisted that in establishing a new republican government " Congress must follow implicitly the definition supplied by the Declaration of Independence," and, " after excluding all disloyal persons, take care that new governments are founded on the two fundamental truths therein contained : first, that all men are equal in rights; and secondly, that all just government stands only on the consent of the governed." He had the satisfaction at this session of seeing these doctrines adopted. His persistence, as before and afterwards, was finally rewarded, and impartial suffrage became the accepted principle of his party.

The first step was taken when, on December 13, 1866, a bill giving the suffrage to colored men in the District of Columbia passed the Senate. Sumner said nothing until the third day of the debate, when he explained briefly why he voted against an amendment giving women the suffrage, and against another imposing an educational qualification. Of the first he said : " That question I leave untouched, contenting myself with the remark that it is obviously the great question of the future, — at least one of the great questions, — which will be easily settled whenever the women in any considerable proportion insist that it shall be settled," an observation fraught with practical wisdom. Of the second : " In voting against an educational test, I do not mean to say that under other circumstances such test may not be proper. But I am against it now." His reason was thus stated : " To my mind nothing is clearer than the present necessity of suffrage for all colored persons in the disorganized States. It will not be enough if you give it to those who read and write ; you will not in this way acquire the voting force needed there for the protection of the Unionists, whether white or black." This bill passed the House, was vetoed, and passed over the veto.

The next day Mr. Wade moved to take up the bill for the admission of Nebraska, which had failed at the last session. Sumner again opposed it, because the proposed constitution gave only white men the right to vote. Gratz Brown offered the proviso which Sumner had offered at the previous session, and in the debate some of his Republican associates, impatient at Sumner's opposition, became quite angry. Sumner in reply was courteous and gentle, but inflexible in his resolution that no new State should be admitted "with the word 'white' in its constitution." "It passes my comprehension," he said, "how we can require equal rights in the rebel States, when we deliberately sanction the denial of equal rights in a new State completely within our jurisdiction and about to be fashioned by our hands." Some Republicans wished the State admitted to strengthen the party in the Senate, and various reasons were given for the inconsistency which Sumner pointed out, such as the insignificant number of negroes in Nebraska, and the fact that the enabling act under which Nebraska had been organized as a State did not require impartial suffrage. The debate lasted several days until interrupted by the holiday recess, during which Sumner stirred up much opposition by letters. When the discussion was resumed an amendment, offered by Mr. Edmunds, was adopted, making the act take effect upon the fundamental condition that there should be "no abridgment or denial of the exercise of the elective franchise or of any other right to any person by reason of race or color, excepting Indians not taxed." The bill passed the Senate on January 9, was amended in the House by requiring the assent of the Nebraska legislature, and became a law after a veto. The bill to admit Colorado was amended by adding the same proviso, and was passed without debate.

On the next day the Senate passed a bill, already passed by the House, forbidding the denial of suffrage in the Territories on account of race or color. Thus another step was taken and Congress again adopted Sumner's view. The final battle occurred when a bill " to provide for the more efficient government of the insurrectionary States " passed the House and was laid before the Senate. This created five military districts in the South without any requirement as to suffrage and with no exclusion of those who had supported the Confederacy. The Senate began the discussion on February 15, 1867, when great differences of opinion were developed. What followed was thus narrated by Sumner to Bright : —

" I do not know that I have mentioned to you how the requirements of universal suffrage in the new constitutions came to be readjusted in our reconstruction bill. The bill as it came from the House was simply a military bill. In the Senate several amendments were moved in the nature of conditions of restoration. I did not take much interest in them, as I preferred delay, and therefore was content with anything that secured this, believing that Congress must ultimately come to the true ground. In the confusion which ensued a caucus of Republican senators was called. Then Mr.

Sherman moved that all the pending propositions be referred to a committee of seven. Of this committee he was chairman; I was a member. In the committee I insisted that the existing governments should be declared invalid; adopted. Then that the States in question be designated simply ' rebel States;' adopted. Then that in the new constitutions there should be no exclusion from suffrage on account of color. This was voted down; only one other member of the committee sustaining me, Mr. Sherman being strongly averse. When the committee reported their bill to the caucus, I stated my objections and moved my amendment in an enlarged form, to the effect that in the new constitutions all citizens with a proper residence should be voters. In moving it I simply said that it was in our power to decide this question, and to supersede its discussion in the Southern States; that if we did not decide it every State and village between here and the Rio Grande would be agitated by it. It was dinner time and there was impatience for a vote, which was by the ayes, standing and being counted, and then the noes. There were two counts, seventeen ayes to fifteen noes; so this important requirement was adopted. Mr. Sherman, as chairman of the committee, was directed to move the amended bill as a substitute for the pending measure, and it was passed by the usual Republican majority. That evening in caucus some few saw the magnitude of the act, and there was corresponding exultation. Wilson wished to dance with somebody. I have given you this narrative because it concerns an important event, and will show you how business with us is sometimes conducted."

The bill was passed after an all-night session at an early hour in the morning, and finding its passage sure, Sumner, tired out, left before the vote.

Thus was won the great battle for equal rights. It is interesting in reading the debates on this and other questions of reconstruction to observe that, though they were often hot and not infrequently acrimonious, the differences were those of honest men. His opponents were often exasperated by Sumner's persistence and his somewhat tedious reiteration of arguments drawn from the principles of our government; but no one can doubt their sincerity. At no period in the history of our government have the debates in Congress been conducted upon a higher plane or been less marred by the kind of argument known as "buncombe," than when Sumner, Fessenden, Grimes, Trumbull, and their associates were seeking to settle the questions growing out of the civil war.

Ever on the watch against any encroachment upon liberty, Sumner at this session called attention to the system of peonage in New Mexico, and a bill to abolish and forever prohibit it was passed.

After the question of suffrage was decided, the most important act of the session was the Tenure of Office law. The President had used the offices so openly to buy support, to punish his opponents and reward his friends, that Congress felt it necessary to check the abuse. To this end a bill was reported which required the consent of the Senate to the removal of any officer whose appointment was subject to confirmation. It gave the President, during the recess, power to suspend such officers, but made it his duty to give his reasons to the Senate at its next session, when, if the Senate failed to concur, the officer was reinstated. Sumner tried to make it more sweeping, by providing that the consent of the Senate should be necessary to the appointment of a large number of officers, where it was not required by existing law, and by limiting the terms of such officers appointed after July 1, 1866. He contended that these subordinates were as much entitled to protection as were those to whom the bill applied, and that the additional labor imposed upon the Senate was not to be weighed against the duty of preventing injustice. He urged his amendment persistently, but was defeated. In one of his speeches he said : —

" I return, then, to my proposition, that the duty of the hour is protection to the loyal and patriotic citizen. But when I have said this, I have not completed the proposition. You may ask, Protection against whom ? I answer plainly, Against the President of the United States. There, sir, is the duty of the hour. . . . There was no such duty on our fathers, there was no such duty on recent predecessors in this chamber, because there was no President of the United States who had become the enemy of his country." For these words he was called to order, but he insisted upon his language and the point of order was overruled. Later he used yet more pointed language: " Do not forget that we stand face to face with an enormous and malignant usurper, through whom the Republic is imperiled, — that Republic which, according to our oaths of office, we are bound to save from all harm." Mr. Reverdy Johnson, in reply, suggested that this expression of opinion disqualified Sumner to sit on any impeachment of the President; but Sumner repudiated this idea at once, saying: " What right have I to know that the President is to be impeached? How can I know it? And let me add, even if I could know it, there can be no reason in that why I should not argue the measure directly before the Senate, and present such considerations as seem to me proper, founded on the misconduct of that officer." It was quite apparent already that the contest between President and Congress might result in extreme measures.

Mr. Sumner supported a proposed amendment to the Constitution, making the term of the president and vice-president six years, and making the president ineligible for reëlection. He wished even to abolish the electoral college for reasons thus stated: —

" Such an amendment would give every individual voter, wherever he might be, a positive weight in the election. It would give minorities in distant States an opportunity of being heard in determining who shall be chief magistrate. Now

they are of no consequence. . . . I know nothing
that would contribute more to bring all the people
. . . into one united whole, than to make the President directly eligible by their votes."

In a letter to W. W. Story during this session,
Sumner expressed his views of the political situation : —

"Congress is doing pretty well ; every step is
forward. The next Congress, which will probably
meet on the 4th of March, will be still better inspired. All that is possible will be done to limit
the executive power. It is possible that the President may be impeached. If we go forward and
supersede the sham governments set up in the rebel
States, we encounter the appointing power of the
President, who would put in office men who sympathize with him. It is this consideration which
makes ardent representatives say that he must be
removed. Should this be attempted, a new question will be presented."

The expiring Congress, feeling it unsafe to leave
the President unwatched during the usual recess,
provided that the new Congress should meet on
March 4, and the session beginning on that day
lasted till the 30th of the month. On March 7
Mr. Sumner presented the usual resolutions em-
bodying his views as to the work which demanded
the attention of Congress. His requirements were :
the vacation of the existing state governments ; the
creation of provisional governments, from which
every disloyal influence should be excluded ; the

establishment of free public schools ; and measures
to secure a piece of land for every head of a family
among the freedmen. A few days later he moved
the consideration of the resolutions and a debate
ensued, in which Sherman, Fessenden, Frelinghuysen, and other Republicans indicated dissent.
Sumner felt that without education or land the
freedmen would be at the mercy of their former
masters, and he thought it of the first importance
to provide the machinery for the creation of new
state governments. He urged his resolutions earnestly and claimed that the power to give the negroes
land was found in the necessity of the case. He
failed to point out any constitutional way in which
Congress could take land from its owners and give
it to the freedmen, and it is not surprising that his
resolutions never came to a vote. In the heat of
argument he reminded his opponents that they had
differed from him before and had insisted that steps
were unconstitutional or impossible which they had
afterward supported. This line of argument was
made more irritating by his Democratic opponents,
who taunted the Republicans with the fact that
what he proposed was always eventually done.
Perhaps the experience to which they alluded made
him more impatient than hitherto, for as a rule
he was singularly courteous in debate. His criticism was a serious matter to less known men, backed
as he was by a strong body of supporters all over
the country who followed his lead implicitly, and
it is not strange that some of those whom he con-

demned were aggrieved by his tone, and that their resentment weakened his position in the Senate. It is probable that dislike, created in these days of his domination, helped his removal from the committee on foreign relations a few years later.

A bill to amend the reconstruction act was introduced almost as soon as the new Congress met, and in the debate Sumner insisted that a majority of the registered voters in each State should vote on the question of holding a convention, and that voting at all popular elections should be by ballot. The latter proposition was defeated. He himself offered as an amendment the proviso: " That the Constitution shall require the legislature to establish and sustain a system of public schools open to all without distinction of race or color."

By making it a condition that no seceded State should be admitted whose Constitution did not contain this clause, he hoped to secure public and impartial education in the South. He thought that the power under which all other conditions were imposed warranted this one, and of its wisdom and necessity he entertained no doubt. The Senate divided equally upon his amendment and it was lost, to his bitter disappointment. In advocating it he explained his plan of reconstruction, which was to make the States adopt constitutions which would insure good government and equal rights. His policy was far-reaching and deserved success. In following him so far as to require impartial suffrage, Congress was doubtless influenced by the necessity of creating a loyal electorate, and securing the lives, the rights, and the property of loyal men, white and black.

In the light of all that has happened since, many think the policy unwise which at once changed the slaves into citizens. No one should criticise the legislation adopted unless he has studied the condition of the Southern States at the close of the war, and has realized the difficulties which beset any course. It is easy to point out the evils which negro suffrage caused, but far greater evils would probably have occurred had negro suffrage been refused. A community just conquered, demoralized by a long war, prostrated by the loss of property and lives, sullen, disloyal, and filled with hatred and contempt for the new freedmen and their own loyal white neighbors, was a hotbed in which trouble of every kind found root easily and grew rapidly. No law could prevent it. Only the slow passage of years, the death of those too old to learn, the birth of a new generation, the replacement of men born slaves by men born free, could make these communities peaceful and prosperous. Friction between the two races in their new relation was inevitable.

It was clear that the slavery question would never be settled until the negroes were recognized as citizens, equal before the law with their white neighbors. Had President Johnson's reconstruction prevailed, they would have remained virtually slaves. The laws passed by his legislatures were skillfully devised to secure this result, and the consequence would have been disorder and bloodshed. Politicians needing votes would have sought to get them by giving the suffrage to the negroes, and they would have offered in this way a constant temptation to agitators. It was better to cut deep at once, to extirpate the cancer utterly, and having done all that law could do by giving the freedmen equal rights, to let them gradually learn, as they must, how to use them. No people can learn self-government while governed by others. Years were needed more than laws. It was to hasten this process that Sumner insisted on education, and he seems wiser than his opponents. His terms would not have irritated the masters more than those imposed, while they would have given the freedmen the one thing needed to fit them for their places as citizens.

The conditions which the war left, no matter what the legislation, required as representatives of the government the most honest, wise, and patient men that could be obtained; men whom freedmen and masters could trust and respect, and who could understand and deal considerately, if firmly, with a stricken community. Instead the government was represented by mere adventurers, ignorant, foolish, corrupt, and wholly unfitted for their work. No matter what the policy, it must fail if administered by such men. Without brains and character no form of government is good. With these absent and every element of disorder present, it is not strange that the reconstructed States were unhappy. But in considering the course of Sumner and his associates, we may well pause before we attribute to a policy, in itself just, evils which sprang inevitably from the condition of the community, and which were increased by the men who were placed in power during reconstruction.

This first session of the Fortieth Congress adjourned on March 30, but before the resolution of adjournment was adopted there was a struggle between those who wished to adjourn till the following December and those who were afraid to trust the President so long. Among the latter was Sumner, who urged the importance of not leaving the loyal men without protection, and spoke of the President as follows : —

"You must not forget that the President is a bad man, the author of incalculable woe to his country, and especially to that part which, being most tried by war, most needed kindly care. Search history, and I am sure you will find no elected ruler who, during the same short time, has done so much mischief to his country. He stands alone in bad eminence."

Repeated differences between the houses resulted in adjournment till the first Wednesday in July, when, in the absence of a quorum, the presiding officers were to adjourn their respective houses without day.

CHAPTER XX

THE Senate held a special session for executive
business from the 1st to the 20th of April, at which
the treaty for the purchase of Alaska was ratified.
Sumner first learned of the treaty late in the evening of Friday, March 29, at the State Department.
It was signed on the morning of the 30th and on
the same day it was sent to the Senate. The committee on foreign relations reported it favorably,
Mr. Fessenden alone dissenting. On April 9
Sumner spoke for three hours in favor of ratification and the treaty was ratified, only Mr. Fessenden and Mr. Morrill voting in the negative.
The injunction of secrecy was removed, and Sumner
was requested to write out his speech, which had
been made from scanty notes. After the adjournment he devoted some six weeks to informing
himself and to amplifying his speech, which when
finished was a miracle of information on the subject of Alaska, gathered from sources of every
kind, of which many were in foreign languages,
and some in Russian were translated for his use.
It was he who gave the name of Alaska to the

whole territory. He wrote to John Bright on
April 16, 1867 : —

" The Russian treaty tried me severely ; ab-
stractedly I am against further accessions of territory, unless by the free choice of the inhabitants.
But this question was perplexed by considerations
of politics and comity and the engagements already
entered into by the government. I hesitated to
take the responsibility of defeating it."

In a note to the speech as published in his works
he says : " Mr. Sumner was controlled less by
desire for more territory than by a sense of the
amity of Russia, manifested especially during our
recent troubles, and by an unwillingness to miss
the opportunity of dismissing another European
sovereign from our continent, predestined, as he
believed, to become the broad, undivided home of
the American people."

His influence doubtless carried the treaty ; or, to
speak more accurately, his opposition would have
killed it. In his speech he did not allude to the
doubts of which he wrote to Mr. Bright, but spoke
of the cession as an extension of republican institutions. He was doubtless satisfied by the fact
that there was practically no population to consult.
To use his own words : " The immense country is
without form and without light, without activity
and without progress. . . . Its life is solitary and
feeble. Its settlements are only encampments or
lodges." He estimated the number of Russians
and Creoles at about 2500, the number of abori-

gines within the jurisdiction of the Fur Company at about 8000, and of those outside at between 40,000 and 50,000, and these he compared to our Indians. It was clearly impossible to ask or obtain the consent of so insignificant and scattered a population, with no national life and no relation to government. He, however, took occasion to guard against further annexation, saying : —

"This treaty must not be a precedent for a system of indiscriminate and costly annexation. Sincerely believing that republican institutions under the primacy of the United States must embrace this whole continent, . . . I cannot disguise my anxiety that every stage in our predestined future shall be by natural processes, without war, and I would add even without purchase. There is no territorial aggrandizement worth the price of blood. Only under peculiar circumstances can it become the subject of pecuniary contract. Our triumph should be by growth and organic expansion in obedience to 'preëstablished harmony,' recognizing always the will of those who are to become our fellow citizens. All this must be easy, if we are only true to ourselves."

As the pressure of domestic difficulties was gradually relieved, the questions growing out of England's course during the war began to receive attention, and negotiations were begun looking to a settlement. The English government saw its mistake, and aware of the latent exasperation in the United States became anxious to remove a source of danger to international peace. Sumner's speeches during the war had made perfectly apparent the grounds of our feeling, but England did not realize that we proposed to make claims as a nation on account of losses caused by her action.

Sumner took a deep interest in this question and his attitude upon it never changed. His correspondence shows the development of the controversy. Thus he wrote to Mr. Bright on August 8, 1865: "General Grant was here last week. . . . He cared little whether England paid 'our little bill' or not; upon the whole, he would rather she would not, as that would leave the precedent of her conduct in full force for us to follow, and he wished it understood that we should follow it. He thought that we should make more out of the 'precedent' than out of the 'bill,' and that Boston especially would gain. . . . I need not say that I dissented from his policy most resolutely. I told him that our true object should be to bring the two countries into relations of harmony and good-will; that this could not be done if one nation was watching an opportunity to strike, and the other was standing on guard; that the truest statesmanship was to remove all questions, and to that end I wished the precedent rejected."

On December 25, 1865, he wrote to George Bemis: "Sir F. Bruce, at dinner Saturday evening, said to me that England would fight before she would pay a dollar or consent to arbitration."

On December 24, 1866, almost exactly one year

after saying that England would never arbitrate, Sir F. Bruce told Sumner that he had left with Seward a letter from Lord Stanley "accepting arbitration in the 'Alabama' case," and asked whether this country would, upon this basis, "proceed to a general settlement of reciprocity, fisheries, and everything else."

On May 27, 1867, Sumner wrote to Mr. Bright: "I have just perused the correspondence between Mr. Seward and Lord Stanley on the 'Alabama' claims. There is a deadlock, the legacy of Lord Russell. The British government offers arbitration, but insists upon excluding the fundamental question on which our claims rest — namely, the right, morally and legally, of the recognition of the rebels as belligerents on the ocean. We are willing to arbitrate, provided the whole case is submitted. I think that the correspondence, when published, will rally the whole country. . . . Thus far I have avoided saying anything on this question in the Senate, because I was anxious to secure time for an amicable adjustment. The next Congress will debate it fully, unless meanwhile in some way it is settled."

Sumner took no pains in his correspondence to disguise the views which he was soon to express publicly.

Congress convened in July, 1867, in accordance with the resolution of the last session. The Republican senators in caucus voted to do no business during this session except such as was necessary to secure the execution of the reconstruction laws already passed. Their decision was embodied in a rule of the Senate and prevented Mr. Sumner from bringing forward legislation on the subject of suffrage and other measures which he had much at heart. Sumner vigorously opposed the adoption of the rule, insisting that there was public business of great importance which the Senate had no right to neglect, and repudiating the claim that he was bound as a senator by the decision of the Republican caucuses. His opposition was unavailing, but his argument for individual independence deserves attention. He justly characterized the caucus as "a meeting of friends for consultation and harmony, where each gives up something with a view to a common result, but no man gives up a principle, no man gives up anything vital." The opposing view makes the caucus a convenient instrument by which the minority of a legislative body controls the majority, and dominates the conscience and judgment of the best members.

The principal measure of the session was a bill to strengthen the reconstruction laws and to limit the power of the President. When this bill was under discussion, Mr. Sumner offered an amendment, that " every constitution in the rebel States shall require the legislature to establish and maintain a system of public schools open to all without distinction of race or color." This was excluded under the rule. He offered another amendment, " that no person shall be disqualified as member of any board of registration by reason of race or color." In advocating this he expressed his belief that under the existing law a colored person might be a senator of the United States. This amendment was rejected by a tie vote, but at a later stage of the bill was adopted. Other amendments were excluded under the rule.

He endeavored to obtain consideration for a bill, introduced by him at the last session, to secure the franchise to colored citizens all over the country, which he had advocated by letter during the recess. Again the rule proved a barrier, nor would the Senate suspend it on his motion. He succeeded, however, by unanimous consent, in bringing up his bill to prevent the exclusion of any person from office in the District of Columbia on account of race or color, and, amended in form, this was passed. The President refused to sign it, and as Congress adjourned before the expiration of ten days from its passage it failed to become a law. It was again brought forward by Mr. Sumner and passed at the December session, but by the refusal of the President to sign it and the adjournment of Congress for the holidays, it again failed. It had a like experience once more in the session which ended March 4, 1869, but it finally became a law by the signature of President Grant. At every stage of its checkered career Mr. Sumner was its sponsor and persistent advocate. An attempt by him on July 19, 1867, to strike the word " white " from the naturalization laws was referred to a com mittee, and not reported till February, 1869, too late for consideration.

The adjourned session of Congress met on November 21, and during the holiday recess Sumner moved into his new house on the corner of Vermont Avenue and Lafayette Square, which was his home till his death. He gathered here the books, autographs, and works of art which he had collected during his life, and while he was in Washington entertained freely. He was a most agreeable host, and at his table were to be met the most interesting men of the time. Here, for example, Dickens met his great admirer Stanton, who paid him a high compliment when he said: " During the war I always kept ' Pickwick ' under my pillow. Often and often I went to bed with my mind so full of anxiety after bad news of battles or campaigns that sleep seemed impossible, but two chapters of ' Pickwick ' never failed to divert my thoughts so that I could sleep, and it was the only book in the language that would do it." Seward was a frequent guest; and, unmindful of his previous misadventures as a prophet, tempted fate again by saying: " In thirty years Mexico will be the capital of the United States." Here Mr. Evarts, coming to dinner on Sunday, after a day's work upon the answer of the President to the articles of impeachment, excused his breach of the commandment by saying: " Is it not written that if thine ass falleth into a pit, it is lawful to pull him out on the Sabbath day?" Here Motley was a frequent guest while a candidate for the English mission. Here the diplomatic corps were constantly welcomed, and political opponents like Caleb Cushing and William Beach Lawrence engaged in literary and diplomatic discussion. Here Emerson and Agassiz made him visits. It was a pleasant house, and, when he first occupied it, he was at the very height of his reputation and power on both sides of the ocean.

In the brief session which began on November 21, little was done; but it is amusing to find Sumner opposing a resolution to fix the final adjournment one half hour before the beginning of the regular session, on the ground that in that half hour the President might make appointments and suspensions which, under the Tenure-of-office Act, might stand till the close of the next session.

The regular session of Congress began on December 2, 1867, and was at first uneventful. In February Sumner opposed the admission of Mr. Thomas, senator-elect from Maryland, because he had permitted and aided his minor son to join the Confederate army, which was such aid to the rebellion as should prevent his taking the oath of office. It was a strict construction of the law, but it prevailed.

In August the President had removed Secretary Stanton, whose presence in the Cabinet was regarded by the Republican leaders as a great safeguard. The feeling against the President had been gathering force for some time, and now led his opponents in the House to propose his impeachment, but the House would not direct it. On January 13, 1868, the Senate refused to concur in the suspension of Stanton, and on February 21 the President removed him in direct violation of the Tenure-of-office Act. Mr. Stanton refused to go, acting upon the advice, among others, of Sumner, who, hearing of the President's action, wrote from his desk in the Senate: "Stick, Stanton, stick." The President, after trying in vain to make General Grant take the place, appointed General Lorenzo Thomas secretary of war *ad interim*. For a time it seemed that Mr. Stanton would be expelled by force, and that the President would obtain control of the army through a plastic person of his own choice. Congress was excited to immediate action, and on February 24 the House voted to present articles of impeachment. Thaddeus Stevens, advanced in years and feeble in health, but looking the ideal Roman, announced this action to the Senate with singular impressiveness, as if he were discharging a sad duty, though it was a result for which he had long labored, and the element of personal triumph could not have been absent from his mind.

The Senate began its sessions as a court of impeachment on March 5, and from then until May 11, when the final votes were taken, the trial was its chief business. The principal charge was the removal of Mr. Stanton, but some of Mr. Johnson's scandalous and violent language in attacking

Congress was made the ground of a distinct article.
The examination of the witnesses was conducted
mainly by General Butler for the prosecution, and
by Mr. Evarts for the defense. The former lost
his sense of proportion and, as he admitted, conducted himself as if he were trying a criminal case
in a Middlesex County court room. He forgot
that his success depended upon winning the doubtful senators like Fessenden, Trumbull, and Grimes,
and these were alienated by his methods, while
they were much impressed by the argument of
Judge Curtis for the defense. The managers insisted that the proceeding was in its nature political, while the counsel who defended the President
sought to make it absolutely judicial, and invoked
the rules which would govern a trial that might
result in the punishment of the offender and not
merely in his removal from office. Remember-
ing that the law provides adequate machinery for
the punishment of offenders, while impeachment
is designed to relieve the people from the dangers attending the abuse of official power, a strong
argument may be made for the former view. It
is the danger to the country, rather than the
guilt of the defendant, which the prosecution must
establish. The balance of power was held by
three or four lawyers, who felt that they were sitting as judges and who tried the question of the
President's guilt or innocence with strictness. The
counsel for the defense addressed them in language which commanded their respect, while they

had no sympathy with the looser methods and theories of the prosecution. It was training and temperament which separated these men from their associates and saved the President.

This is not the place to describe the events of the trial, but no one who heard it can forget the wonderful impression which the brief argument of Mr. Groesbeck made upon the Senate and the audience. Beginning at noon, his voice an hour later had become so husky as to be almost inaudible. An earlier recess was taken on that account, and when he began again his voice gradually cleared, until during the last hour he addressed a crowded but absolutely still chamber. No senator wrote on his desk, no page was summoned, no conversation could be heard in gallery or cloak room, and a silence prevailed almost unknown in the Senate, while every one listened with rapt attention to each word that the speaker uttered. It was an oratorical feat which had no parallel at that trial, and few in the experience of the Senate.

At the outset the question arose whether Senator Wade, the president *pro tempore* of the Senate, could take the oath as a member of the court of impeachment, since in the event of the President's conviction he would succeed to the office. Sumner showed that there was no authority for the objection, and paid Mr. Wade this high compliment: —

"Put in one scale these interests, so dear to the heart of the patriot, and in the other all the personal temptations which have been imagined, and

I cannot doubt that, if the senator from Ohio holds these scales, the latter will kick the beam."

A few weeks later the chief justice, presiding, threw the casting vote, when the Senate was equally divided on some question of procedure or evidence. Sumner would not let this claim of right pass unchallenged, and argued that the right to " preside " gave no right to vote. He gathered copious authority in support of his contention, which he sustained also by comparison with the provision giving the vice-president the right to preside *and* give the casting vote; at the same time he took occasion to speak most pleasantly of Chief Justice Chase.

After the vote the different senators prepared their opinions upon the case, and Mr. Sumner stated his views at some length, taking the ground that the proceeding was a remedy against political offenders. He insisted that the acts charged were to be interpreted by the President's whole course in office, and that " if on any point you entertain doubts the benefit of those doubts must be given to your country," whose safety is the supreme law. Seeing clearly the danger to which all the great interests of the country were exposed while the President continued in office, he voted without hesitation for conviction, and while it is now clear that no especial harm was done during the brief remnant of Mr. Johnson's term, and many feel that a dangerous precedent was avoided, we may hereafter find that a not less dangerous precedent was

established, and learn to consider the doctrine of
Sumner the safer for the country.

After the trial Congress returned to reconstruction, and Sumner made a strong speech, repeating
his argument in favor of the right to impose fundamental conditions when States are admitted to
the Union. Congress adopted this view, and a bill
was passed admitting Arkansas upon the fundamental condition that there should never be in the
State any denial of suffrage or of any other right
on account of race or color, except to " Indians not
taxed." A few days later an act admitting North
Carolina, South Carolina, Louisiana, Georgia, Alabama, and Florida was passed, with fundamental
conditions that they should not deprive " any citizen or class of citizens of the State of the right
to vote by the constitution thereof," and should
ratify the Fourteenth Amendment, and with some
further requirements. The same policy was pursued with the other States, and in 1870 Virginia,
Mississippi, and Texas were admitted upon similar
fundamental conditions.

By various letters at this time Sumner encouraged the election of colored men to Congress, believing that nothing could so effectually establish
their absolute equality as citizens, and that such a
conspicuous example was worth more than speeches
or statutes. His advice was soon taken, and he
had the pleasure of welcoming a colored senator
from Mississippi.

CHAPTER XXI

THE civil war left a legacy of debt and financial disturbance which has been ever since a prolific source of trouble. During the year 1867 and early in 1868 the plan of paying the bonds of the United States in the demand notes called "greenbacks" was supported by various politicians. Mr. Sherman, chairman of the Senate committee on finance, had maintained in the Senate the right to do this. In May, 1868, the Republican National Convention had passed a resolution in favor of paying all debts of the government "in the utmost good faith, . . . not only according to the letter, but to the spirit of the laws" under which they were contracted. This, however, like many another campaign declaration, was not too definite, and when a bill to fund the national debt came before the Senate Mr. Sumner on July 11, 1868, expressed his views fully. He stated as the two objects of our policy the reduction of taxes and the substitution of specie for unconvertible paper, and claimed that these objects could only be attained by keeping the public faith "above all question or suspicion." From this impregnable ground he attacked the propositions to tax the bonds, and to pay them in irredeemable paper, showing that both were clear violations of public faith. The speech was a welcome reinforcement to the cause of public honesty, and increased Sumner's strength with conservative men.

A few days after this speech a bill containing some extraordinary provisions came before the House. The recent triumph over the Confederate armies and our great military strength did not tend to foster discretion in Congress. Questions had arisen as to the effect of naturalization in this country. Foreign governments took the ground that no one could, as against the country of his birth, assume a foreign citizenship, and upon this theory they arrested our naturalized citizens, held them to military service, and otherwise treated them as still their own subjects. It must be admitted that then, as since, many of these naturalized citizens were more interested in the affairs of their native land than in those of the United States, and that they used our citizenship only as a shield against the consequences of seditious enterprises. They were foreigners in feeling and conduct while successful in their plots, and became citizens of this country only when they failed. But the unfriendly course of European governments had left a feeling here which induced sympathy with their disaffected subjects and made many Americans willing to seize any pretext for aiding them. Prominent in this class were certain Irish Fenians, whose purposes were actively hostile to England. General Banks, the chairman of the committee on foreign affairs of the House, though he came into public life as a vigorous opponent of the foreigners and Catholics among us, now espoused their cause, and seemed bent on committing this country to a reckless policy. He had carried through the House a bill which, as Sumner wrote to Mr. Bright, " was Seward's work," asserting the American doctrine that any man may assume a new citizenship and thereby dissolve his old allegiance. To this was added a section empowering the President, when any citizen was arrested by any foreign government in denial of this right, to suspend commercial relations with such government and to arrest and detain any citizen of such government found within our jurisdiction.

Mr. Sumner reported a substitute for this provision, directing the President, when any naturalized citizen should be arrested, to report the circumstance to Congress for its action, and taking from him all power of reprisal. He supported this in a speech exposing the absurdity and barbarism of the House bill, saying : —

" Suppose the law is passed, and the authority conferred upon the President. Whom shall he seize ? What innocent foreigner ? What trustful traveler ? What honored guest ? It may be Mr. Dickens, or Mr. Trollope, or Rev. Newman Hall, or it may be some merchant here on business, guiltless of any wrong and under the constant safeguard of the public faith.   Permit me to say, sir, that, the moment you do this, you will cover the country with shame, of which the present bill will be the painful prelude." Mr. Conness, himself of Irish birth, in reply charged Sumner with indifference to the rights of foreign-born citizens who happened to be white and not black. But Sumner met the charge completely by recalling his position at the time of the Know-Nothing excitement, thereby well illustrating how he who resists the folly of the hour is sure to find in time that his course is vindicated and his influence increased.

The bill had passed the House by a vote of 104 to 4, men like Garfield, who had opposed it vigorously, voting for it.   Eighty or more others did not vote.   Sumner kept it in committee for two months and then led in opposing its monstrous provisions. The result was that his substitute was carried in the Senate by a vote of 30 to 7, though an amendment was passed against his opposition, which authorized the President to use all methods except war to effect the release of any American citizen unjustly arrested by a foreign government.   These votes in House and Senate show the feeling of the hour, which Sumner resisted.   Without this contemporary record it would be impossible to believe that such a measure could pass the House of Representatives.

At this session treaties with Germany and Bavaria were ratified which recognized our claim, and these were followed by like treaties with the other European powers, so that the rights of our naturalized citizens were established on a sure foundation.

The Republican convention of Massachusetts unanimously nominated Sumner for reëlection to the Senate, by a resolution which approved his course in the warmest language. This nomination was ratified by the legislature, and he was elected in the following January by an almost unanimous vote. After his nomination he made one speech, delivered at Cambridge, in which he stated the issue of the campaign thus: " *Shall the men who saved the Republic continue to rule it, or shall it be handed over to rebels and their allies?* " and the statement was the only argument needed in those days. He insisted that the defeat of Grant meant the nullification of the reconstruction acts, declared by the Democratic convention to be " unconstitutional, revolutionary, and void." On the financial question he went further, and urged the possibility and the duty of resuming specie payments on July 4, 1869. He repeated his argument against any breach of the contract with the public creditor, and concluded with propositions that cannot too often be repeated : —

" A republic is where every man has his due. Equality of rights is the standing promise of Nature to man. . . . In harmony with the promise of Nature is the promise of our fathers, recorded in the Declaration of Independence. It is the two-fold promise; first, that all are equal in rights;

and, secondly, that just government stands only on
the consent of the governed, — being the two great
political commandments on which hang all laws
and constitutions. Keep these truly and you will
keep all. Write them in your statutes ; write them
in your hearts. *This is the great and only final
settlement of all existing questions.*"

Sumner had taken no part in nominating Grant.
From a statement published by Mr. Forney it would
appear indeed that in November, 1867, he opposed
his nomination, in a conference held to consider
the situation, when General Babcock and other
close friends of Grant favored it. Sumner doubted
his qualities as a civil administrator, but the popular feeling made the nomination inevitable, and
Sumner did not publicly dissent. In November he
wrote to Dr. Lieber : " Grant will be our President
with infinite opportunities. I hope and believe he
will be true to them."

During the summer of 1868 President Johnson
appointed Reverdy Johnson minister to England,
and in a letter to Mr. Bright, Sumner thus spoke : —
" He hopes to settle all outstanding questions. I
think he will be successful on the naturalization
question. But I do not see signs of accord on the
other question." This passage is quoted because it
was afterwards suggested that Sumner had misled
Bright into thinking that Johnson fully represented
the feeling in this country on the Alabama question.

The last session of the Fortieth Congress began
on December 7, 1868.

The most important action at this session was the adoption by Congress of the Fifteenth Amendment. Although impartial suffrage had been required in the Southern States by the fundamental conditions imposed on their readmission, it was deemed wise to secure it in the States which had not sceded, and to place the result of the war beyond the reach of legislative action by constitutional amendment. Accordingly, after much discussion of the exact phraseology, the amendment was adopted by Congress on February 25, 1869. Its ratification by the States was announced a little more than a year later.

To the policy of this amendment Mr. Sumner was strongly opposed. He was satisfied that Congress had power to secure impartial suffrage by legislation, and he thought that to propose the amendment was to admit that the power did not exist. If after Congress had made this admission the States should fail to ratify the amendment, the opportunity to secure equal rights would be lost. He thought that the proposal therefore exposed the cause to great and unnecessary peril. He urged these views upon the Senate with great persistency, and he presented them again in a speech against the amendment, wherein he spoke with great sadness and strong feeling, seeming to consider that his opponents were defending wrong by throwing doubt upon the power of Congress under the Constitution. He failed to convince them, and their practical wisdom was proved by the ratification of the amendment, while his fears were not realized. In the result he rejoiced as heartily as any one.

This was the session of Congress preceding the inauguration of a new administration, but the usual struggle over the new cabinet did not occur. General Grant, possibly from his experience in the army, had conceived a profound distrust of politicians, and at the outset evidently expected to conduct his administration without consulting the leaders of the party which had elected him. He seemed to regard his Cabinet as his staff, and was governed largely by personal considerations in selecting it. Yet he soon came under the influence of politicians belonging to the very class which he at first distrusted, with results unfortunate alike to the country and to himself. Sumner's manners and methods never could have attracted Grant, and the attitude of the two men towards public questions was radically different even when they agreed in opinion. Sumner was suggested for secretary of state, but he never countenanced the idea. He felt, as he wrote to Dr. Lieber just after the election: " The headship of the first committee of the Senate is equal in position to anything in our government under the President; and it leaves to the senator great opportunities."

General Grant never spoke to him on the subject or consulted him about the Cabinet, though their relations were pleasant. Sumner was not, however, confident that Grant would be a successful president, and his doubts were shared by other leading statesmen.   He wrote to Whittier on February 26, 1869 : " Stanton says that he hears of declarations by Grant in favor of economy, retrenchment, and the collection of the revenue, but nothing about the rights of man to be maintained in all their fullness ; but I hope for the best."

At this session the treaties negotiated by Reverdy Johnson with Lord Clarendon relating to naturalization, the San Juan boundary question, and the Alabama Claims were sent to the Senate. Sumner took pains to ascertain the views of General Grant, who showed his feeling that the settlement of the main questions pending with England should be left for the new administration. The consideration of the Claims treaty was accordingly postponed.   Sumner tried to prepare Mr. Bright for adverse action, in a letter of January 19, 1869 : —

" I finish this letter at my seat in the Senate. Last evening I met General Grant at dinner and conversed with him briefly on the new treaties. I would not commit him, and do not think that he has any very precise policy.   He did not seem to object to the naturalization and San Juan negotiations, but I think he had a different feeling with regard to the Claims convention.   He asked why this could not be allowed to go over to the next administration ?   This morning I called up the subject in my committee.   There was nothing but general conversation, in the course of which it was remarked that Great Britain had never appreciated the wrong, the terrible wrong done to us, not only in the cases of the ships destroyed, but also in driving our commerce from the ocean. You know that I have never disguised the opinion that the concession of belligerent rights was wrongful."

In 1867 Mr. Seward negotiated a treaty with Denmark by which the United States were to buy the island of St. Thomas for $7,500,000, if the inhabitants by vote consented to the transfer. When the treaty was first sent to the Senate, at the session beginning December 2, 1867, this assent had not been obtained nor were the papers which Mr. Sumner at once called for sent to the Senate for several weeks. Meanwhile the impeachment of the President had been voted, and the treaty was laid over till the next winter. It was now considered. General Raasloff, one of the Danish ministers and a most attractive man, who came to Washington in order to urge its ratification, was kindly treated by Sumner and others, and given every opportunity to present his case; but the committee on foreign relations was unanimously opposed to the project, and in this represented the opinion of the country. Consideration for Raasloff, to whom failure meant political ruin, induced them to keep the treaty in committee until after the inauguration of Grant, when it was laid upon the table, the entry in the records being that "this was equivalent to a rejection and was a gentler method of effecting it." This action accorded with the opinion of the new President.

CHAPTER XXII

GRANT'S ADMINISTRATION : THE ALABAMA CLAIMS

SUMNER'S last term in the Senate began on March 4, 1869, when General Grant was inaugurated. The oldest senator in continuous service, he occupied a place of great consideration and influence. The cause to which he had devoted his life had triumphed, and equality of rights seemed established in this country under the protection of the Constitution. Having been in opposition during the larger part of his senatorial career, he was now in full sympathy with the party in power and among its recognized leaders. His former associates, Chase and Seward, were no longer Republicans, which made his position in the party more conspicuous. There was no man in public life whose career had been so long, so distinguished, so consistent, as his, or who to so great an extent led the conscience of the country. Emerson wrote at this time : " Wherever I have met with a dear lover of the country and its moral interests, he is sure to be a supporter of Sumner. Sumner's moral instinct and character are so exceptionally pure that he must have perpetual magnetism for honest

men ; his ability and working energy such that
every good friend of the Republic must vote for
him." This position, won by the constant labors
and sacrifices of eighteen years, was exceptional,
and he might well look forward to a period of dignified repose, free from the strain of active political
contest and from the fearful anxieties of the struggle with slavery, — a period in which his experience
and accumulated wisdom would make his counsels
respected, and in which he could exert a strong influence in the conduct of the government. These
anticipations were not to be realized. His last
term of service was to be marked by a series of
conflicts with his own party associates, more bitter
to him than any he had known, and was to be saddened by personal differences which clouded the
rest of his life.

At first his relations with the administration
were most cordial. Hamilton Fish, who after
Elihu Washburne's brief service of a week became
secretary of state, was an old and intimate friend.
With Judge Hoar, the attorney-general, his friendship was even closer ; while Mr. Boutwell, the secretary of the treasury, was, among leading Republicans, the one most uniformly in sympathy with
Sumner. Indeed, there was no one in the Cabinet
with whom he was not on pleasant terms, though
some of its members were little known to him.
The President's first choice for secretary of the
treasury was Alexander T. Stewart of New York,
but after his nomination it was found that he was

ineligible under the law of 1789, which provided
that no incumbent of this office should "directly
or indirectly be concerned in carrying on the
business of trade or commerce." Mr. Sherman
at once introduced a bill to repeal this provision,
asking unanimous consent to its immediate consideration. Mr. Sumner objected, and when, a
little later, the President sent a message urging
legislation which would exempt Mr. Stewart from
the prohibition and Mr. Sherman introduced a
bill for this purpose, Sumner repeated the objection. He thus prevented instant action, and on
reflection the proposed legislation was abandoned.
It is doubtful if some of Mr. Sumner's more
conspicuous services were followed by so many
private letters of thanks as was this simple action.
There is, however, reason to think that General
Grant was irritated thereby, though his feeling
was not manifested.

The diplomatic appointments were the subject of
much conference between Mr. Fish and Mr. Sumner, but it does not appear that Sumner's wishes
were always regarded. He recommended Mr.
Motley as minister to England, but the appointment was probably due to other considerations.

The Johnson-Clarendon treaty for the settlement of our claims against England came before
the Senate at its special session. Reverdy Johnson's effusive expressions of good-will towards
England and a desire that the new administration
should deal with the question created a feeling

against ratification, and the committee on foreign
relations unanimously agreed in an adverse report.
Sumner, however, had sounder reasons for opposing
the treaty, and on April 13, 1869, he stated them,
putting the case of the United States against England in its extreme form and in severe terms.
The treaty, he said, did not settle the pending
questions; "it is nothing but a snare." His reason
was that it was only an ordinary "claims convention," providing for the adjustment of individual
claims on both sides, but leaving untouched the
great wrong to the United States as a nation.
Therefore, he said, "it cannot be for the interest
of either party" that it be ratified, since both
desired a final settlement.

He claimed that our real grievance lay in the
concession to the rebels of ocean belligerency,
when they had no ships, no ports, no prize courts,
and were in fact not belligerents at sea. This enabled the Confederacy to build and equip ships of
war and to buy munitions in England, in short it
made England a Confederate arsenal, and saved
blockade runners from being treated as pirates.
He dwelt on the negligence which allowed the Alabama to escape, and on the shelter accorded to her
in English ports, which made her in fact an English
ship warring upon us under English protection.
He recalled the fact that the proclamation of
neutrality was signed on the very day that Mr.
Adams landed in Liverpool, and claimed that the
offense was far worse because England departed

from her settled policy of hostility to slavery in thus helping men who were fighting to establish it.

"The blockade runners," he said, "were kindred to the pirate ships. . . . When, after a long and painful siege, our conquering troops entered Vicksburg, they found Armstrong guns from England in position; and so on every field where our patriot fellow citizens breathed a last breath were English guns and munitions of war, all testifying against England. The dead spoke also — and the wounded still speak."

Individual losses were trifling compared with the national losses caused by England's conduct. Among these he counted the loss of our carrying trade, the injury to our shipbuilding interest, and the expense of the war during the period by which England's action prolonged it.

Mr. Sumner stated his own position thus: "For several years I have carefully avoided saying anything on this most irritating question, being anxious that negotiations should be left undisturbed to secure a settlement which could be accepted by a deeply injured nation. The submission of the pending treaty to the judgment of the Senate left me no alternative. It became my duty to consider it carefully in committee, and to review the whole subject. If I failed to find what we had a right to expect, and if the just claims of our country assumed unexpected proportions, it was not because I would bear hard on England, but because I wish most sincerely to remove all possibility of strife between our two countries; and it is evident that this can be done only by first ascertaining the nature and extent of difference. In this spirit I have spoken to-day. . . . The attempt to close this great international debate without a complete settlement is little short of puerile."

Notwithstanding its few pacific words the speech seemed hardly calculated to promote a settlement. England had reluctantly consented to arbitrate, and now her most conspicuous friend among American statesmen replied that her concession was idle, and that the claims of the United States exceeded in character and magnitude anything that her statesmen had imagined possible. In it Sumner took no new position; his opinions had already been stated fully, and in fact our government had taken the same ground; but the English had not realized what we meant. As Sumner wrote to Lieber somewhat later: " I have made no demand, not a word of apology, not a dollar! nor have I menaced, suggested, or thought of war. . . . My object was simply to expose our wrongs as plainly, but as gently, as possible. . . . To my mind our first duty is to make England see what she has done to us."

Sumner accomplished this object completely. He instructed England, and he satisfied America. The people of the United States felt that his presentation of the case was adequate. The administration, the Senate, and the public approved his words. The treaty was rejected by a unanimous vote, and Sumner acquired a controlling influence in the settlement of the controversy. In England the speech was received with indignation by the public, with sorrow by some of his friends, and with resentment by others. He was regarded as an enemy of England. Even John Bright complained, and the Duchess of Argyll wrote: "For the first time I am silenced when you are spoken about. I understood you through the war. I do not now."

After the first feeling of wrath subsided, however, England awoke to the fact that the questions growing out of her course during the civil war must be settled; that the grievance of this country was real and its sense of wrong deep, and that such a feeling was a danger not to be ignored. The result was the Joint High Commission. Two years later Sir Stafford Northcote wrote to Mr. Sumner, after reading the speech again: "Though I must own your speech was somewhat sharp, I verily believe that it taught us a valuable lesson in that respect, and that we may say of it, *fidelia vulnera amantis.*"

Mr. Sumner's course was justified by the event, and the words, which seemed likely to prevent an adjustment, paved the way to a real settlement as he intended. His views were met in the later treaty, his positions were maintained by our counsel at Geneva, and if the arbitrators rejected our claims for "indirect damages," it is one thing to lose after a fair trial, and quite another to be denied a trial altogether. It was not money but the recognition by England that her course was at least questionable which was desired. England's consent to arbitrate all our claims was such a recognition and was what we asked. That conceded, reconciliation was substantially accomplished.

During the early months of the new administration the secretary of war, General Rawlins, a close friend of the President, endeavored to secure the recognition of the insurgent Cubans as belligerents. The President was inclined to follow this advice, and Mr. Sumner exerted all his influence against it. Not only did the conditions fail to justify it, but premature recognition would have embarrassed us seriously in our controversy with England. Backed by Mr. Fish and Judge Hoar, Sumner's arguments prevailed, and were repeated publicly when at a later day the question became more pressing.

Mr. Fish consulted him freely upon the instructions to Mr. Motley, especially as to the difficulty of making the proclamation of belligerency a ground for claim against England, while it was still uncertain whether the President would not recognize the Cubans as belligerents. Sumner was determined that our position against England should not be affected by any such consideration, and succeeded in having the instructions so drawn as to present the case against England substantially in accordance with his speech upon the Johnson-Clarendon treaty. His relations with the administration at this time were stated by Mr. Fish himself in a dispatch to a New York newspaper, which he dictated : —

" Mr. Sumner, as chairman of the Senate committee on foreign relations, was consulted constantly during the preparation of these instructions ; and when they were completed he not only expressed his entire approval of the course Mr. Motley was intended to pursue, but signified that the policy thus marked out was as firm and vigorous as our foreign relations would now justify. In fact at no time has Mr. Sumner been in closer accord or in more direct sympathy with the policy of President Grant than at present, and rumors of disagreement are entirely unfounded."

Evidently the secretary of state saw that there was danger even in a rumor that Sumner disapproved the policy of the department.

Sumner left Washington shortly after June 15, entirely satisfied with the situation, for he wrote to Motley on that day : " England must listen and at last yield. I do not despair of seeing the debate end, (1) in the withdrawal of England from this hemisphere, (2) in remodeling maritime international law. Such a consummation would place our Republic at the head of the civilized world."

Indeed at that time the cession of Canada, in satisfaction of our claims, was suggested by Mr Fish to the English minister, who replied, as Sumner writes in a private letter, that " England did not wish to keep Canada, but could not part with it without the consent of the population."

After leaving Washington Sumner visited Mr. Fish, among others, and continued to urge vigorous action in the negotiations with England. At his suggestion Caleb Cushing was consulted in drawing the instructions to Mr. Motley, which were sent on September 25, and were described by Lord Clarendon as "Mr. Sumner's speech over again."

On September 22 Mr. Sumner presided at the Republican convention in Massachusetts, and made a speech upon the political situation, in which he reasserted the positions which he had taken already on reconstruction, finance, and the pending questions with England. He spoke also of our relations with Spain and Cuba, dealing with the problem which has confronted the country steadily for years, and which has now taken a new phase, admitting that the Spanish power was "an anachronism," and that the day of European colonies had passed in this hemisphere, but contending that "the true course of the United States" was "to avoid involving ourselves in any way," that the sound rule was "non-intervention, except in the way of good offices." He said that by international law "nations are not left to any mere caprice. There is a rule of conduct which they must follow, subject always to just accountability where they depart from it." Under that law "belligerence is a 'fact' attested by evidence. If the

' fact ' does not exist, there is nothing to recognize. The fact cannot be invented or imagined, it must be proved. No matter what our sympathy, what the extent of our desires, we must look at the fact."

In speaking of the question with England, he said : " Sometimes there are whispers of territorial compensation, and Canada is named as the consideration. But he knows England little, and little also of that great English liberty from Magna Charta to the Somerset case, who supposes that this nation could undertake any such transfer. And he knows our country little, and little also of that great liberty which is ours, who supposes that we could receive such a transfer. On each side there is impossibility. Territory may be conveyed, but not a people. I allude to this suggestion only because, appearing in the public press, it has been answered from England." He expressed his belief, however, that eventually a union between Canada and the United States would come by mutual desire.

During this autumn he delivered his lecture on " Caste " before audiences all over the Eastern States. It was intended as an appeal to public opinion against the prejudice of race and in favor of equal rights. His conclusion indicates what his attitude would have been on some later issues : —

" To those who find peril in the growing multitudes admitted to citizenship I reply, that our Republic assumed these responsibilities when it declared the equal rights of all men, and that just government stands only on the consent of the governed. Hospitality of citizenship is the law of its being. . . . If the Chinese come for labor only, we have the advantage of their wonderful and docile industry. If they come for citizenship, then do they offer the pledge of incorporation in our Republic, filling it with increase. Nor is there peril in the gifts they bring. As all rivers are lost in the sea, which shows no sign of their presence, so will all peoples be lost in the widening confines of our Republic, with an ocean-bound continent for its unparalleled expanse, and one harmonious citizenship, where all are equal in rights, for its gentle and impartial sway."

In November, shortly before the reassembling of Congress, Mr. Fish wrote him that Mr. Thornton, the British minister, had expressed the anxiety of his government to settle the pending question, and had asked for some intimation as to terms. "I answered," wrote Mr. Fish, "somewhat vaguely; but he evidently wished . . . to obtain something more definite, — which I was not willing to give, until I could have the opportunity of consulting with you to know what your committee and the Senate will agree to. When will you be here? Will you either note what you think will be sufficient to meet the views of the Senate and of the country, or will you formulate such a proposition?" In such cordial relations with the administration Sumner began the session of Congress which opened on December 6, 1869. Mr. Fessenden's death during the recess had left a vacancy in the committee on foreign relations, which was filled by Mr. Schurz, who was from this time in close accord with Mr. Sumner.

The reconstruction question came again before the Senate in January, 1870, when a long debate occurred on a bill to admit Virginia. Sumner, believing that the reconstructed government was in the hands of disloyal men, urged investigation. An amendment was moved, that action by the legislature of Virginia at any time, rescinding its ratification of the Fifteenth Amendment, should exclude the State from representation in Congress and remand it to its provisional government. Governor Morton of Indiana and Mr. Sumner supported this, insisting that Congress would always have the power to enforce the conditions on which the States were admitted. Sumner said : " No one of these States, by anything that it may do hereafter, can escape from that far-reaching power." If this position can be maintained, a question may arise as to the power of Congress over the recent action of certain Southern States, by which the right of suffrage is taken from ignorant colored men but preserved to equally ignorant white men.

The amendment was lost ; but fundamental conditions were attached to the bill, imposing the test oath on state officers and securing impartial suffrage, equal eligibility to office, and equal school privileges. "Good faith" in the adoption of a republican state constitution, and in the ratification of the Fourteenth and Fifteenth Amendments,

was also made " a condition precedent to representation of the State in Congress." Sumner took
part in the debate, supporting every proposition
calculated to insure a loyal government and absolute equality of rights, but not voting for the bill,
even as amended, because he felt that it endangered the rights and security of loyal people.

Mississippi was admitted at this session upon the
conditions already imposed on Virginia. The passage of this act was followed by the admission of
Mr. Revels, a colored man, as one of the senators
from Mississippi, an event which Sumner hailed as
forever setting at rest the question of equal rights.
With this session the reconstruction period practically ended, and though the battle for equal rights
was not yet over, the recognition of the principle
in the reconstruction legislation was due to Sumner's untiring persistency.

At this session he struck another blow at discrimination on account of color, when a bill was
pending to amend the naturalization laws so as
to prevent certain election frauds. Much to the
disgust of Mr. Edmunds, who was in charge of
the bill, he offered an amendment striking the
word " white " from all statutes relating to naturalization. The session was approaching its end, and
the amendment meant a discussion, for it opened
our citizenship to the Chinese as well as to men of
African descent. Hence, doubtless, Mr. Edmunds
considered it ill-timed, and opposed it. Mr. Sumner answered that he had twice tried to pass his

amendment as a separate bill and would not forego
this opportunity. The amendment was at first
adopted, whereupon a proviso excluding Chinese
was moved. The debate continuing, Sumner was
attacked by Conkling for pressing his amendment.
The day was July 4, and Sumner did not fail to
take advantage of the coincidence in reply, quoting the Declaration of Independence, and continuing : —

"The great, the mighty, words of this clause are
that these self-evident, unalienable rights belong to
' all men.' It is ' all men,' and not a race or color,
that are placed under protection of the Declaration. . . . But the statutes of the land assert the
contrary, — they declare that only all *white* men
are created equal."

Sumner's amendment was finally rejected, on
account of the feeling against the Chinese ; but an
amendment extending the privilege of naturalization to persons of African birth or descent was
adopted, and the bill passed. It certainly was
strange that among all nations of color, preference
should be given expressly to the African, so lately
deemed the lowest among the races of men.

Sumner firmly believed that financial reconstruction was essential to repair the wounds of the war,
and amid the contest over the admission of Virginia he introduced a bill to authorize the refunding of the national debt, " to extend banking
facilities, and to establish specie payments." This
he supported in a careful speech, and afterwards

in debates upon this and other financial measures
he took an active part. These speeches were direct
and business-like discussions of the subject, entirely
free from the tone into which he was sometimes
betrayed when speaking on questions of human
rights. His plans involved refunding at a lower
rate of interest by the issue of long-time bonds,
substituting for the " greenbacks " an equal amount
of national bank notes so distributed as to provide
for the necessities of districts where the currency
was insufficient, and direct legislation looking to
the resumption of specie payments. He recognized
those evils which still confront us, and his remedies might have avoided much subsequent trouble.
Some of his recommendations, indeed, were in substance adopted shortly afterwards; but the replacement of the " greenbacks " by bank circulation
properly distributed and secured, though recognized
as necessary by the best financial authorities, is
still to come.

Always in favor of everything that aided education and the diffusion of knowledge, he made an
elaborate speech in favor of one-cent postage, which
must remain a permanent contribution to the discussion of postal systems and a convincing argument for the lowest rates. When Mr. Fessenden's
death was formally announced in the Senate he
spoke of him in terms of cordial appreciation,
showing that their sharp differences had not affected his respect for his eminent associate. He
opposed the continuance of the income tax as a

war tax no longer needed, unequal and vexatious. By sheer persistence he secured a pension for Mrs. Lincoln in spite of a unanimous report against it from the committee. These were among his miscellaneous labors.

CHAPTER XXIII

THE most important contest of the session in its effect on Sumner personally arose over the treaty for annexing San Domingo. This part of Hayti had long been torn by the feud between Baez and Cabral, rivals for the presidency and alternately successful. In 1868 Baez was in control, but Cabral threatened his supremacy. When out of power Baez had sought aid from the United States. Now, being in office, he sent an envoy to this country in the hope of gaining support, and resolutions for the annexation of San Domingo, or a protectorate, were introduced in the House during Mr. Johnson's administration, but were not discussed.

After General Grant's accession Baez applied to him, and he was persuaded that the annexation of San Domingo was desirable. He kept the negotiations in his own hands and selected his secretary, General Babcock, as his representative. In May a man-of-war was sent to the several Dominican ports in order to learn the popular feeling, and in July General Babcock was dispatched with instructions, signed by Mr. Fish, to inquire as to the island, its resources, and the condition of its affairs. Secretary Robeson placed a man-of-war at his service, instructed if necessary to give him " the *moral* support of its guns; " and in September, acting absolutely without authority, Babcock executed with Baez a treaty of annexation involving the payment by this country of $1,500,000 for defraying the debt of San Domingo. Babcock signed as the aide-de-camp of the President, and his protocol stated that the President " promises privately to use all his influence in order that the idea of annexing the Dominican republic to the United States may acquire such a degree of popularity among members of Congress as will be necessary for its accomplishment."

The President ratified his action and sent him back to San Domingo in November, backed by three men-of-war. There he made two treaties, one for the annexation of San Domingo and one for a lease of Samana Bay, and in behalf of the President guarantied San Domingo against foreign interference until the treaties were ratified. Babcock forthwith declared his intention to take possession of Samana Bay and to raise the American flag there, and he instructed the naval commander to protect the government of San Domingo against any attack, especially from Hayti. This meant that the navy should keep Baez in power against Cabral until the bargain by which Baez sold his country was ratified by the United States. These instructions were confirmed by Secretary Robeson, who kept a large force in the waters of San Domingo and directed the admiral in command, not only to "protect" the "Dominican government against any power attempting to interfere with it," but to "visit Samana Bay and the capital and see the United States power and authority secure there." He was directed also to notify the government of Hayti that the United States would protect San Domingo, and the peremptory order was added: "If the Haytians attack the Dominicans with their ships, destroy or capture them." The navy of the United States was thus placed at the disposal of Baez, to protect him against his own subjects as well as foreign enemies, while war was threatened against Hayti, a friendly power; and these things were done without authority from Congress.

The country was in no mood for annexing a hotbed of revolution with a population like that of San Domingo. The rejection of the St. Thomas treaty was fresh in the public mind, and the arguments against the annexation of San Domingo were much stronger. But even had annexation been desirable, the manner of securing the treaty, the doubts as to the authority of Baez, the absence of popular consent, the extraordinary proceedings of Babcock, and the arbitrary use of the navy, added much to the opposition. Had President Johnson done these things, he could not have escaped impeachment. But the great popularity of Grant, the public confidence in his honesty, and the feel-

ing that his training had not fitted him to understand the illegality of his action, made men
indulgent to his errors; nor was the Republican
party inclined to quarrel a second time with a
president of its own selection.

Sumner's first knowledge of these transactions
was in January, 1870, when President Grant called
at his house one evening while he was at dinner
with J. W. Forney and B. P. Poore, one the secretary of the Senate, the other a well known newspaper correspondent. They were both present at
the interview which followed. The President made
some reference to treaties about San Domingo, but
gave no clear idea of their terms or object. He
said that they would come before the committee on
the judiciary, and therefore he wished to see Mr.
Sumner as its chairman, a mistake in the name of
the committee, which indicated General Grant's
lack of familiarity with the Senate. Sumner turned
the conversation to Governor Ashley of Montana,
of whose removal he wished to speak, but the
President brought it back to the treaties and made
some inquiry intended to ascertain Sumner's attitude towards them. Sumner's reply, as he repeated
it to Mr. Schurz next day, was: "Mr. President,
I am an administration man, and whatever you do
will always find in me the most careful and candid
consideration." The President afterwards claimed
that Sumner promised his support, and it is probable that he misunderstood Sumner's language,
interpreting what was said by his own strong

wishes and not anticipating opposition. It is incredible, however, that Mr. Sumner pledged himself to support the treaties without having seen them, and with no knowledge of their contents. In such matters he was extremely cautious, and where the " Black Republic " was concerned he would have been especially so ; for to preserve its independence was to him a matter of great importance. Nor would he ever have consented to any treaty which annexed territory without the consent of the inhabitants.[1] The attitude which he had just taken on the annexation of St. Thomas, his political creed, the whole habit of his life, were such as to make the alleged promise impossible.

Sumner was a man of his word and absolutely truthful. It is therefore of no slight importance that, from the moment of the interview until the treaties were rejected, he never by word or act indicated the least consciousness of any pledge to support them, while on the contrary his opposition was frank and consistent. It is impossible to resist the conclusion that this opposition to a scheme which the President had at heart seemed to him, with his ideas of military discipline, like rank insubordination. Experience has shown that a president bent upon enlarging the country's boundaries is apt to take a deeper personal interest in the project than in questions of domestic policy, and to treat opposition as personal disloyalty. To Grant this was especially easy, for he felt that, as the head of

[1] See his remarks upon the annexation of Canada, *ante*, p. 372.

the Republican party, he had a right to command its members, and he was peculiarly impatient of resistance. Finding Sumner opposed he became irritated, and in his irritation gave to the interview at Sumner's house a character which it did not deserve. It became a subject of bitter controversy; but its importance was exaggerated. Had no interview occurred the President would have been equally indignant at Sumner's attitude.

When the treaties were referred to the committee on foreign relations, the first meeting, on January 18, 1870, made it clear that the committee would report against them. Only one member said anything in their favor. At Sumner's suggestion the committee proceeded deliberately, so that their action might be taken with due respect to the President, and Sumner withheld his own opinion for a while that each member might act upon his own judgment. During the consideration he learned from the assistant secretary of state, and afterwards by inquiry at the Navy Department, how our navy had been employed and by what means the treaties had been secured. He was shocked at the discovery that " we were engaged in forcing upon a weak people the sacrifice of their country." From that moment his position was taken. He did not call upon the President and state his views, because, as he afterwards said in the Senate : " On careful reflection at the time I did not regard it as expedient. I thought it more gentle and considerate to avoid discussions with him, being assured

that he would ascertain the judgment on annexation through the expression of public sentiment in
the newspapers and various reports."

The opposition angered the President, and he
exerted all his influence to carry his point. He
sent two messages to the Senate urging ratification, on March 14 and on May 31. He argued
with members of the committee; he visited the Capitol, and interviewed senators. In a word he did
all that General Babcock had pledged him to do,
and his influence, especially with the new Southern
senators, was very great. Mr. Fish urged Sumner
not to oppose the President, and the efforts of the
administration continued up to the final vote. On
March 15 the treaties were reported adversely,
Senators Harlan and Morton dissenting from the
report in which Sumner, Patterson, Schurz, Cameron, and Casserly joined, though Cameron reserved the right to vote for ratification in certain
events. Mr. Ferry moved that the debate be in open
session, but the motion was defeated upon Sumner's
suggestion that, though he favored open sessions, it
was unwise to change an established rule when it
might seem to be done with reference to a particu-
lar treaty. Sumner opened the debate in a speech
of four hours, in which he discussed the whole subject, but "expressed confidence in the President's
entire honesty." No partisan of the President who
heard it ever complained of its tone, while several
spoke of it in terms of admiration. He opposed on
obvious grounds, such as the difficulty of dealing

with the population, the likelihood of our being
tempted into further annexation, the chronic rebellion existing there, the expense and trouble, and the
wrong to the colored man involved in taking away
the independence of Hayti. After a debate run-
ning through some weeks the treaty was laid aside
until June 29, when after a brief discussion the
vote was taken on June 30, and the Senate being
equally divided the treaty was rejected.

The day after the vote Mr. Motley was removed
from his place as minister to England. This was
clearly meant as a punishment of Sumner, who was
Motley's friend, and had favored his appointment.
The President's friends learned his purpose and
some protested against the removal before it was
made. Senator Wilson wrote an urgent letter
against it, saying : " His removal will be regarded by the Republicans of Massachusetts as a
blow not only at him, but at Mr. Sumner."

The tone and manner of the removal, and the
testimony from contemporary witnesses, leave little
doubt that Mr. Wilson was right. Till then Mr.
Sumner had said or done nothing to indicate any
hostility to the President, and though indignant at
an act which seemed intended to influence impro-
perly the action of senators, he now gave no public
expression of his feeling. He could not, however,
fail to recognize in the act a meaning which was
apparent to the President's own supporters. In
letters to intimate friends he spoke of it, but more
in sorrow for Motley than in wrath on his own
account.

Sumner's first public speech after the adjournment of Congress was in Faneuil Hall, where he presided at a meeting held to ratify the state nominations, and urged the voters of Massachusetts to maintain the Republican party, saying : " So long as anybody assails the Declaration of Independence the Republican party cannot cease its patriotic labors." The speech contained no reference to the administration or to the treaties, and no hint of any difference with the President.

At the next session the President in his annual message reiterated his conviction that the interests of the country demanded the ratification of the San Domingo treaties, and he recommended the appointment of commissioners to negotiate a new treaty for the acquisition and an appropriation for their expenses. He said : " I now firmly believe that the moment it is known that the United States have entirely abandoned the project of accepting as a part of its territory the island of San Domingo, a free port will be negotiated for by European nations in the Bay of Samana, — a large commercial city will spring up, to which we shall be tributary without receiving corresponding benefits, and then will be seen the folly of our rejecting so great a prize." Thirty years have elapsed since these words were written, and no great foreign city has sprung up on the Bay of Samana. The cry is ancient that acquisitions, useless or worse to us, are much desired by other nations, but experience has never proved it true.

An attempt was made at the outset of the session to change the committee on foreign relations, in order to get a body more favorable to the project. The first suggestion was to drop Sumner or Schurz, but it was decided to leave them and to substitute Conkling for Patterson. The committee thus changed was reported to the caucus, but Sumner objected and the change was abandoned.

The first move was made by Sumner, who, on December 9, offered a resolution calling for all the correspondence and instructions relating to the former treaty, the directions given to our naval officers, and other information. On December 12 Senator Morton offered resolutions authorizing the President to appoint a commission with authority to inquire into matters bearing upon annexation. The latter resolution was taken up first and pressed to a vote, without reference to a committee which was refused. It was treated by its supporters as a resolution of inquiry, and the commission contemplated by it was very different from that which the President wanted. It was an attempt to temporize. Sumner opposed it vigorously on December 21, pointing out that it was unnecessary, since the President already had power to appoint commissioners and money enough in the secret service fund to pay their expenses. He argued that the only effect of the resolution was to commit the country, and that it was offered for this purpose. He discussed the history of the rejected treaty, criticised Baez, and condemned the use of the

navy, which had been employed to keep Baez in
power that he might sell his country. He did not
attack the President personally, but he criticised
the course of the administration, and described the
whole project as an attempt to deprive a feeble
people of their independence by methods unjustifiable in law or morals. He spoke evidently with
strong feeling, and his speech, though in form
merely an attack upon a policy, was in effect an
arraignment of the President. He was absolutely
right in his positions, but his language and manner
were unfortunate, and he excited a feeling which
made it harder to attain his object. His opening
sentence was : —

"The resolution before the Senate commits Congress to a dance of blood. It is a new step in a
measure of violence. Already several steps have
been taken, and Congress is now summoned to another."

Addressing the Vice-President, he said : —

"Go to the President, I ask you, and address
him frankly with the voice of a friend to whom he
must hearken. Counsel him to shun all approach
to the example of Franklin Pierce, James Buchanan, and Andrew Johnson; tell him not to allow
the oppression of a weak and humble people;
ask him not to exercise war powers without authority of Congress; and remind him, kindly,
but firmly, that there is a grandeur in justice and
peace beyond anything in material aggrandizement,
beyond anything in war. . . . I am not insensi-

ble to the commercial and material prosperity of
my country. But there is something above these.
It is the honor and good name of the Republic,
now darkened by an act of wrong. If this territory so much coveted by the President were infi-
nitely more valuable than it is, I hope the Senate
would not be tempted to obtain it by trampling on
the weak and humble."

This speech led to sharp replies, and Sumner
answered, repeating what he had in fact said to
the President in the interview at his house, and
declaring that his "language was precise, well-con-
sidered, and chosen in advance." It was entirely
characteristic of Sumner that he did not see how
his words were calculated to irritate the President.
At the close of his last speech during the debate he
insisted: "I said nothing to arraign Grant," and
disclaimed any disposition to do so. But it was
impossible for him to feel so strongly as he did
without making his feeling apparent, even though
his language was impersonal. His words were
those of one outraged at a wrong and determined
to expose it as a matter of duty, though not willing
to call names. The President recognized and undoubtedly exaggerated Sumner's feeling; he felt
himself attacked, and from that moment his hostility to Sumner was settled.

The debate became very bitter, and Sumner was
sharply criticised by Conkling, Edmunds, Carpenter, Chandler, and others, who attributed his attitude to personal resentment. It is certainly true

that he was indignant with the President for treating his opposition as a personal matter, and his indignation undoubtedly affected his speech. It is not true that any personal feeling led him to oppose the treaty, or to condemn the acts by which Baez was supported and the treaty negotiated. The President's purpose and methods were bad, and Sumner was sure to oppose them, though his language might have been more persuasive.

When Sumner made this speech he was familiar with the facts disclosed by the records of the State and Navy Departments; but the country was ignorant of them, so that the justice of his criticisms was not apparent. His resolution of December 9 was intended to elicit these facts, and after the passage of Morton's resolution it was taken up on January 4, and passed without a division. Another resolution, calling for orders and facts relating to the naval force then in the waters of San Domingo, was also passed on February 15, and the answer to these brought out the whole history which had inspired Sumner's speech.

Meanwhile Morton's resolution was taken up in the House on January 9, under a suspension of the rules, and was passed the next day, General Butler leading for the administration. It was, however, amended by a provision that it should not be considered as committing Congress to the policy of annexation, whereby its real purpose was defeated. The Senate at once passed it as amended and the commission was appointed. Their report was in line with the President's recommendation, but led to no action.

A contest with the administration involving so much personal bitterness, and the disturbance of long-established relations, was a serious strain upon Sumner. Age and unremitting labor began to tell upon his strength. During much of the session he suffered from some difficulty in his throat or lungs, which gradually weakened him until, on February 18, he had an attack of *angina pectoris*, his old trouble, which was very severe, and kept him from the Senate for a week. His condition after this attack is described by Wendell Phillips : —

"The doctors say the only policy is rest; the more he 'll take, the better health, and the better chance of life prolonged. I argued and prayed, so did we all. . . . The Russian minister said to me, ' Make him rest — he must. No man in Washington can fill his place, — *no man, no man*. We foreigners all know he is honest. We do not think that of many.' "

Sumner's relations with Mr. Fish had continued unchanged, notwithstanding the controversy over San Domingo, and on December 23, after his speech in the Senate, Sumner dined at Fish's house. On January 9, 1871, the President sent to the Senate the papers relating to the recall of Motley, among which was a letter, in which Motley alluded to the statement that he was removed on account of Sumner's opposition to the treaty. Fish's reply was that this rumor originated " in a source bitterly, personally, and vindictively hostile to the President," clearly indicating Sumner, and continued : —

" Mr. Motley must know — or, if he does not know it, he stands alone in his ignorance of the fact — that many senators opposed the San Domingo treaty openly, generously, and with as much efficiency as did the distinguished senator to whom he refers, and have nevertheless continued to enjoy the undiminished confidence and the friendship of the President, — than whom no man living is more tolerant of honest and manly differences of opinion, is more single or sincere in his desire for the public welfare, or more disinterested or regardless of what concerns himself, is more frank and confiding in his own dealings, is more sensitive to a betrayal of confidence, or would look with more scorn and contempt upon one who uses the words and the assurances of friendship to cover a secret and determined purpose of hostility."

These words were absolutely without excuse, and conveyed a charge against Mr. Sumner unwarranted by any statement of facts made by Mr. Fish or his defenders. No one else, who had known Mr. Sumner so long and so well as Mr. Fish had done, would have believed Mr. Sumner capable of duplicity, nor can any motive for it be suggested. The object of duplicity is to deceive, and Mr. Sumner's opposition to the treaty was open, so soon as he understood its provisions. Nothing could be gained by a promise of support broken at once, and it is perfectly clear that no promise was ever given. The whole nature, training, experience, and standards of Grant and Sumner made it easy for them to misunderstand each other. Mr. Fish had no such excuse for misrepresenting him, and it is charitable to believe that he did not, in writing to Motley, fully appreciate how his words would read if published. At all events he understood afterward what they meant; for three days later, though nothing but the publication of the letter had occurred to change his relations with Mr. Sumner, he sent Mr. Patterson to inquire how Mr. Sumner would receive him if he called upon public business. Sumner replied: "That should the secretary come to my house he would be received as an old friend, and that at any time I should be at his service for consultation on public business; but that I could not conceal my deep sense of personal wrong received from him absolutely and without excuse."

Fish accordingly called, and the two had a frank and full conversation upon the Alabama claims; but a few days later Sumner refused to recognize Fish at dinner.

The Forty-first Congress expired on March 4, and its successor met on the same day and remained in session until May 27. In the debate on the Morton resolution in December, Conkling had indicated that Sumner was to be removed from the chairmanship of the committee on foreign relations, and this was done when the committees were elected at the beginning of the new Congress.

Howe, Nye, and Pool, a majority of the caucus committee, reported a list of committees, putting Cameron in Sumner's place and making Sumner chairman of the committee on privileges and elections. Sherman and Morrill of Vermont, the other members of the committee, dissented. In private conversation, Howe said that Sumner had offended the President by the tone of his opposition to the San Domingo treaty. In the caucus he said that, as a majority of the Senate favored annexation, the committee should be constituted in sympathy with this feeling. After some debate in the caucus the report was adopted, though Trumbull, the Morrills, Ferry of Connecticut, Wilson, Logan, Schurz, and others opposed it. Hamlin, Edmunds, Conkling, Chandler, Howe, Carpenter, and the strong personal following of the President were in the majority. When the report was moved in the Senate on March 10, Schurz opposed it. Howe, replying, paid a high compliment to Sumner's " management of the affairs of that committee in the years that have passed," and even said: " If senators insist upon it, I will admit that the senator from Massachusetts could, under happier circumstances, fill it better than anybody else."

After a debate, which was one long testimonial to his fitness and which exposed the wrong that was done him, the report was adopted. The Senate refused to stand by Sumner, but yielded to executive influence and removed him. It is not proposed to discuss the reasons which, in the contro-

versy over the matter, were subsequently alleged
to justify this action. These were afterthoughts,
not suggested at the time, and disproved when they
were brought forward. The only reason alleged
in the discussion was that Sumner's personal relations with the President and secretary were not
good, whereby the public business might suffer.
The charge, made later by Mr. Fish, that Sumner
had delayed action on treaties, was disproved by
the Senate records, when the injunction of secrecy
was removed. It is not proposed, however, to
discuss Mr. Fish's action. For the purposes of
this biography it is enough to chronicle the fact
that Sumner's opposition to the San Domingo
treaty, in which he was fully supported by the
opinion of the country, led to his removal at the
instance of the administration from the place which
he adorned. The whole chapter illustrates the
condition of our politics at the time, and is not
pleasant reading for a patriotic American.

The press and the public condemned the act of
the Senate, and it is perhaps sufficient to record
the judgment of Mr. Blaine, then the speaker of
the House, as given years afterward. He was
not naturally in sympathy with Sumner, though in
active opposition to some of his opponents : —

" Many senators were compelled, from their sense
of obedience to the decision of the majority, to
commit an act against their conceptions of right,
against what they believed to be justice to a political associate, against what they believed to be

sound public policy, against what they believed to
be the interest of the Republican party." Mr.
Sumner's "bearing was distinguished by dignity
and magnanimity. He gave utterance to no complaints, and silently submitted to the unjustifiable
wrong of which he was a victim."

The Joint High Commission to consider all
pending questions between Great Britain and this
country was then in session, and Sumner was removed from his position at the very crisis when a
question which he had made his own came up for
settlement. Mr. Blaine's statement is true. He
bore himself with dignity and made no complaint,
simply excusing himself from service on the new
committee. The documents called for by his resolutions of January and February were sent to the
Senate, and the facts which had led him to oppose
the President were thus laid before the country.
On March 24 he introduced a series of resolutions
reciting these and calling for the withdrawal of our
naval forces from San Domingo pending negotiations, and for the disavowal of the threats uttered
by our naval officers to the government of Hayti
and of all hostile action taken by them upon the
island. The employment of our navy to maintain
Baez was condemned " as morally wrong," as a
violation of international law, as "an infraction of
the Constitution of the United States and a usur-
pation of power not conferred upon the President,"
and as "unauthorized violence utterly without support in law or reason, and proceeding directly from

that kingly prerogative which is disowned by the Constitution of the United States."

Against a vigorous attempt to prevent it, Sumner gained the floor and delivered a speech, which had been prepared carefully and was far stronger than his previous one, because it was more temperate and impersonal. He now proved his facts by the official records, and the severity lay in the facts and the law. He declared that " the navy of the United States, acting under orders from Washington, has been engaged in measures of violence and of belligerent intervention, being war without the authority of Congress." This he certainly established, and he made it evident how little the administration had regarded the legal limitations of executive power, and with what reckless violence the attempt at annexation had been conducted. He told the story of the Dominican adventurers who were trying to sell their country, and the case of Mr. Hatch, an American citizen, who was arrested and imprisoned to prevent his using his influence against annexation, because, said Baez, " a few weeks' restraint would not be so inconvenient to him as his slanderous statements might become to the success of General Grant's policy in the Antilles."

The most direct attack upon Grant was this : —

" It is difficult to see how we can condemn, with proper, whole-hearted reprobation, our own domestic Ku-Klux with its fearful outrages, while the President puts himself at the head of a powerful

and costly proceeding operating abroad in defiance
of international law and the Constitution of the
United States. . . . Nor should I do otherwise
than fail in justice to the occasion, if I did not
declare my unhesitating conviction, that, had the
President been so inspired as to bestow upon the
protection of Southern Unionists, white and black,
one half, nay, sir, one quarter, of the time, money,
zeal, will, personal attention, personal effort, and
personal intercession, which he has bestowed on
his attempt to obtain half an island in the Carib-
bean Sea, our Southern Ku-Klux would have existed in name only, while tranquillity reigned
everywhere within our borders."

This was inserted on the morning of the speech,
and might better have been omitted. A debate
followed, in which Sumner was attacked personally
by the President's friends, and ably defended by
Schurz.

On April 5 the President sent the report of the
commission to Congress with a special message.
Morrill of Vermont replied to it, and then the San
Domingo project was abandoned, as it was found
impossible to get the necessary support in Congress. Again Sumner had helped to keep the
country right, though at terrible cost to himself.

Shortly after this Sumner spoke in favor of a
measure to stop the outrages of the Ku-Klux Klan,
standing in this case with many who had opposed
him; but after the defeat of the San Domingo
proposition the most important work of the session

was the treaty of Washington. His relation to the questions pending with England and the knowledge that the country was behind him gave him an influence unaffected by his removal from the chairmanship of the committee. He conferred with the English commissioners often and freely, and in the Senate he made the leading speech in support of the treaty. He offered, indeed, certain amendments, to secure immunity for private property on the ocean and other ameliorations of war, but he did not press them. The new treaty was in substantial harmony with his views, and thus the result of the session was gratifying to him.

His health called for rest, and he spent the summer and autumn in visits and literary labors. During this autumn General Butler made his first attempt to win the Republican nomination for governor of Massachusetts. His campaign was extraordinary, and the prospects of his success were at one time so good that Sumner and Wilson were induced to throw their influence against him, which was done by the publication of a statement, prepared by Sumner and assented to by Wilson, in which they expressed their regret at his course, and their opinion that " his nomination as governor would be hostile to the best interests of the Commonwealth and the Republican party." The hostility of the administration had not yet weakened Sumner's influence in Massachusetts, and it was believed that his action defeated Butler, who from this time was his enemy.

Henry Wilson

CHAPTER XXIV

CIVIL RIGHTS: GRANT'S RENOMINATION

THE second session of the Forty-second Congress began in December, 1871. An attempt was made to reconcile the President and Sumner, but the President did not receive it favorably, though he had become reconciled to General Butler and was much under his influence. It does not appear that Sumner was cognizant of the effort.

The lines were forming for the campaign of 1872, and the question of the President's renomination was beginning to press. On December 21 Sumner proposed a constitutional amendment making the President ineligible for reëlection, with a resolution which was in itself a stump speech in favor of the proposition. This amendment had been reported by the judiciary committee of the Senate in 1867. As the preamble of Sumner's resolution recited, it had been three times recommended by President Jackson; President Harrison, in accepting his nomination, had supported it; Henry Clay had urged it; the Whig party in 1844 had made it a plank in their platform; Senator Wade had proposed it at the end of his senatorial term, and De Tocqueville had dwelt on the danger arising

from the desire of the President to be reëlected.
The proposed amendment by its terms was not to
take effect until after March 4, 1873, so that it
could not prevent President Grant's renomination,
but in effect it was an argument against that action.
Certainly, if the facts were as stated in the resolution, there was every reason for selecting a new candidate.   It was Sumner's habit to use this method
of influencing public opinion, and undoubtedly he
now had this in view.   The President's friends all
opposed the resolution, but its purpose was accomplished when it was presented and printed.   It
showed his probable position in regard to the next
nomination.

At this session Sumner began in earnest the last
great struggle of his life to secure the protection
of equal rights by national statute.   He had introduced what became known as the " supplementary
civil rights bill " in May, 1870, but at the end of
the session the committee on the judiciary reported
against it.   He introduced it again in January,
1871, and again an adverse report was made.   In
March, 1871, he again offered it, and on his motion
it was ordered to lie on the table.   At this session a resolution limiting legislation to certain subjects was passed against Sumner's protest, and this
prevented the consideration of his measure.   On
December 20, 1871, the Senate had under consideration an amnesty bill, and Mr. Sumner moved
his civil rights bill as an amendment.   The first
section of this bill declared : " That all citizens

of the United States, without distinction of race, color, or previous condition of servitude," were entitled to " equal and impartial facilities and accommodations from common carriers, innkeepers, managers of theatres and other places of public amusement, the officers of common schools and other public institutions of learning, supported or authorized by law, and the officers of church organizations, cemetery associations, and benevolent institutions incorporated by public authority." The other sections prescribed penalties, gave the courts of the United States jurisdiction to enforce the act, forbade the exclusion of jurors by reason of race, color, or previous condition of servitude, and annulled every state law inconsistent with the act.

A long discussion ensued between Mr. Sumner and Senator Hill of Georgia, which brought out the Southern point of view very clearly. Hill thought that distinct accommodations in public conveyances, inns, and schools, if equally good, were all that the colored race could ask. Sumner insisted that the distinction was an indignity to which no man should be subjected, saying : —

" How often shall I say that this is no question of taste, — it is no question of society, — it is a stern, austere, hard question of rights ? . . . I may have whom I please as friend, acquaintance, associate ; . . . but I cannot deny any human being, the humblest, any right of equality. He must be equal with me before the law, or the promises of the Declaration of Independence are not yet fulfilled."

A point of order was overruled, and then the amendment was defeated by one vote. Sumner renewed his motion when the bill was reported to the Senate, and on January 15 supported it by an elaborate speech, which put the argument largely on moral grounds, ignoring those legal objections which led the Supreme Court in after years to declare the act unconstitutional. He easily showed that evils existed, and that the civil rights of colored men were not recognized in the South. He insisted that if the Civil Rights Act was constitutional, this supplemental measure was equally so, and that since the Thirteenth and Fourteenth amendments had made the colored man a citizen, well-settled law compelled innkeepers and common carriers to treat him as such. He argued against the prejudice of color, placing himself on Rousseau's proposition: "It is precisely because the force of things tends always to destroy equality that the force of legislation should always tend to maintain it;" and he contended that before rebels were restored to rights and privileges which they had forfeited, they should be compelled to give their colored fellow citizens the equal rights which belonged to them, thus making his amendment a condition of amnesty. It is impossible to do more than indicate his line of argument. He contended for what was right, and relied on arguments which appealed to moral convictions, but which were not calculated to meet the constitutional doubts of men who, like himself, were in favor of equal rights, but who were unwilling to exceed their power. In fact, the constant reiteration of moral considerations, whose force is admitted, inevitably irritates men who are considering a legal question, nor is the irritation diminished if the argument is presented in sonorous phrase. Mr. Sumner's amendment was adopted by the casting vote of the Vice-President, but the amended bill was defeated.

On May 8 another amnesty bill came from the House, and Sumner again moved to amend by striking out all after the enacting clause and inserting his bill. This was lost by the casting vote of the Vice-President. Sumner then moved it as an addition, and it was adopted by the same vote. The bill thus amended failed, as had its predecessors. On May 10 Sumner again introduced his bill with some slight changes. On May 21, when a bill to extend the provisions of the so-called " Ku-Klux Act " was pending, and an all-night session was ordered, Sumner, who was unwell, left the Senate. In his absence, on motion of Carpenter, his civil rights bill was taken up and passed, amended by inserting a substitute, which did not provide against discrimination in schools, churches, cemeteries, or juries, and which was in other respects imperfect. A protest was made against this action in Sumner's absence, and he was sent for by friends, but arrived too late. An amnesty bill was under consideration, which he tried to amend by adding his bill, but his amendment was rejected and the bill passed, Sumner

protesting. He then moved a reconsideration of
the vote which had been taken, but without success, and after a vigorous speech, in which he
charged that the rights of the colored race had
been sacrificed by the Republican majority in the
Senate, the discussion closed. The amnesty bill
became a law; the civil rights bill was not considered in the House. Three days before the session ended he moved his bill as an amendment to
the civil appropriation bill, but it was ruled out of
order, and so Congress adjourned without action on
the subject. The next session Sumner was unable
to attend, but on the first day of the Congress
which met on December 1, 1873, he again introduced his bill, in a new draft, but the same in
effect.

The debates just alluded to show that Sumner's
mind was tired and that ill health was telling
upon him. He could not discuss the question to
which he had devoted his life without repeating
himself. His brain worked in channels which had
been worn deep by use, and he could not escape
from the lines of thought, or even the phrases, with
which he had grown so familiar. In his contest
with younger men like Carpenter and Conkling,
and among associates of whom some were inclined
to treat him with scant respect, there was something
pathetic in his efforts to make them feel what was
so clear and so vital to him. From this discussion
no one can get any just idea of Sumner's power.
It is a sick and weary man, animated by high pur-

pose and with indomitable resolution, struggling against obstacles of which his own weakness was not the least. The form remained, the will and purpose were there, the vigor and life were beginning to fail.

None the less Mr. Sumner took a leading part during the session in other matters. He felt keenly the methods and practices which discredited the administration, and it was not in his nature to let them pass unchallenged. On February 12, 1872, he introduced a resolution for a select committee to investigate the sales of ordnance stores made by the government during the Franco-German war, and said that the United States had fallen under the suspicion of violating the neutrality laws, and that therefore there should be an investigation. This led to a long and sharp debate, for any reflection on the government during Grant's administration was at once resented by his supporters, who felt that his renomination was at stake. The fact undoubtedly was that during this war large amounts of arms and ammunition were sold by the War Department to agents of the French government, and were sent to France. The only authority for this lay in the statute authorizing the sale of arms and munitions of war, which were "damaged or otherwise unsuitable;" but the arms sold were of our best, and ammunition was manufactured at our arsenals for the purpose. The original purchasing agents were Remington & Co.; but after their admitted relations with the French government made further sales to them imprudent, later ones were made to a small country lawyer, who lived in Ilion, where the Remingtons were established in business. The sales amounted to 425,000 arms and 54,000,000 cartridges, and the amount of money involved was more than $4,000,-000. The circumstances were suspicious, the transaction was illegal, and there was good reason to suspect corruption; therefore the demand for an investigation was manifestly proper. The debate was very animated, Sumner and Schurz speaking for the investigation, while Carpenter, Conkling, Edmunds, Morton, Frelinghuysen, and others defended the War Department. Sumner and Schurz were charged with want of patriotism, with laying the United States open to claims from Germany, and with being " emissaries and spies " of foreign nations. Schurz took the more active part, and carried off the honors of the debate. Sumner closed the case, on February 28, with a dignified and able presentation of the facts and the law. It attacked no one and was free from personality, but it left no doubt that an investigation must be had. The supporters of the administration did not dare to prevent it, and his resolution passed, the preamble having been laid on the table with his consent.

In reply to attack he said, " The objection of Senators is too much like the old heathen cry, 'Our country, right or wrong.' Unhappy words, which dethrone God and exalt the Devil! I am for our country with the aspiration that it may be always right; but I am for nothing wrong. When I hear of wrong, I insist at all hazards that it shall be made right, knowing that in this way I best serve my country and every just cause."

The opponents of the investigation next undertook to stifle it by appointing a committee, upon which was placed no Republican who favored the inquiry and only one Democrat. Sumner, attacked by *angina pectoris* and disabled for a fortnight, declined to serve on the committee, and Schurz was denied a seat on it, though permitted to attend its sessions and examine the witnesses. Both were invited to testify and Sumner came, but protested against being examined. He was then subpœnaed and submitted to examination, but under protest because the confidential communications on which he had acted were privileged, and because the committee was made up, in violation of parliamentary law, from persons who did not favor the inquiry. He was entirely willing to testify, though treated with scant courtesy by members who resented his protest.

The report, in which all the Republican members joined, exonerated the War Department, and so accomplished the result for which the committee was organized; but no impartial person can read the evidence and feel satisfied with this conclusion. The report was discussed in the Senate, but without final action, and the episode remained as one count in the indictment which many Republicans were framing against the forces of which the President was at once the leader and the instrument.

President Grant had used his appointing power very freely to benefit his relatives and personal friends, and he was surrounded and influenced by politicians who did not command the public confidence. In the San Domingo affair he had shown an obstinacy, a disregard of law, and an impatience of opposition, which had shaken the confidence of many; and the corruption in the departments and among his close friends, which in his second administration led to scandals without precedent in our history, was beginning to be generally suspected. At the same time it was clear that the power of the executive would be used to compass his renomination and election, as it had been used in behalf of the politicians whom he favored. The Republican party as a whole was so much swayed by the prejudices and passions of the war, Grant's personal popularity was so great, the Democratic party was so thoroughly discredited, that the chance of successfully opposing him either in the Republican convention or at the polls was very slight, but many Republicans felt it a public duty to oppose him, and among these were the very best of the Republican leaders, as for example, Trumbull and Schurz. A convention of Republicans opposed to Grant was called to meet at Cincinnati on May 1, and the movement was supported by influential newspapers like the New York "Tribune," the Chicago "Tribune," the Cincinnati "Commer-

cial," and others. It was rich in leaders, its principles were sound, it was entirely patriotic, the
need for it was imperative, but it was unfortunate
in its choice of a candidate, and its chance of permanent influence was lost when its nominations
were made. The Republicans who had taken
prominent part against Grant had expended some
of their influence in so doing. A man of unquestioned character and ability was needed, who would
command the respect of the country, and who had
not been weakened by political antagonisms. Such
a man was Charles Francis Adams, but unhappily
he spoke of the new movement somewhat con-
temptuously and seemed indifferent to the questions at issue. Sumner's name was suggested, but
not with his approval, and finally the choice fell
upon Horace Greeley, a man of unquestioned ability, high character, and intense earnestness, but
erratic and impulsive. His personal peculiarities
and his foibles invited ridicule, and the people
hardly treated him as a serious candidate. The
movement therefore failed, though Greeley was also
nominated by the Democrats and received more
than four ninths of the popular vote, which showed
the strength of the opposition to Grant.

Sumner was urged to join this political movement before the convention at Cincinnati; but
though in cordial sympathy with the opposition to
Grant and in close relations with Trumbull and
Schurz, he was reluctant to leave the Republican
party and hoped that Grant might be defeated in

the Republican convention. He indeed sent to Mr.
F. W. Bird a draft of the platform, which, so far
as it demanded the equal rights of all, and declared
that emancipation and enfranchisement were finally
and forever secure, was in substance adopted; but
he refused to declare his position until after the
convention had adjourned. Against many and
urgent appeals from both sides he preserved absolute silence when the prospects of the new movement were brightest, but after its failure, and when
Grant's election seemed certain, he took his position. His reasons for hesitation were given in a
letter to Mr. Bird written late in May: —

" Nor have I ever given a hint to a human being
as to my future course. My right hand has never
spoken it to my left. Of this I shall not speak
until I can see the whole field, and especially the
bearing on the colored race. I mean to fail in
nothing by which they may be helped; therefore
all stories as to what I shall do, or shall not, are
inventions. Nobody will know my position sooner
than yourself. I honor you constantly. But I
seek two things: (1) the protection of the colored
race, and (2) the defeat of Grant."

It was hard for him to sever his political relations
with his party and especially with men like his colleague Wilson, who had been his warm supporter
when he was first elected and who had been in substantial harmony with him during their long association in the Senate. His feelings were stated in
the speech by which he attempted to defeat the

nomination of Grant, making his opportunity un-
expectedly on May 31 by moving to postpone the
consideration of an appropriation bill. He spoke
to a full Senate, and among the listeners were three
members of the Cabinet and the President's private
secretaries. It was published under the title of
" Republicanism *v.* Grantism," and it was the inconsistency between these which Sumner tried to
show. He began thus : —

" I have no hesitation in declaring myself a member of the Republican party, and one of the strait-
est of the sect. I doubt if any senator can point
to earlier or more constant service in its behalf.
I began at the beginning, and from that early day
have never failed to sustain its candidates and to
advance its principles. . . . To such a party, with
which so much of my life is intertwined, I have no
common attachment. Not without regret can I see
it suffer ; not without a pang can I see it changed
from its original character, for such a change is
death. Therefore do I ask, with no common feeling, that the peril which menaces it may pass away.
I stood by its cradle ; let me not follow its hearse."

He then pointed out that the party had become
" the instrument of one man and his personal will,"
recounting the history of the San Domingo treaty.
The general tenor of the speech may be gathered
from a part of the introductory statement : —

" Not only are Constitution and law disregarded,
but the presidential office itself is treated as little
more than a plaything and a perquisite. . . .

Here the details are ample, showing how from the beginning this august trust has dropped to be a personal indulgence, where palace cars, fast horses, and seaside loiterings figure more than duties ; how personal aims and objects have been more prominent than the public interest ; how the presidential office has been used to advance his own family on a scale of nepotism dwarfing everything of the kind in our history, and hardly equaled in the corrupt governments where this abuse has most prevailed ; how in the same spirit office has been conferred upon those from whom he had received gifts or benefits, thus making the country repay his personal obligations ; how personal devotion to himself, rather than public or party service, has been made the standard of favor ; how the vast appointing power conferred by the Constitution for the general welfare has been employed at his will to promote his schemes, to reward his friends, to punish his opponents, and to advance his election to a second term ; how all these assumptions have matured in a personal government, semi-military in character and breathing the military spirit."

The speech amplified fully the details of this general outline. It condemned the President unsparingly, and its charges were true, though it was possible to put a much more charitable interpretation upon the facts than Sumner adopted. Grant's unfitness and the dangers involved in his reëlection were clear to Sumner, and he determined to make them equally clear to the country. Yet it was an ineffectual speech. It was too elaborate, too much encumbered with historical matter. It dealt too much in generalities and sweeping accusations. If it had recognized President Grant's services and his good qualities, it would have carried more weight. From the standpoint of the practical politician it was a failure, — the attempt and not the deed, which "confounds." Grant was not a Cæsar, as Sumner painted him. There was no fear that he would overthrow our form of government. The real peril was that unchecked corruption would lower the public standards, and undermine that respect for the traditions of honorable government upon which free institutions rest; and this danger was realized.

Sumner's speech provoked bitter replies in the Senate and adverse criticism from all supporters of the Republican party. He must have been disappointed in its effect and pained to see the unswerving allegiance of the party to an unfit man. Nothing is harder to bear than the sense of hopeless failure, coming at a dangerous crisis to a man who knows that he is right, but is wholly unable to impress his convictions on others. Many friends, even while recognizing his sincerity, could not but feel that his vision was distorted by his personal wrongs, and that his judgment was consequently at fault. Among these were George William Curtis, Mrs. Child, Whittier, Phillips, and others, whose doubts were especially disappointing. Garrison bitterly attacked him in successive articles.

Many of these lived to learn that Sumner was right, and perhaps to regret all the more keenly that he did not present his argument more effectively.

Though he had opposed Grant he had not yet declared his readiness to support Greeley; but after the Republican convention had unanimously nominated Grant, the next step was necessary. He was urged by Republicans to remain silent, by the friends of Greeley to speak, and finally, on July 29, he announced his decision in a reply to a request for advice from a committee of colored men. He dwelt upon Grant's indignity to the colored race in San Domingo and his neglect to help them by supporting the civil rights bill; he repeated the charges of his speech; he contrasted the training of Greeley and Grant and their careers, and finding in Greeley a lifelong Republican and a consistent friend of the negro, he advised them to support him, declaring that he proposed to do so.

Immediately after the publication of this letter Mr. Blaine, then the speaker of the House, wrote to him an open letter, charging him with being false both to his party and his principles, and pointing out that he was in singular alliance with Confederates and allies of Preston S. Brooks.

Sumner replied effectively and somewhat tartly:

"You are greatly concerned about the company I keep. To quiet your solicitude, I beg leave to say that, in joining the Republicans who brought forward an original Abolitionist, I find myself with

so many others devoted to the cause I have always
served, that I had not missed you until you hastened
to report absence. . . . You entirely misunderstand me when you introduce an incident of the
past, and build on it an argument why I should
not support Horace Greeley. What has Preston
Brooks to do with the Presidential election?
Never, while a sufferer, did anybody hear me
speak of him in unkindness; and now, after the
lapse of more than half a generation, I will not
unite with you in dragging him from the grave,
where he sleeps, to aggravate the passions of a
political conflict, and arrest the longing for concord."

In this letter he met the charge that a Democratic victory would mean a reaction against the
rights of the colored race, asserting that, with
Greeley and a Congress elected upon the Democratic platform, equal rights would be safe.

The session, with its sharp personal conflicts,
and the strain attending the severance of his relations with the administration and his party, had
overtaxed his strength, and when it closed he
found himself with a feeble and irregular heart,
and other indications of exhaustion. He was in no
condition for a presidential campaign, in which his
feelings were so much enlisted, and his physicians
advised Europe. He took this advice, and sailed
on September 3. He was anxious to make one
speech in Faneuil Hall before he left, but under
medical advice he abandoned the idea, deterred

not by the fear of death, but by the danger of paralysis or some form of mental disability. He accordingly wrote his speech, and it was published about the time of his departure. It began: " While recognizing party as an essential agency and convenience, I could not allow it to restrain my conscience against what seemed the requirements of public good; " and then stated the arguments for Greeley and against Grant simply and directly. He said that his first inclination was not to vote at all, but that his doubts were removed when the Democratic party accepted a Republican platform, " the best ever adopted, with a Republican candidate who was the most devoted Republican ever nominated, thus completely accepting the results of the war, and offering the hand of reconciliation." The speech does not appear to have produced any new effect upon the public mind. His opposition to Grant had long been declared, and it was easy to misrepresent his motives. On reaching England he learned, to his great surprise and annoyance, that he had been nominated as the Democratic candidate for governor of Massachusetts, and he at once cabled a positive refusal.

He spent a month in Paris, meeting American friends, and many distinguished Frenchmen. He devoted himself to the galleries, and to buying works of art, books, bronzes, china; but he could not forget the abuse of which he had been the target, and to which he alluded sadly in his letters Returning to London he was entertained pleasantly by old and new English friends, but he and they alike felt that it was his last visit, and there was evidently that undercurrent of sadness which inevitably attends the partings of later life. He passed a night with John Bright, who wrote of the visit: "There was great gentleness in all he said, with a sadness and a melancholy, which left upon us the impression that he felt himself seriously ill, and that his work of life was nearly ended."

The trip seemed to help him, but his health was by no means restored, and he was urged to prolong his stay. His sense of duty, however, called him back to the Senate, and he sailed on November 14, reaching New York on the 26th and Washington on the 29th, the day of Mr. Greeley's death, which was a serious shock to him.

When the session opened he was so ill that he asked to be excused from service on committees, and from December 19 until the following March he was not in his seat at all, nor did he after December 18 take any part in the business of the Senate. On the opening day of the session he offered the following bill: —

"Whereas the national unity and good-will among fellow citizens can be assured only through oblivion of past differences, and it is contrary to the usage of civilized nations to perpetuate the memory of civil war: Therefore, — *Be it enacted*, That the names of battles with fellow citizens shall not be continued in the Army Register, or placed on the regimental colors of the United States."

He attempted without success to press his civil
rights bill and his bill to secure equality in the
schools of the District, and spoke briefly on minor
topics. In his eulogy of his former associate, Gar-
rett Davis, and in some remarks prepared to be
spoken of Horace Greeley there was an apparent
recognition that his own end was near, and a gentle kindliness which was pathetic. Smarting from
the wounds inflicted by former friends he felt the
beauty and the uses of charity. Such was his work
for the session.

The bill just quoted provoked an unexpected re-
sponse. Already in 1862 and 1865 he had introduced similar propositions without exciting adverse
criticism, and his purpose was clearly reasonable.
His position cannot be stated better than in these
words of Carl Schurz in his eulogy : —

" Let the dead man have a hearing. This was
his thought: No civilized nation, from the republics
of antiquity down to our days, ever thought it wise
or patriotic to preserve in conspicuous and durable
form the mementos of victories won over fellow
citizens in civil war. Why not ? Because every
citizen should feel himself with all others as the
child of a common country, and not as a defeated
foe. All civilized governments of our days have
instinctively followed the same dictate of wisdom
and patriotism. . . .

" Should the son of South Carolina, when at
some future day defending the Republic against
some foreign foe, be reminded by an inscription on

the colors floating over him that under this flag
the gun was fired that killed his father at Gettys-
burg? Should this great and enlightened Republic, proud of standing in the front of human progress, be less wise, less large-hearted, than the
ancients were two thousand years ago, and the
kingly governments of Europe are to-day? . . .

"Do you want conspicuous mementos of your
victories? They are written upon the dusky brow
of every freeman who was once a slave; they are
written on the gate-posts of a restored Union; and
the most glorious of all will be written on the faces
of a contented people, reunited in common national
pride."

Now it happened that in December, 1872, the
legislature of Massachusetts was holding an extra
session. A country member introduced a resolution condemning the senator's bill, and the committee to which it was referred gave him a private
hearing. On the last day of the session this resolution was reported by half the committee, and
after a debate, in which Sumner's purpose was
wholly misrepresented by those who favored the
resolution, it was passed. The legislators feared
the anger of the veterans, and this fear carried the
resolution. As adopted it described Sumner's bill
"as an insult to the loyal soldiery of the nation"
and as "meeting the unqualified condemnation of
the people of the Commonwealth."

This astonished Sumner, who wrote: "I cannot
understand this tempest. The resolution which is

treated so severely is an old inhabitant. I have already brought it forward in substance twice before this last motion. . . . I know that I never deserved better of Massachusetts than now. It was our State which led in requiring all safeguards for liberty and equality; I covet for her that other honor of leading in reconciliation."

His own bill was not taken up in the Senate, for he wished to take part in the debate and his health rendered this impossible. The leaders of Massachusetts, however, rallied to his support, and when the new legislature met in January, 1873, an attempt was made to have the resolution of censure rescinded. A very strong petition was presented, supported by energetic speech and action; but the movement failed, owing largely to the efforts made by members of the previous legislature, who wished not to be discredited so promptly and who argued that one legislature could not reverse an expression of opinion by another. Party feeling, fear of " the soldier vote," desire to propitiate the administration, carried the day, and it was a year before the legislature of Massachusetts removed the blot which the legislature of 1872 had placed upon the good name of the State.

Such action from his own State, coming when he was prostrated by disease and discouraged by the political situation, naturally hurt Mr. Sumner, but did not change his purpose. He was determined to persuade Massachusetts, and wrote: " How a cultivated heathen could differ from me I

do not understand.   History is full of examples to
sustain me ; only the sea and tiger are as blind
and senseless in ferocity as party hate.   I long to
state the case."

Unhappily his strength was not sufficient for
the undertaking.   During the whole winter he suffered from recurring attacks of *angina pectoris*
with constant nervous pains, sleeplessness, and general weakness.   From the time when he left the
Senate in December until May he was substantially
confined to the house, and employed himself in
reading and chatting with his visitors, keeping his
mind as free from disturbing thoughts as possible.
He wrote one or two brief letters for publication
favoring equal civil rights, but he was substantially
withdrawn from public life.   He was naturally depressed in spirits by his sickness, and there was
nothing in the political situation or prospect to
encourage him.   Even men in full health were
saddened by the acts and tendencies of the day.
At a time when his great and unselfish services
should have surrounded him with respect and
honor, it was hard to feel that his influence was
weakened, and that the legislature of his own State
was hostile.

Nor was it so much the condemnation of himself
as the uncivilized attitude of the Commonwealth
which depressed him.   The change which the four
years of Grant's administration had wrought in
the character of the Republican party, and in his
own position, was bitter to the taste.   Add to this

the death of old friends like Seward, Chase, and Greeley, the paralysis of Wilson, the retirement of others from public life, and it is not surprising that he felt the increasing isolation of advancing years. A host of friends were busy in writing him letters of regard and sympathy, and these were very pleasant, but his position was inevitably lonely. When the Senate met in special session on March 4, 1873, he went to present the credentials of Governor Boutwell, his new colleague, but he was not invited to the caucus of the Republicans, and was substantially without party relations. Nothing was neglected that could make him feel the consequences of opposing the President.

Sumner refused to visit Europe again, as his friends advised, and reached Boston on August 2, feeling very much better. He spent the autumn there and in visits, writing occasional letters upon public questions.

He grew stronger for a while, so that he could enjoy the society of his friends; he went to the Saturday Club and other like social organizations; he occasionally spoke briefly, avoiding controversial topics and leaving on all who met him an impression of gentleness and kindliness. He renewed early acquaintances, some of whom had been estranged from him by political differences, and it seemed as if, having abandoned the consideration of political questions, he returned to the simple friendliness of his youth. It was the pleasant evening of his life, his last visit to his native State. He

was cordially received, and the general expression
of respect and regard, which met him everywhere,
made him feel that he was appreciated at home
and dispelled the sense of injustice and wrong
which had clouded the previous winter. He learned
on her own soil that Massachusetts did not condemn him and that the resolution of the legislature
did her as much injustice as it did him. He was
assured on every hand that his reëlection to the
Senate was certain, and he returned to his seat
refreshed in body and cheered in mind by touching
again his native earth.

CHAPTER XXV

THE LAST SESSION

SUMNER had borne himself during this period with entire dignity. He had made no complaints, had in no way discussed his party relations, but had simply, so far as his health permitted, proceeded as before. His absence from the Senate and the known condition of his health had permitted exasperation to subside, so that on his return he found his associates disposed to welcome him with cordiality. He was not recognized as a Republican, owing to the opposition of the senators who assumed to represent the administration, and as a member of the Democratic party he was given inferior places on two unimportant committees. He was again where he stood when he entered the Senate, with such influence only as came from his personal character and arguments.

He showed how great was the improvement in his health by at once introducing several measures, including his civil rights bill; the bill to secure equality in the schools of the District; a bill for the payment of the French spoliation claims; a bill to hasten specie payments; a proposition for the election of the president by popular vote for

one term; and one for international arbitration.
His programme indicated no sense of failing power
or desire to avoid controversy; it showed, on the
contrary, a resolute determination to deal with all
the more important questions before the country.

On the second day of the session he moved to
take up his civil rights bill, saying that it had
been well considered and would require no debate.
Objection was made and a reference urged.   Sumner asked for speedy action, but the Senate refused.
Later a motion to refer it to the committee on the
judiciary was made, which Sumner opposed.   He
recited the action repeatedly taken on the bill by
the committee since its first introduction in May,
1870, and urged that the committee could not further enlighten the Senate, which itself had fully
debated and indeed passed the bill.   He appealed
personally to Edmunds, to join him in supporting
the measure, saying: " My desire, the darling
desire, if I may say so, of my soul, at this moment,
is to close forever this great question, so that it
shall never again intrude into these chambers, —
so that hereafter in all our legislation there shall
be no such words as ' black' or ' white,' but that
we shall speak only of citizens and of men."

Finally, on a promise from Mr. Frelinghuysen,
in which Edmunds joined, that the bill should be
reported promptly, Sumner consented to the reference.   It was his last speech on the subject.   Before the bill was reported, he died; but after his
death it passed the Senate with some changes, and

ultimately became the law, only to be declared unconstitutional by the Supreme Court, which construed the Fourteenth and Fifteenth amendments
strictly, thereby justifying Sumner's objection to
the wording of these amendments and his advo-
cacy of more sweeping language when they were
under discussion in Congress. He lived to urge
and to see enacted every law which Congress had
the power to pass in aid of equal rights and against
distinctions of color. He proposed and pressed
nearly to enactment, the act which he considered
necessary to complete the work, and its ultimate
failure came from causes beyond his control. All
that man could do he did for the cause so near to
his heart.

This year for the first time he felt that he could
leave the Senate and attend the New England dinner in New York on December 22, and there he
made his last speech outside the Senate. It was a
brilliant occasion, and he was welcomed with the
warmest demonstrations by the whole audience.
The genuine enthusiasm of the distinguished company made Mr. Sumner feel again that his countrymen were not alienated, and it was a pleasant
memory during the few weeks of life that remained
to him.

The rest may be told briefly. After the holiday
recess and his attempt to pass the civil rights bill
Sumner continued in apparently good health until
the beginning of March. He busied himself in
editing his speeches on the civil rights bill, and

in the preparation of his Works. He was prepared to support the nomination of Caleb Cushing for chief justice, believing him well fitted for the position and likely to be sound on questions involving equal rights. When his name was withdrawn and that of Chief Justice Waite was substituted, he made in executive session a speech upon the office and its requirements, with very interesting reminiscences of Marshall and others whom he had known. He spoke on some other matters briefly. The legislature of Massachusetts rescinded in February, 1874, its resolution of censure, and the record of this action was delivered to him on March 6. This was a great gratification, and was the theme of many pleasant letters. His attitude towards the world at this time may be given in the words of a friend : —

" I saw him frequently and familiarly during the last four months of his life, and wish to give my testimony to the gentleness and kindliness of his temper during all that time, and to the fact that he uttered no word of harshness or censure in my hearing concerning any human being."

The clouds which had shadowed the last years had disappeared ; he was at peace with mankind, and his work was done. His comrades in the great battle were passing away, and he was not loath to lay down his burden. Early in March the attacks of *angina pectoris* began to recur. On March 6 he spoke for the last time in the Senate on the bill for the centennial exhibition at Philadelphia. On

the 10th he visited the Senate, where Senator Boutwell presented the resolution of the Massachusetts
legislature, and remained there some time talking
with friends, but complaining of pain. At six
o'clock Henry L. Pierce and B. P. Poore found him
writing letters, and remained to dine with him.
Almost immediately after they left he had a severe
attack of pain, followed by others, which were
deadened by injections of morphine, and from that
time he slowly sank till his death on the afternoon
of March 11.   E. R. Hoar, Carl Schurz, and others
of his friends were with him during the day, and
to Judge Hoar he said several times: " You must
take care of the civil rights bill, — my bill, the
civil rights bill, — don't let it fail ; " and his last
message was: "Judge, tell Emerson how much I
love and revere him ; " and so passed away the man
of whom Emerson said that he had " the whitest
soul of any man I ever knew."

It would be easy to fill a volume with extracts
from the eulogies which were pronounced after his
death, but it may be permitted to preserve at least
a few words from E. R. Hoar, who held his hand
as he died : —

" Wherever the news of the event spreads
through this broad land, not only in this city among
his associates in the public councils, not only in the
old Commonwealth of which he was the pride and
ornament, but in many quiet homes, in many a cabin
of the poor and lowly, there is to-day inexpressible
tenderness and profound sorrow."

Charles Sumner was a great man in his absolute fidelity to principle, his clear perception of what his country needed, his unflinching courage, his perfect sincerity, his persistent devotion to duty, his indifference to selfish considerations, his high scorn of anything petty or mean. He was essentially simple to the end, brave, kind, and pure. In his prime he was a very eloquent speaker, and his unbending adherence to the highest morality gave him insight and power in dealing with great questions and a strong hold upon the moral forces of the country. As Emerson said, he was for many years the " conscience of the Senate."

He was a man of great ability but not of the highest intellectual power, nor was he a master of style. He was not incisive in thought or speech. His orations were overloaded, his rhetoric was often turgid, he was easily led into irrelevance and undue stress upon undisputed points. His untiring industry as a reader had filled his memory with associations which perhaps he valued unduly. Originally modest and not self-confident, the result of his long contest was to make him egotistical and dogmatic. There are few successful men who escape these penalties of success, the common accompaniment of increasing years. A man who is trying to produce definite results naturally and properly wishes to know how far he has succeeded. No one aims at a mark without caring to discover whether his shot hits, and the speaker or writer who is seeking to influence public opinion must know whether his

words tell, in order to guide his future action.
From this proper interest the transition to egotism
is easy.   Sumner's naively simple nature, his confidence in his fellows, and his lack of humor combined to prevent his concealing what many feel but
are better able to hide.

From the time he entered public life till he died
he was a strong force constantly working for righteousness.   He had absolute faith in the principles
of free government as laid down in the Declaration
of Independence, and he gave his life to secure
their practical recognition.   They were not to him
glittering generalities, but ultimate, practical truths,
and in this faith Lincoln and Sumner were one.
To Sumner more than to any single man, except
possibly Lincoln, the colored race owes its emancipation and such measure of equal rights as it now
enjoys.   To Sumner more than to any single man
the whole country owes the prevention of war with
England and France when such a war would have
meant the disruption of the Union.

Such men are rare in the public life of any
nation, and when we depart from the principles
which they believe and practice we may well trem-
ble for the permanence of our government, for, as
Lowell said, this will endure only " so long as the
ideas of the founders remain dominant."

INDEX

INDEX